IMAGES
of America

SANTA CRUZ'S SEABRIGHT

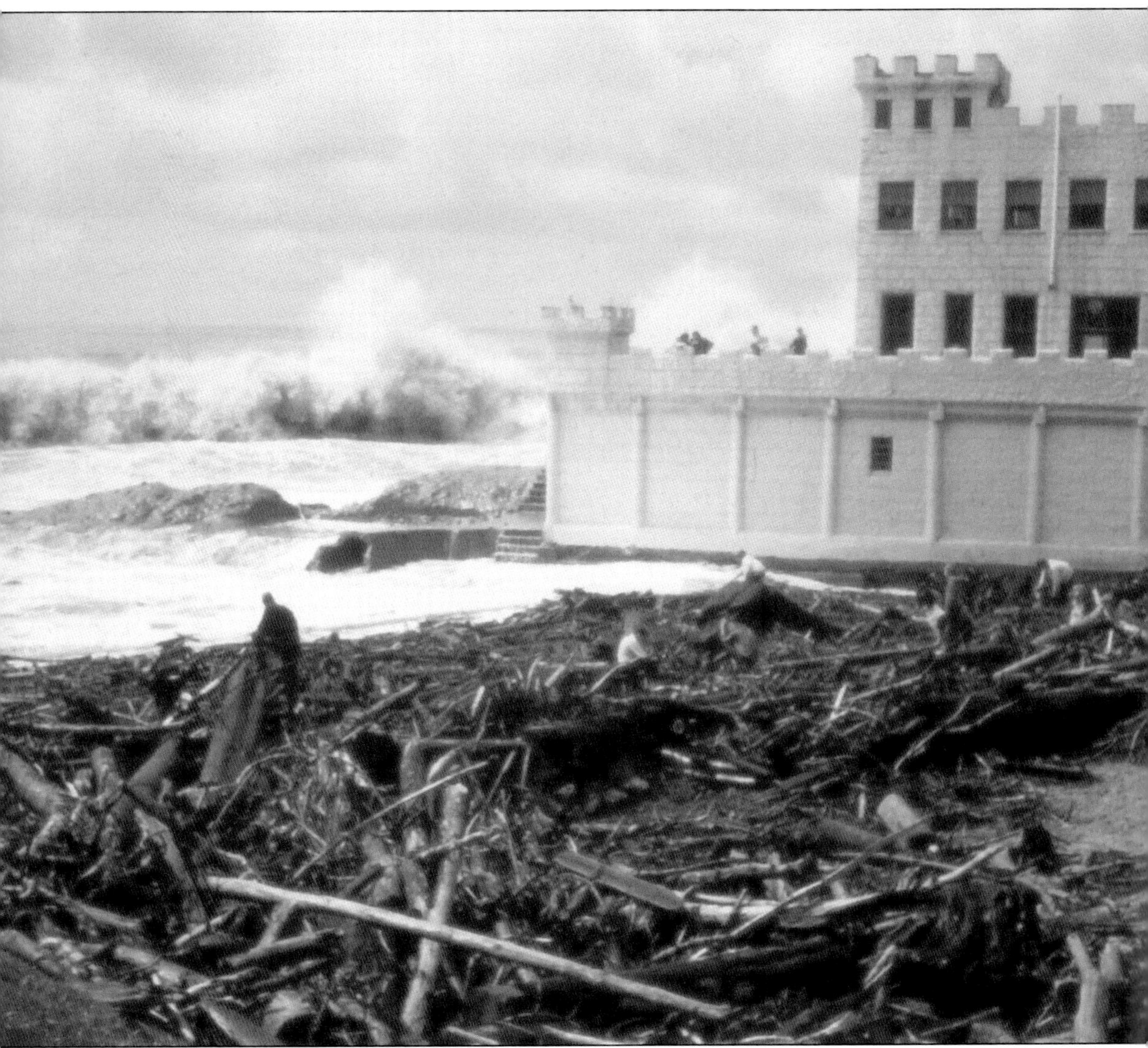

The evolution of the castle on East Cliff Drive—by owner, date, and name of property—is as follows: James Pilkington (1903–1910), Seabright Hot Salt Water Baths; Charles Cushing (1910–1920), Seabright Hot Salt Water Baths; Louis Scholl (1920–1928), Seabright Hot Salt Water Baths; Louis Scholl (1929–1944), Scholl Marr Castle; W.E. Dodge (1944–1945), Casa del Mar; Ivan Netoff (1946–1949), Casa Del Mar; the Lyter family (1950–1954), the Castle; the Russell family (1955–1960), the Castle; the Ritchey family (1960–1967), the Castle. (Courtesy of the Lionel T. Lenox collection.)

On the Cover: Virginia Lenox, caretaker Eileen Livesay, Buddy Lenox, Eileen's friend, and Helen Lenox romp on the beach in 1920. The adults wear rented Seabright bathing suits. This photograph and many others in the chapters that follow are from the Lionel T. Lenox collection. Lionel came to California in the early 1890s and began taking photographs of Seabright in 1914. The family spent summers at their Lake Avenue home, overlooking Woods Lagoon where Lionel and his wife, Alice, retired in the 1950s. Lionel became a professional photographer. Their granddaughter Nancy Lenox, of Aptos, made this exceptional collection available. (Courtesy of the Lionel T. Lenox collection.)

IMAGES
of America

SANTA CRUZ'S SEABRIGHT

Randall Brown and Traci Bliss
with the Seabright Neighborhood Association
and the Santa Cruz Museum of Natural Hitory

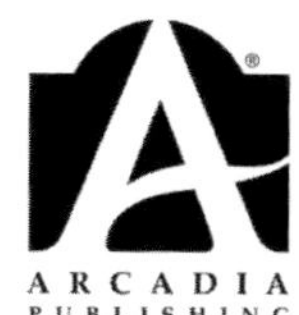

ISBN 978-1-4671-2473-7

Published by Arcadia Publishing
Charleston, South Carolina

Printed in the United States of America

Library of Congress Control Number: 2016959645

For all general information, please contact Arcadia Publishing:
Telephone 843-853-2070
Fax 843-853-0044
E-mail sales@arcadiapublishing.com
For customer service and orders:
Toll-Free 1-888-313-2665

Visit us on the Internet at www.arcadiapublishing.com

This is dedicated to the memory of Bob Halterman and Jim Hammond who wholeheartedly preserved and promoted the history of Seabright.

Contents

Acknowledgments

The Board of the Seabright Neighborhood Association (SNA) committed to this endeavor based on the inspiring work of local historian and Arcadia author Carolyn Swift. Her example and advice led the way. Our major challenge was finding at least 150 historical photographs to supplement the SNA archives. Many individuals and organizations made achieving that goal possible and their names appear with the photographs. The exceptional Lenox, Mee, and Ronnie Trubek collections helped to ensure accurate documentation of Seabright's vibrant social history.

Special recognition is due to the following four organizations that went far out of their way to provide unique images: Santa Cruz Museum of Art and History, Santa Cruz Port District, Santa Cruz Surfing Club Preservation Society, and the Seaside Company. Heartfelt appreciation goes to Heather Moffat and the Board of the Santa Cruz Museum of Natural History for partnering with SNA. We also want to thank the following: Capitola Museum; Covello & Covello; California State Library; Hawaii State Archives; Loon Hill Galleries; Outrigger Canoe Club; Santa Cruz Public Library; Special Collections at the University of California, Santa Cruz; and Joe Michalak, who served as photographer for the final chapter.

We incorporated family photographs and compelling details provided by Mariellen Boone, Larry Dunham, Michael Eck, Reed Geisreiter, Bart Gripenstraw, Don Hall, Marty Mee Dunn, Al Mitchell, Mary Randall Peterson, and Joan Miller, each with deep roots in the community. The names of additional contributors appear within the captions. Our editorial committee—Bill Davis, native Seabrightan Sue Pagen McCrary, and Rod Atchison—added richness and clarity throughout. Local historians Frank Perry and Marion Pokriots gave insightful feedback. Marty Mee Dunn, born and raised in Seabright, did the copyediting. Without the very generous help and expertise of historic preservationists Judith Steen and Joe Michalak, important aspects of this book would not have been possible. *A Gathering of Voices*, *Capitola*, *California Central Coast Railroads*, Newspapers.com, *Santa Cruz Coast*, *Tom Blake: The Uncommon Journey of a Pioneer Waterman*, and *The Sidewalk Companion to Santa Cruz Architecture* also informed the narrative. Please note the following organizations and their abbreviations: Santa Cruz Museum of Art and History (MAH), Santa Cruz Museum of Natural History (SCMNH), and Seabright Neighborhood Association (SNA).

INTRODUCTION

The recorded history of Santa Cruz dates to October 1769 when the expedition led by Gaspar de Portolá passed through the area on its journey of exploration. "Not far from the sea," noted Fr. Juan Crespí, "we came to a river of much water . . . in the middle the water reached to the bellies of the animals. The stream is not distant to the beach . . . We called the river 'San Lorenzo.'" The Spanish troops likely crossed the river near Seabright's eastern cliff, as they reported trouble descending and ascending the steep banks of the stream.

No natives appeared when the visitors arrived, but the area had been settled for many thousands of years by numerous small groups of people speaking similar languages. Experts believe that the inhabitants near the river mouth were known as "Uypi." Their migratory lifestyle depended on the abundant natural resources of the region, with the future Seabright offering a wide variety of seafood and game. Steelhead trout and other fish passed close to San Lorenzo Point on their journeys from river to sea and back. A short distance to the south, the brackish waters of Woods Lagoon attracted flocks of birds—ducks, geese, cormorants, and seafowl—and supported colonies of shellfish, especially clams. Tidal pools and sea rocks provided a special treat, the sea snail known to local Native Americans as *aulon*—translated to Spanish as *abulón* and Anglicized to abalone. The shells of these mollusks were lined with mother of pearl, a shimmering iridescent substance, which, when fashioned into jewelry, became a valuable trade good.

Spanish explorers were especially interested in locating good sources of freshwater, essential to establishing a settlement. They identified land between the San Lorenzo River and the creek they called "Santa Cruz," today's Laurel Creek, as "fit not only for a town but a city." Like the rest of California, the area was first claimed by the Catholic Church, which established a mission on the west side of the river in 1791. The Uypi and other local natives moved into the new establishment; some coming voluntarily, others rounded up by soldiers. Five years later, another settlement, separate from the mission, took shape on the east side of the river, where the Spanish authorities laid out "Villa de Branciforte" along Branciforte Creek near the mouth of the San Lorenzo River.

The signing of the Treaty of Guadalupe Hidalgo in 1848, ending the Mexican-American War, provided quite an opportunity for "American" real estate investors. Unoccupied tracts were considered public lands, available on a first-come, first-served basis. The common pastures of Branciforte, today's Seabright, attracted the attention of the Woods family from Missouri.

The authorities granted land bounded on the east by a creek or ravine and running along the beach to the banks of a lagoon to Mary Ann Silvey Woods in 1849. She secured her claim with a deposit of 12 gold dollars and contributed another $3.63 to record the deed. Settlement had begun. A decade later, the western half of the future Seabright from the San Lorenzo River to Pilkington Creek became the farm of the family that gave the creek its modern name. A century and a half later, this land of grazing cattle and hay fields, overlooking the Monterey Bay, would be a tourist mecca with an expansive state beach, drawing hundreds of thousands of visitors every year.

With railroad construction in the 1870s, the demand for summer recreation intensified. Three competing tent campgrounds gradually gave way to an assortment of quaint beach cottages and elaborate summer homes. By the turn of the century, Northern Californians discovered Santa Cruz as an ideal summer resort and the quiet charm of Seabright became a magnet for developers. Energetic efforts by the culturally minded Improvement Society helped create more and better streets, city utilities, and an elegant library, all of which coincided with expanded automobile travel. The area just west of Woods Lagoon, initially slow to develop, appealed to Central Valley families, eager for a bucolic respite from the relentless summer sun.

The economic boom of the 1920s brought an upsurge in transient tourism, much to the dismay of established residents. At the end of the decade, the popular saltwater bathhouse at the Cove was expanded and transformed into an iconic tourist attraction: a Moorish-style castle. Thereafter, the Cove would always be known as Castle Beach.

Each September, tourists and summer residents returned to their regular lives, creating a rather deserted area that felt forlorn. During World War II, when men joined the war effort, a few resident women remember the "feel of a ghost town." Yet, that all changed with the postwar housing shortage and baby boom. The gradual transition into a year-round community escalated as families with young children moved in, countering the pervasive image of a Seabright for retirees and summer homeowners. Adding to this new mix were itinerant surfers who flocked to the narrow, less-populated beaches throughout the 1950s.

Surfers needed to find a new venue in the 1960s when the Santa Cruz Small Craft Harbor replaced Woods Lagoon. The harbor's west jetty created a profuse accumulation of sand, putting an end to most board and bodysurfing east of San Lorenzo Point. Developers hoped to profit by building high-rise apartments, but with one exception, local opposition stopped these plans. Many Seabrightans welcomed the 1972 creation of the California Coastal Commission (CCC) charged with regulating building height, density, and ongoing beach access. The CCC meant the beginning of a new era when locals could finally rely on a state agency to protect their cherished environment.

Residents coming together to write about Seabright's history actually began in 1983 when the Seabright Neighborhood Association (SNA) published its first issue of the *Seabright News*. In the more than three decades since, the quarterly publication has continued to document compelling aspects of our past. Some previously published stories provided text, topics and ideas for this book that we expanded upon with dozens of interviews. The SNA board assisted with production while simultaneously maintaining the continuity of the *Seabright News*. Led by Bill Davis (president), the board included Rod Atchison, Traci Bliss (historian), Sue Pagen McCrary (museum representative), Sybille Miller (secretary/treasurer), and Nancy Woolf. Many engaging photographs donated by current and former Seabrightans unfortunately did not meet the specifications for this publication but may be used in feature issues of the *News*. All profits from *Santa Cruz's Seabright* will support educational programs at the Santa Cruz Natural History Museum, whose history, as told in these pages, mirrors enduring values of the community.

One

When Seabright Had No Name

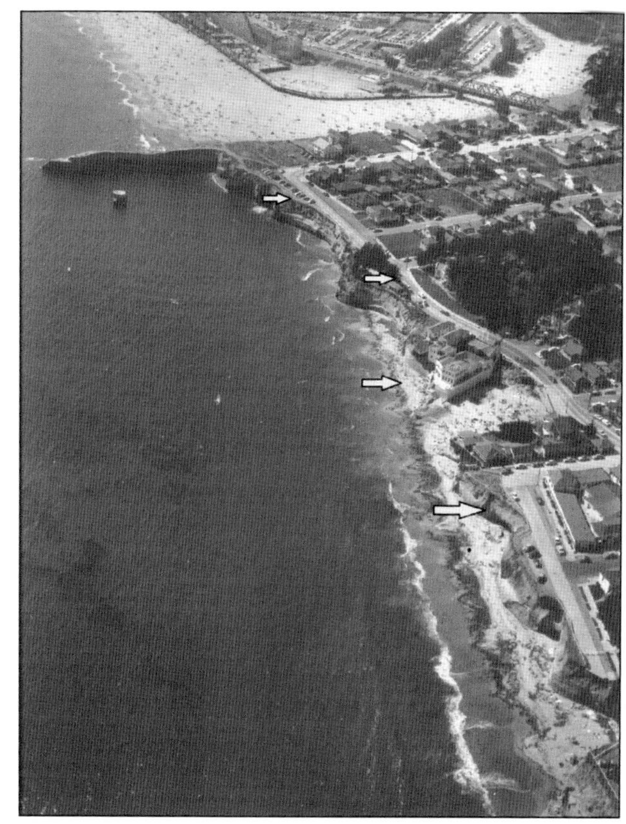

This 1949 photograph shows the Seabright neighborhood coastline, a century after its first pioneers arrived. Beginning at the San Lorenzo Point (top), one first sees a colony of summer homes, then a library-museum (barely visible in a parklike setting), followed by a one-of-a-kind Moorish castle overlooking a sheltered beach, and a row of apartments that catered to surfers. (Courtesy of SNA.)

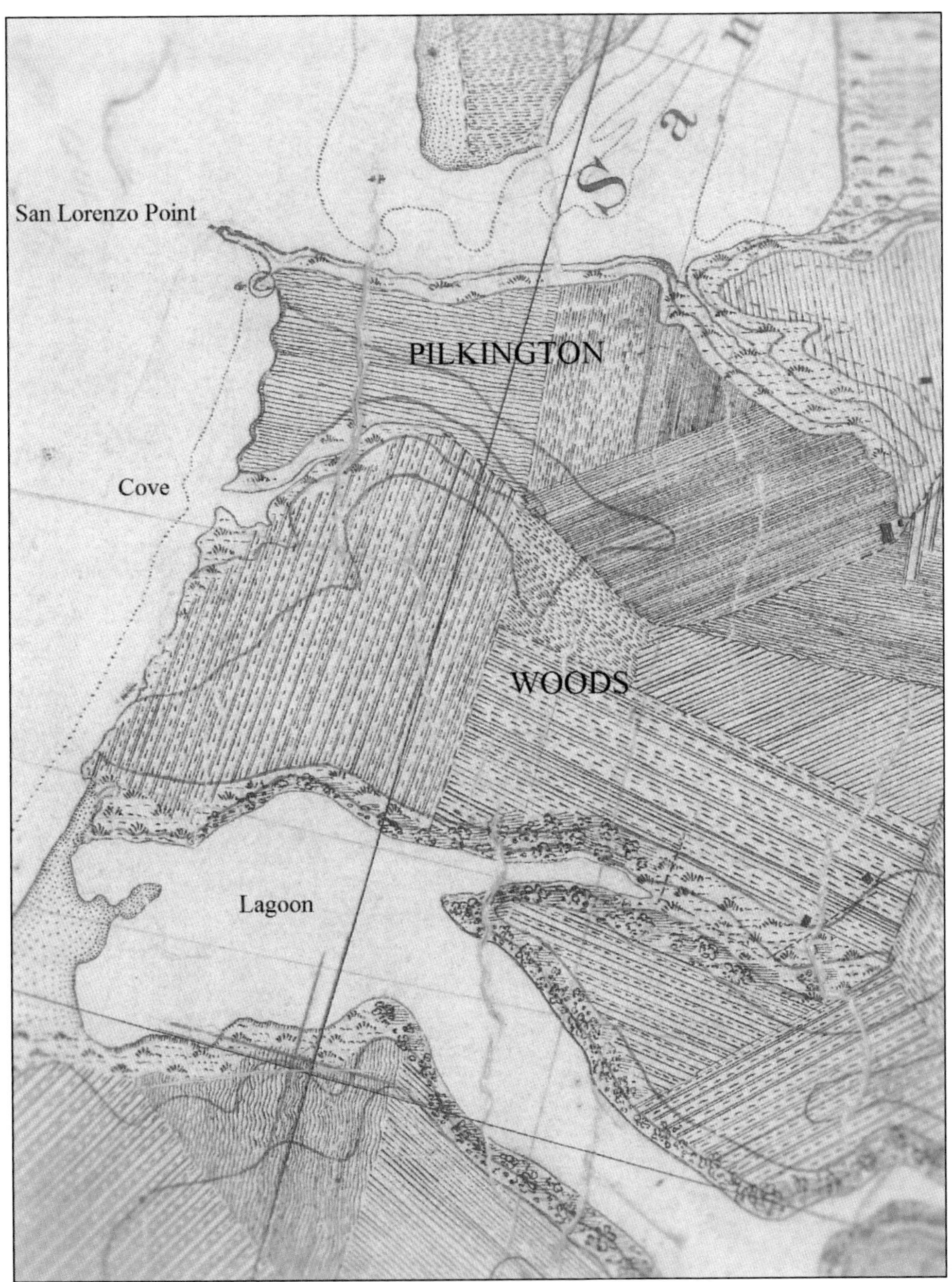

Early on, two families claimed all of what is now Seabright. In 1849, the common pasturelands of the Villa Branciforte were auctioned off. John and Mary Ann Silvey Woods spent their Gold Rush earnings to buy a farm where they raised 11 children. Thomas and Caroline Galbraith Pilkington acquired their ranch from her cousin, a real estate speculator. Both families raised cattle and grew hay on their fields, which reached to Monterey Bay and were divided by a creek emptying into the ocean at the cove. This 1853 map, a product of the US Coastal Survey, shows four key natural landmarks—San Lorenzo Point, the Cove, Woods Lagoon, and, indicated by a dot below the point, Pinnacle Rock. (Courtesy of US Geological Survey.)

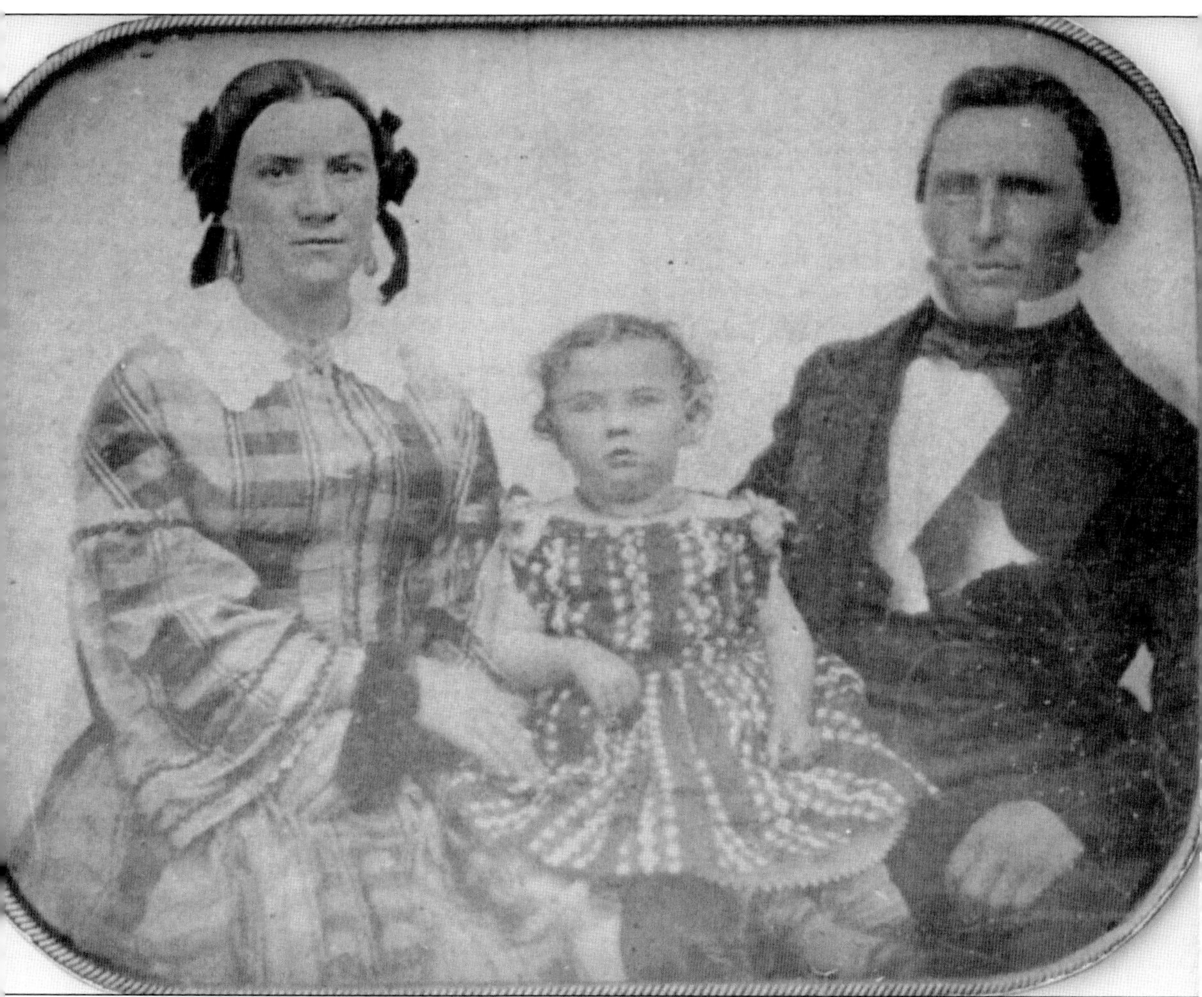

Frederick A. Hihn, seen here with wife, Therese, and daughter Kate, prospered through a series of real estate coups. As early as the 1860s, the visionary business leader imagined Santa Cruz as a railroad center, linked directly to San Francisco and the rest of the country. When transcontinental systems bypassed the local coast, Hihn backed a more modest venture: the Santa Cruz & Watsonville Railroad. The new line, running near the shores of Monterey Bay, cut through farmland, including that owned by the pioneer families, Pilkington and Woods. (Courtesy of MAH.)

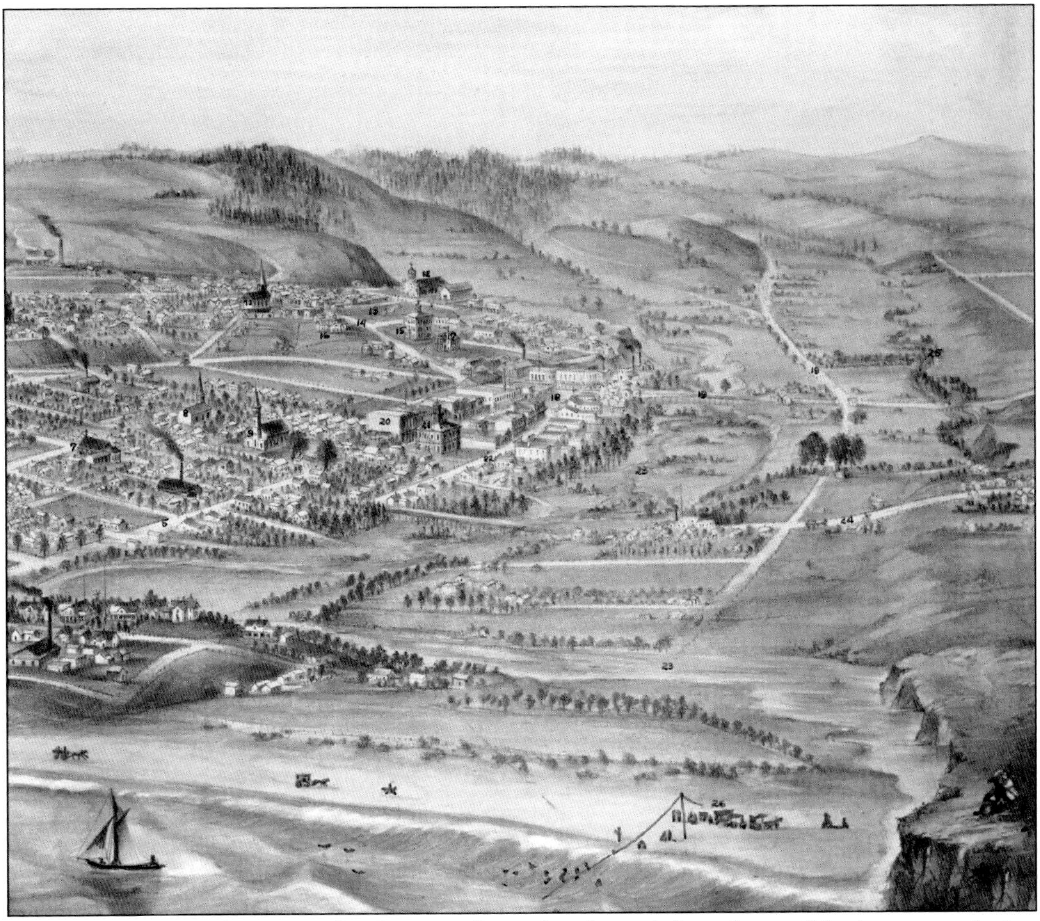

The rock formation known as San Lorenzo Point (on the right) made possible the accumulation of sand at the Santa Cruz Main Beach. Nonetheless, the point was inaccessible from the beach, as shown in this partial view from an early 1870s lithograph by Charles Gifford, of San José. (Courtesy of Traci Bliss.)

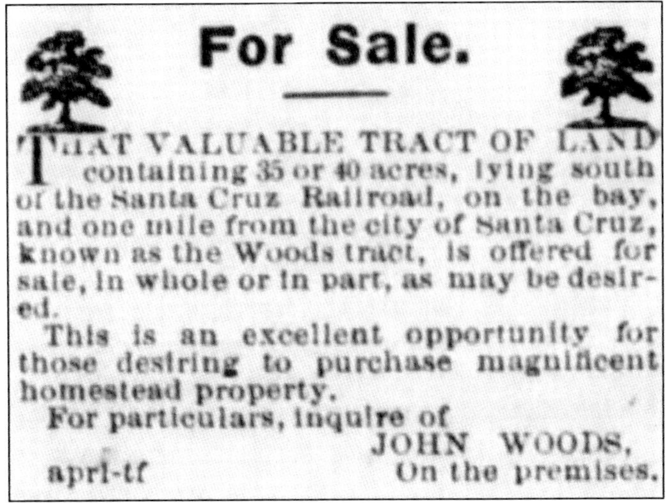

For Sale.

THAT VALUABLE TRACT OF LAND containing 35 or 40 acres, lying south of the Santa Cruz Railroad, on the bay, and one mile from the city of Santa Cruz, known as the Woods tract, is offered for sale, in whole or in part, as may be desired.

This is an excellent opportunity for those desiring to purchase magnificent homestead property.

For particulars, inquire of

JOHN WOODS,
On the premises.

apr1-tf

John Woods gave the Santa Cruz Railroad a right-of-way across the family's land, opening up the future Seabright for development. As soon as the trains began running, John and Mary Ann sold 12 acres of prime land to Hadley B. Doane and 57 acres to Henry Meyrick. (Courtesy of the Brown collection.)

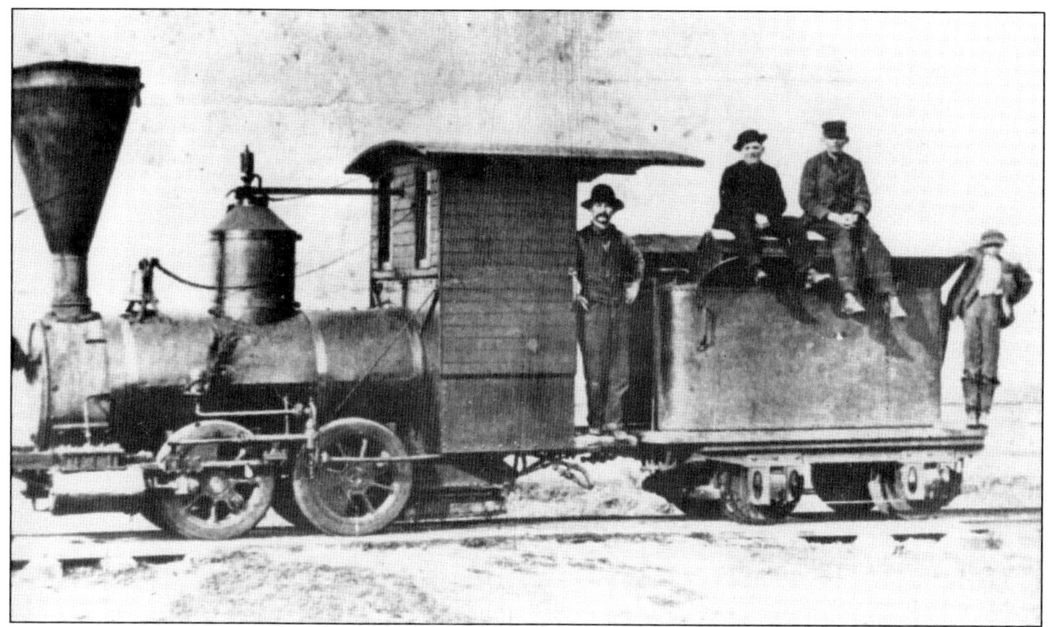

Local journalist Ernest Otto long remembered seeing the Santa Cruz Railroad's first locomotive. "It was a great disappointment. We had seen pictures of eastern locomotives. The *Betsy Jane* did not even have a cowcatcher." She did, however, have an enginehouse when she arrived in 1874—the neighborhood's first building, located on the newly graded Railroad Street, the future Seabright Avenue. (Courtesy of MAH.)

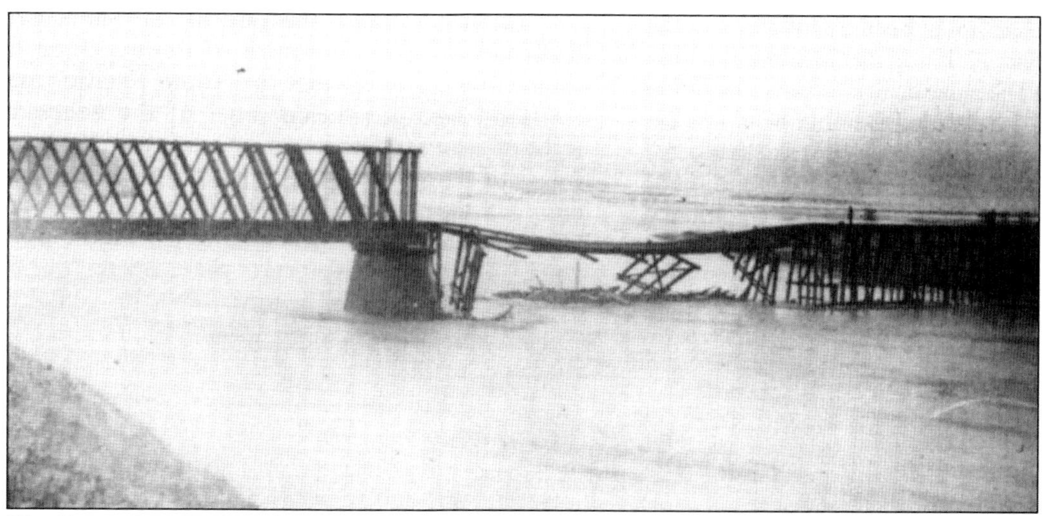

The Santa Cruz Railroad's bridge over the San Lorenzo River collapsed in January 1881, battered by fast-moving logs in a winter storm. His losses mounting, railroad owner F.A. Hihn sold the enterprise to the rapidly expanding Southern Pacific Railroad Company. (Courtesy of the Harold J. van Gorder collection.)

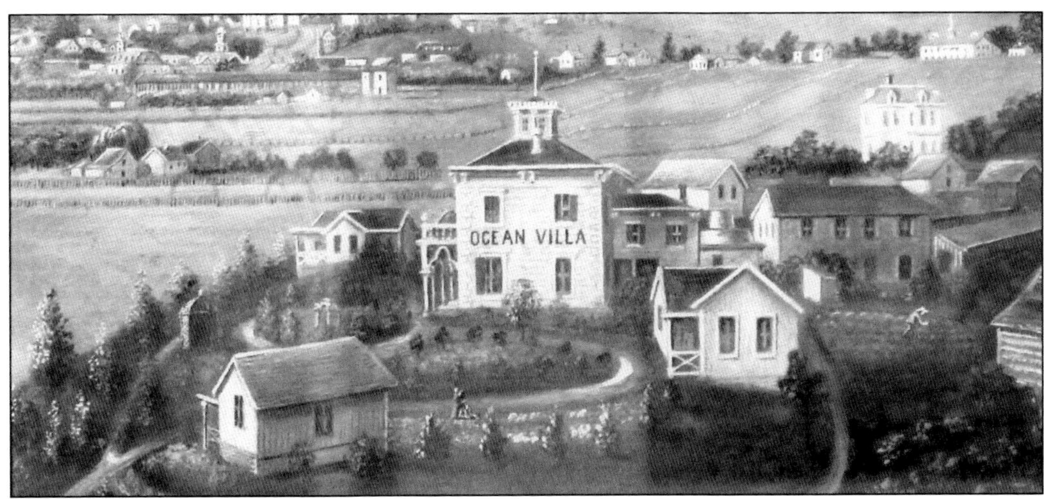

Entrepreneur George Bliss provided lodging for Victorian-era tourists in his charming riverside home and cottages on the east side of the San Lorenzo River. Beginning in 1875, his resort grew to include a villa with an ocean view, seen in this detail from a painting by Leon Trousset. The *Santa Cruz Sentinel* described Bliss's Ocean Villa as "a splendid suburban chateau, built for comfort and utility." To attract "surf bathers," he offered recreational activities on the river. (Courtesy of MAH.)

OPENING OF

CAMP CAPITOLA,

At Hall's Beach, Soquel.

A Ball will be given at the Opening of the above-named camp on

Thusrday, June 18, 1874.

Meanwhile, in the southern portion of the county, tourists were flocking to the Hall family's Camp Capitola. Lulu Hall Green, a 25-year-old widow, persuaded her father, Samuel, to convert his leased beachfront farm into a tenting resort, and the idea won the approval of F.A. Hihn, owner of the land. Hall's Beach continued to flourish as a popular destination for campers from San José and other inland communities, providing impetus to a future Seabright. (Courtesy of the Brown collection.)

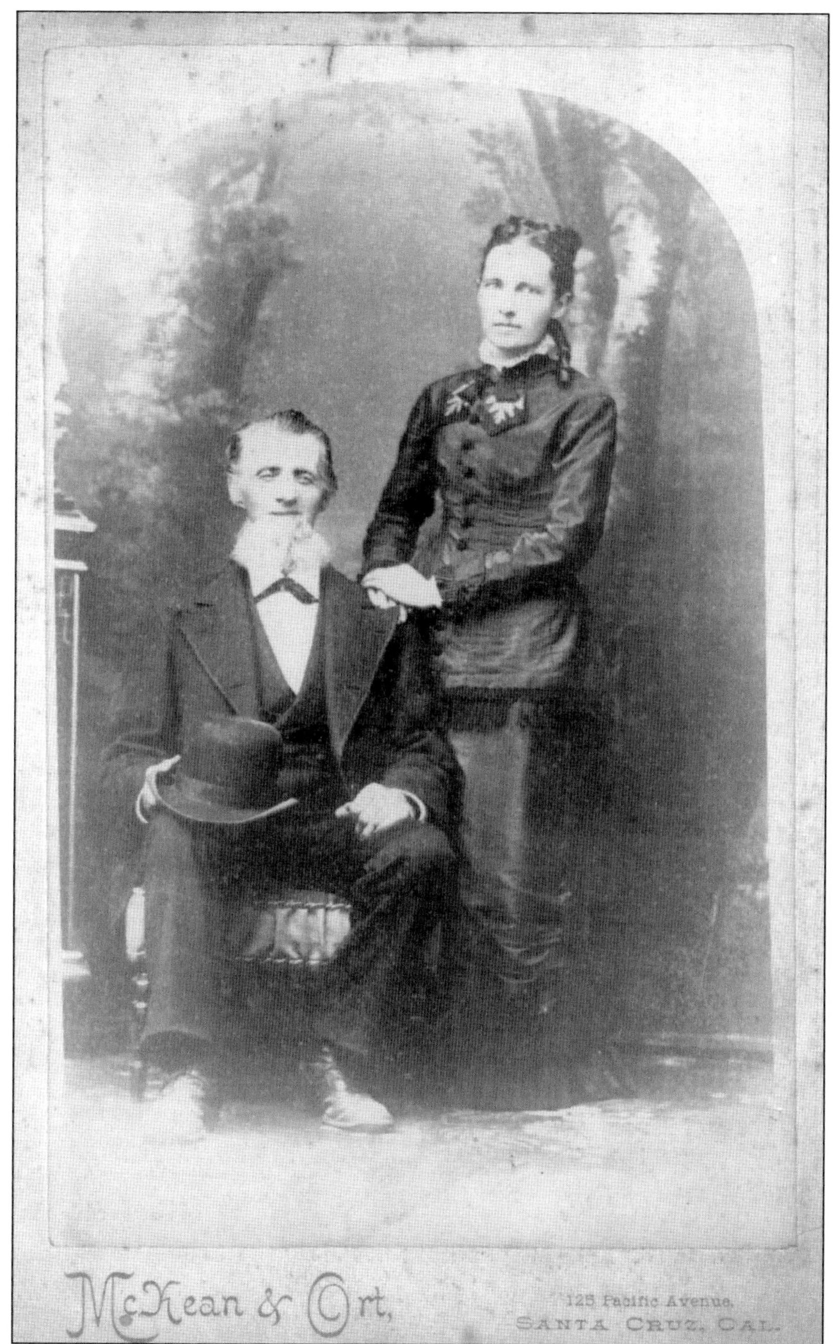

Thomas and Caroline Pilkington lived on a ranch in the heart of what is now Seabright's business district. For 15 years, they raised three children, cattle, and fodder on their 75 acres. After his wife's tragic death in a wagon accident, Thomas thought of a new way to provide for his three teenagers, including daughter Rebecca, shown here with him around 1886. Pilkington and Son, inspired by the successful tourist ventures of Bliss and Hall, created Camp Alhambra in 1878, east of San Lorenzo Point, with direct access to the sheltered local beach. (Courtesy of Special Collections, University of California, Santa Cruz.)

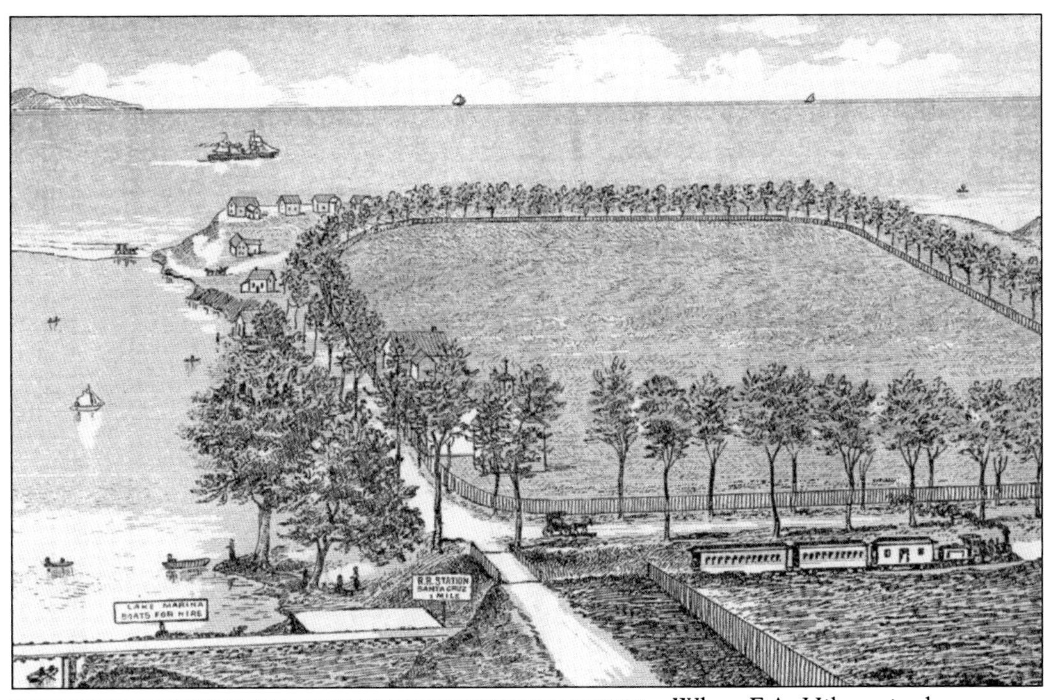

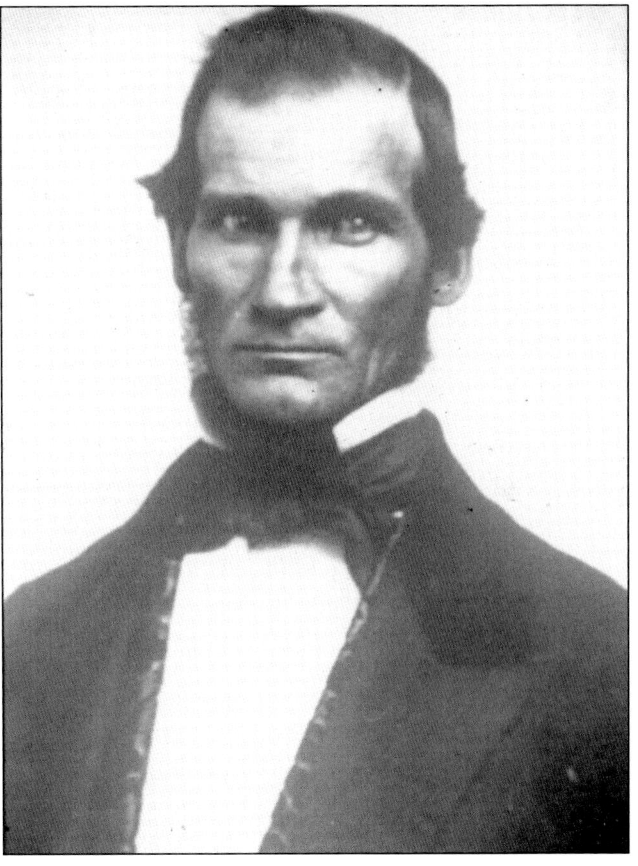

When F.A. Hihn raised Samuel Hall's rent at Camp Capitola, Hall (left) responded by relocating to Seabright, founding Lake Marina, at the edge of Woods Lagoon, now the site of the Santa Cruz Small Craft Harbor. His new enterprise featured a "pleasure drive," dubbed Marine Parade, circling the property. Despite high hopes entertained by Hall's new landlord, Henry Meyrick, Lake Marina closed in 1881 after one season. (Above, courtesy of the Library of Congress; left, courtesy of Capitola Museum)

Despite the failure of Lake Marina, Lulu Hall Green remained charmed by the neighborhood's natural beauty. In the summer of 1881, Thomas Pilkington turned over the operation of Camp Alhambra to Green (seen here) and her parents, Samuel and Rachel Hall, who brought their years of experience managing Camp Capitola. (Courtesy of Capitola Museum.)

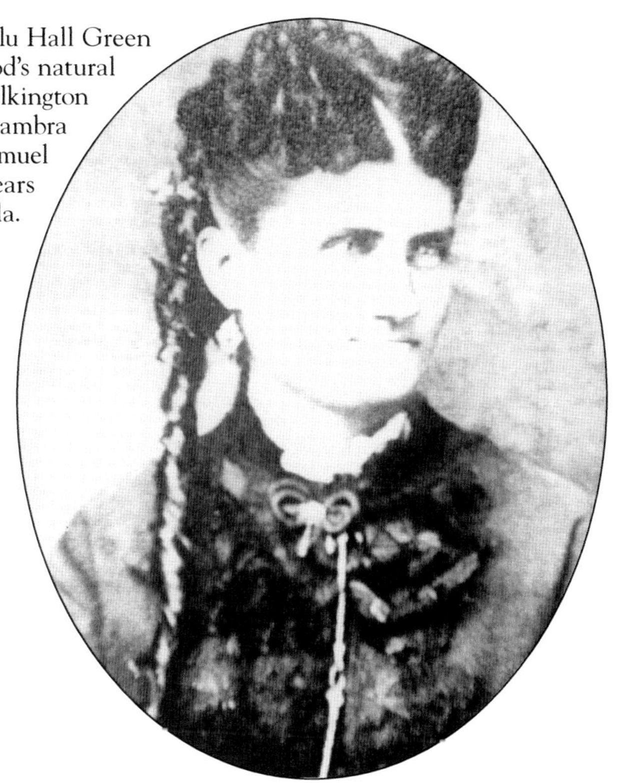

BOARD AND ROOMS

—AT—

ALHAMBRA,

ONE MILE FROM THE SANTA CRUZ Postoffice, **ON THE BEACH**, near **San Lorenzo River**, at Reasonable Rates.

Good Surf Bathing!

NEAR THE HOUSE.

S. A. Hall, Proprietor.

jy2-1m

In 1883, the *San Jose Pioneer* raved about the camp: "Everybody and their grandmothers will go coasting this season. They should all call at Hall's Alhambra. It is the favorite place and will continue to be so." At night, guests gathered at the camp's sheltered beach around its natural fireplace. (Courtesy of the Brown collection.)

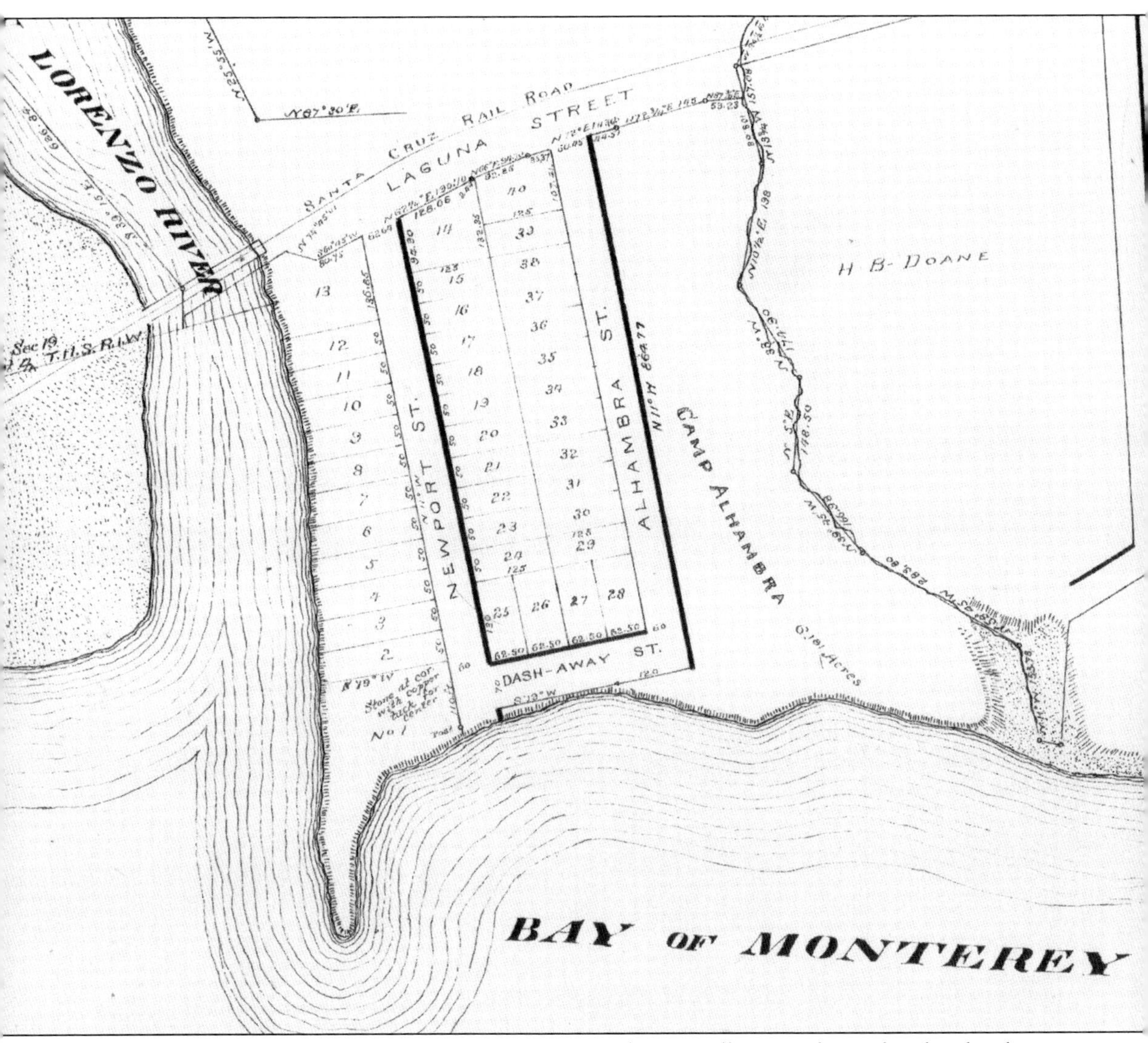

With the Hall family overseeing Camp Alhambra, Thomas Pilkington focused on his development next door—a subdivision of 40 lots, featuring spectacular scenic views of the bay. The plat map shows the railroad at top and Camp Alhambra at center right, extending from the railroad tracks to the beach. (Courtesy of Santa Cruz County Records.)

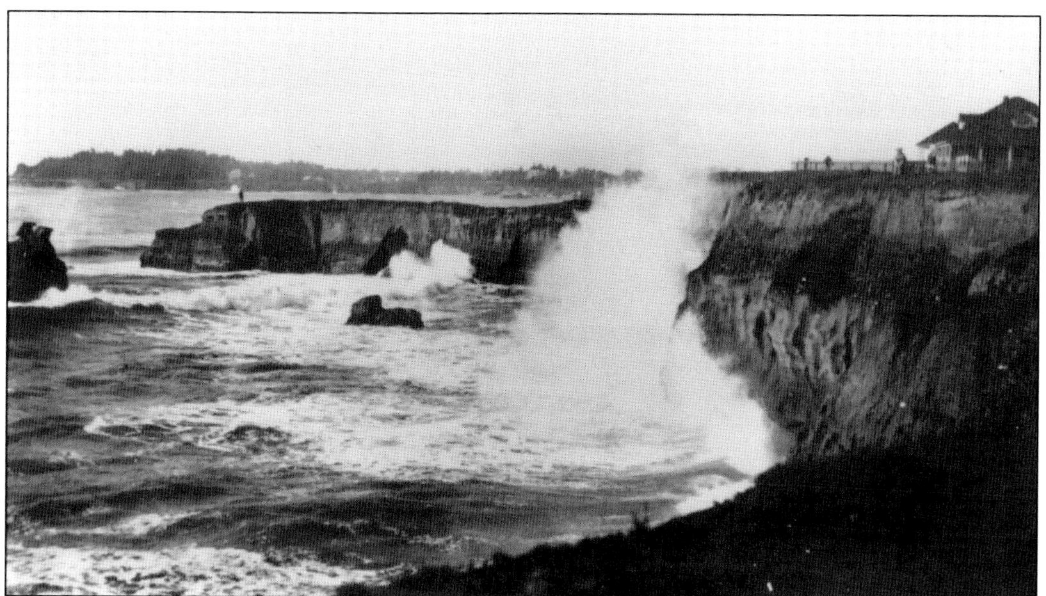

Col. Archibald McKendry, a Civil War veteran, bought Lot No. 1 in the Pilkington subdivision, and constructed its first home at San Lorenzo Point (above right). When fellow forty-niner Foster N. Mott (right) visited from Sacramento, he liked what he saw. Acquiring the Doanes' 12-acre tract adjacent to Camp Alhambra, Mott established Camp Seabright in 1884. A native New Yorker, Mott appropriated the name "Seabright" from the famous Jersey Shore resort. (Above, courtesy of SNA; right, courtesy of California State Library.)

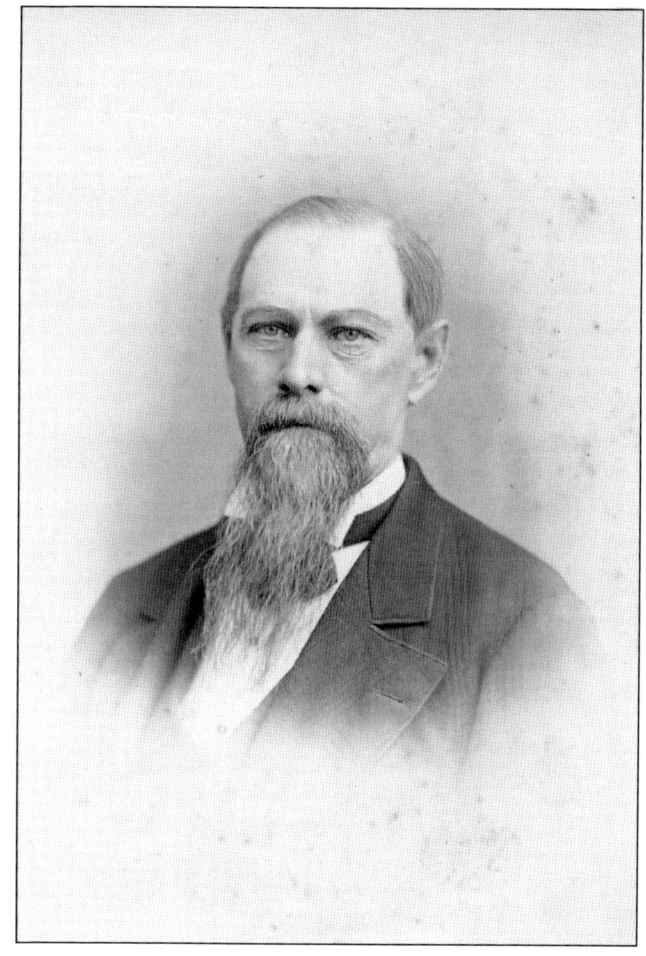

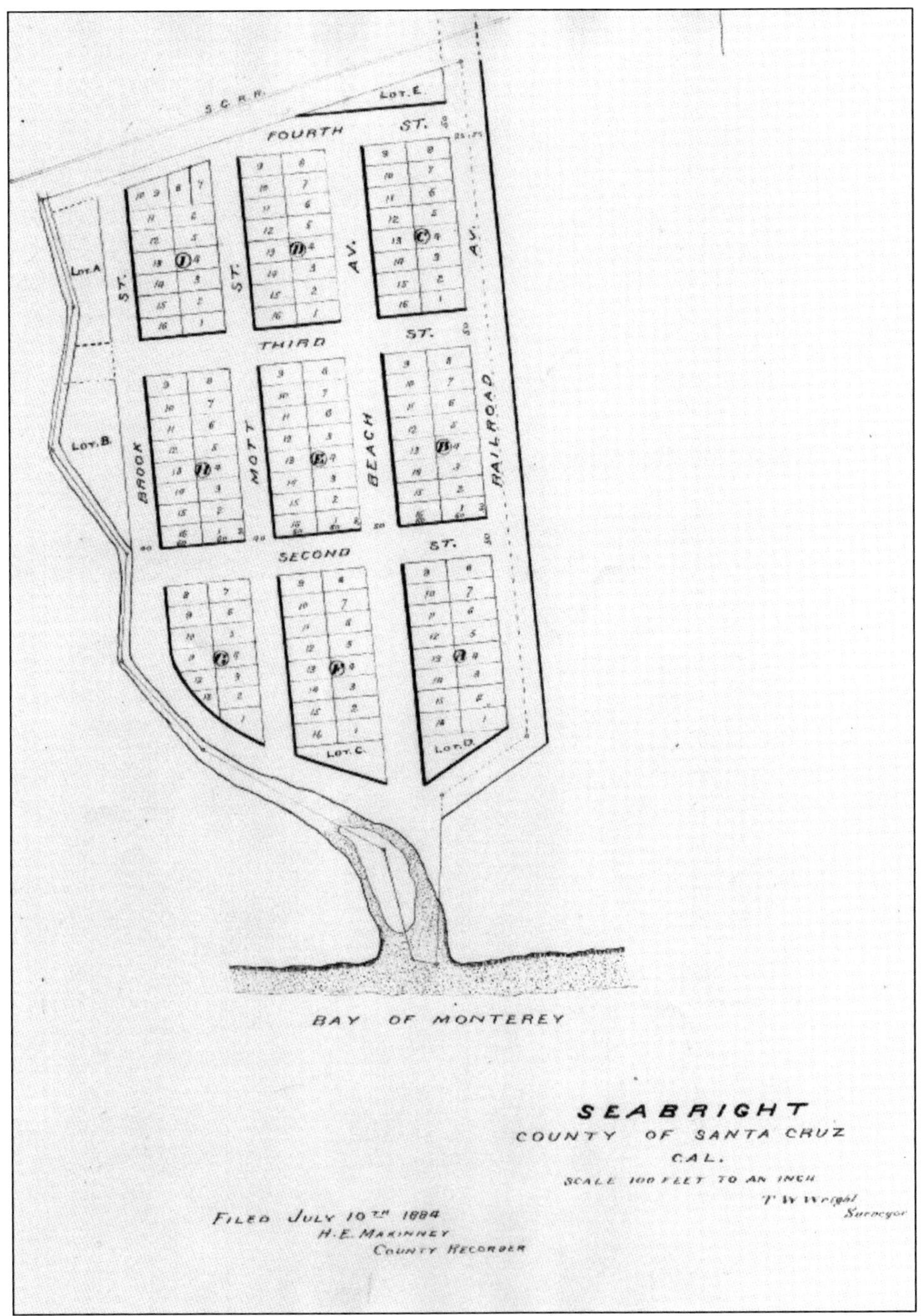

Foster Mott, a peach grower in Sacramento and a raisin farmer in Fresno, followed Pilkington's lead and laid out his own subdivision with close to 150 small cottage lots. Mott offered them at $50 apiece, subject to the following conditions: no business be opened, no barn be raised, and no alcohol be consumed on the premises. Railroad Street, at right, and the brook/ravine, at left, marked the east-west boundaries of the Seabright tract. When Mott's buyers insisted on a place to house their horses, he compromised by providing separate barn lots on Brook Street. (Courtesy of Santa Cruz County Records.)

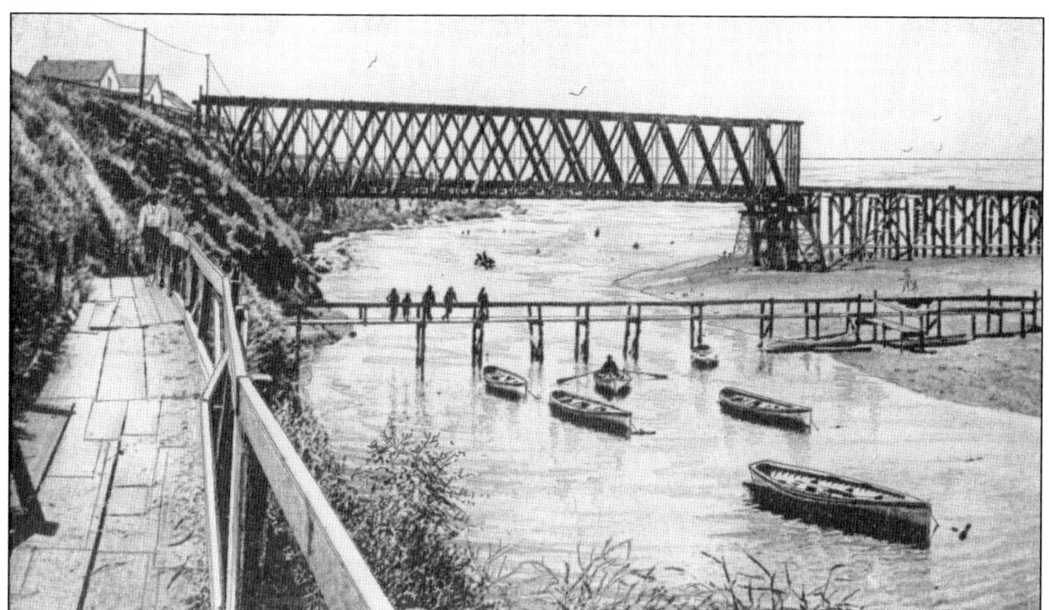

This view of the San Lorenzo River, looking toward the bay, shows George Bliss's 1885 footbridge linking his Ocean Villa and Seabright neighborhood with the Santa Cruz Main Beach. During several summers, brothers Thomas and James Pilkington rented canoes, advertising romantic river excursions under the moonlight. (Courtesy of Santa Cruz Beach Boardwalk Archives.)

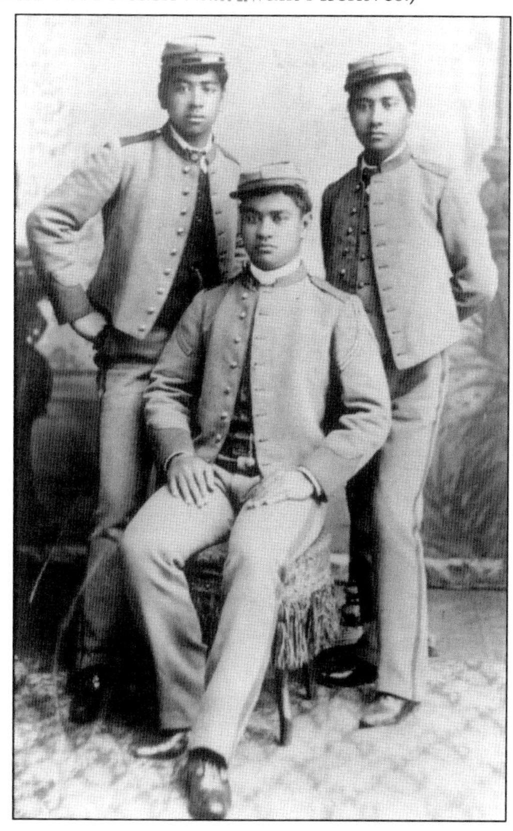

Three Hawaiian princes, on vacation from St. Matthew's Military School in San Mateo, enjoyed the waves where Monterey Bay meets the San Lorenzo River. They are, from left to right, Jonah Kuhio Kalanianaole, Edward Abnel Keli'iahonui, and David Kawananakoa. One afternoon in 1885, the trio gave what the *Santa Cruz Surf* described as "interesting exhibitions of surf-board swimming as practiced in their native islands," introducing the sport to California and the United States in 1885. Their example inspired locals: "The boys who go swimming in the surf at Seabright Beach use surfboards to ride the breakers like the Hawaiians," reported the *Surf* in July 1896. (Courtesy of Hawaii State Archives.)

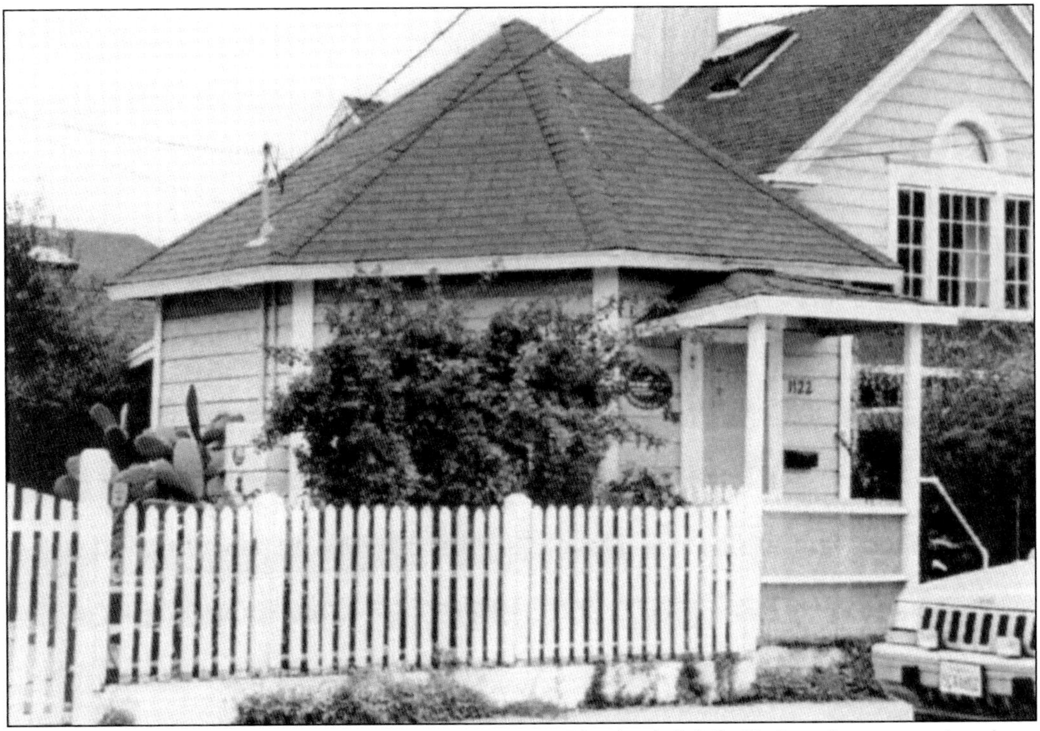

Captivated by Seabright's spectacular ocean view, Elizabeth M.C. Forbes, known to locals as Miss Forbes, purchased Pilkington's Alhambra Lot No. 10 on Newport Street, today 1122 East Cliff Drive, overlooking the San Lorenzo River. The 1886 cottage, Boca del Rio, embodied her preference for octagonal architecture. "Square corners," she asserted, "were wasteful." (Courtesy of SNA.)

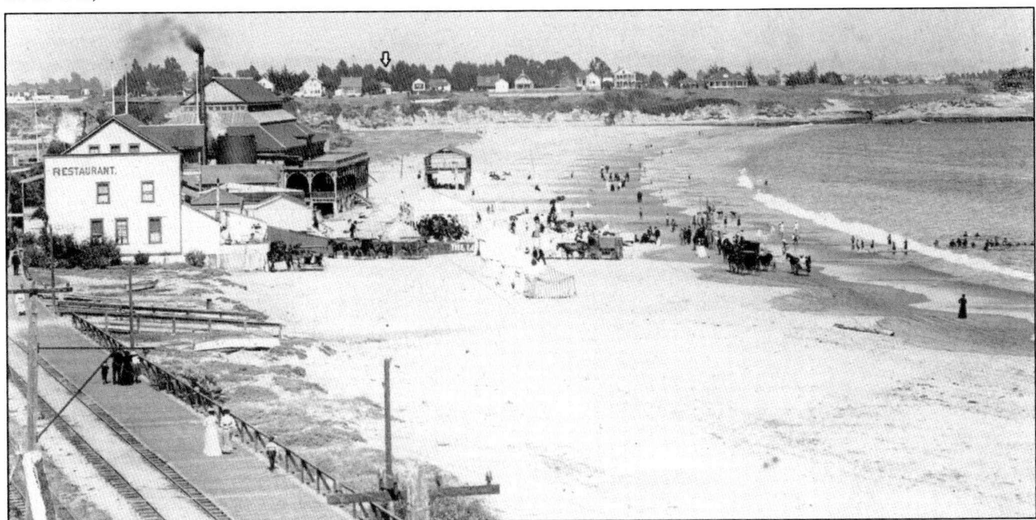

Forbes, a devotee of surf bathing, was known for her routine early morning dips in the bay, with a blue-and-white cape covering her swimming attire. Boca del Rio is seen here at the end of the distant row of houses in Pilkington's subdivision. This c. 1890 photograph also shows recent improvements at the Santa Cruz Main Beach, including increasingly elaborate bathhouses. (Courtesy of MAH.)

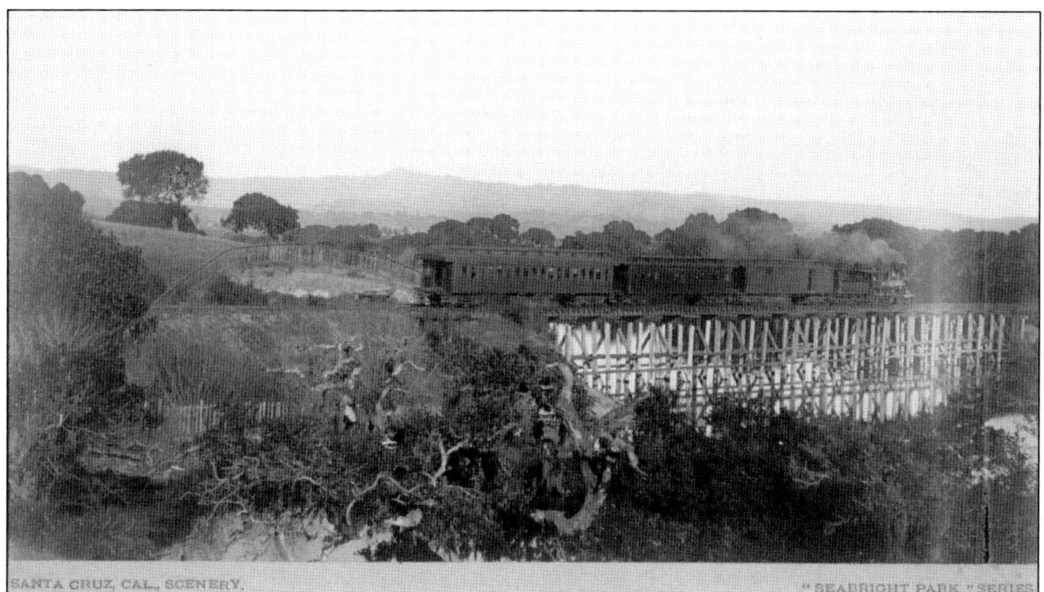

Vacationers and summerhouse-seekers rode the Southern Pacific trains across the Woods Lagoon trestle, en route to Capitola, past the available acres of Henry Meyrick's Seabright Park subdivision. These windswept and water-stressed lots continued to attract more cows than investors. Railroad passengers at this crossing were occasionally startled when the locomotive "hashed" unwary bovines. Meanwhile, on the west side of Railroad Street, the Pilkington and Mott subdivisions prospered. (Courtesy of MAH.)

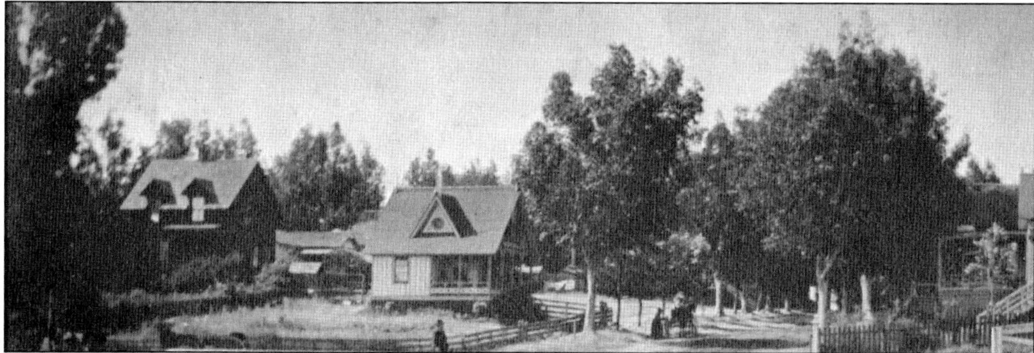

The Southern Pacific Railroad adopted the name "Seabright" for a station stop on Railroad Street in 1886, solidifying the neighborhood's permanent identity. A few blocks away, Mott's lots near the sheltered beach soon became populated with homes, including those of, from left, Susan A. Tyrrell and the McKee family. (Courtesy of MAH.)

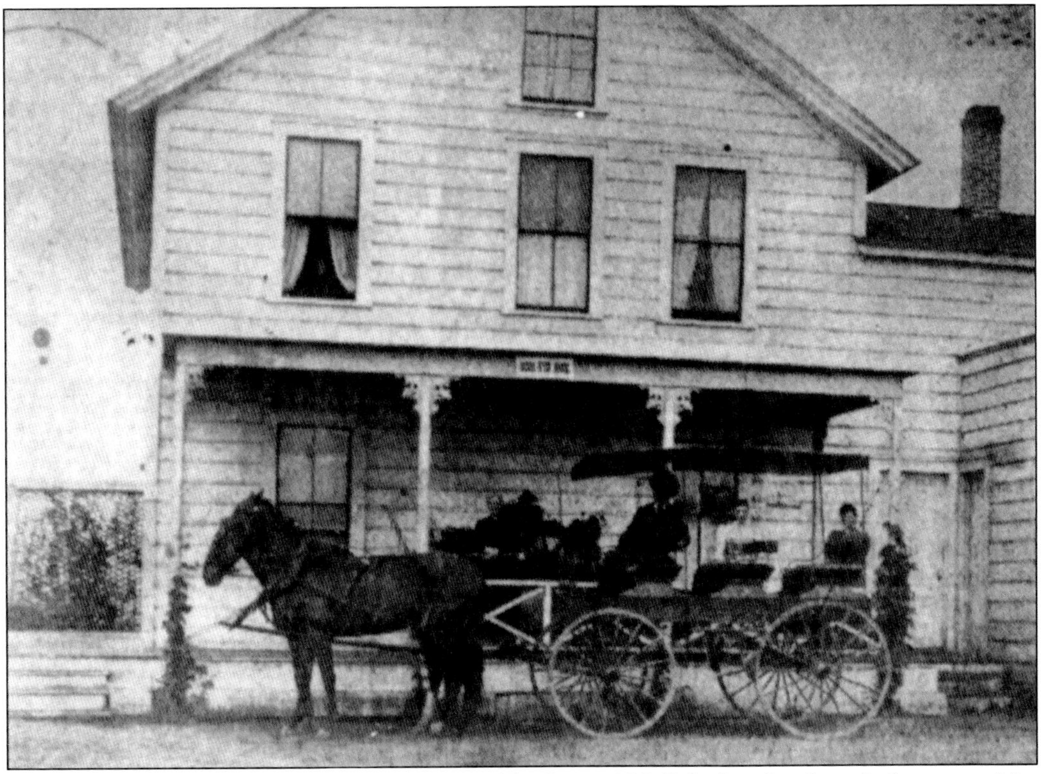

The Ocean View, a lodging house constructed by Samuel Hall for his daughter Lulu, opened for business in 1889. Its front door faced Newport Street, today 1152 East Cliff Drive, with guest rooms overlooking the San Lorenzo River and the Santa Cruz Main Beach. Here, Hall sits in the driver's seat of his touring buggy; his wife, Rachel, granddaughter Ella, and daughter Lulu are on the porch. (Courtesy of the Carolyn Swift collection.)

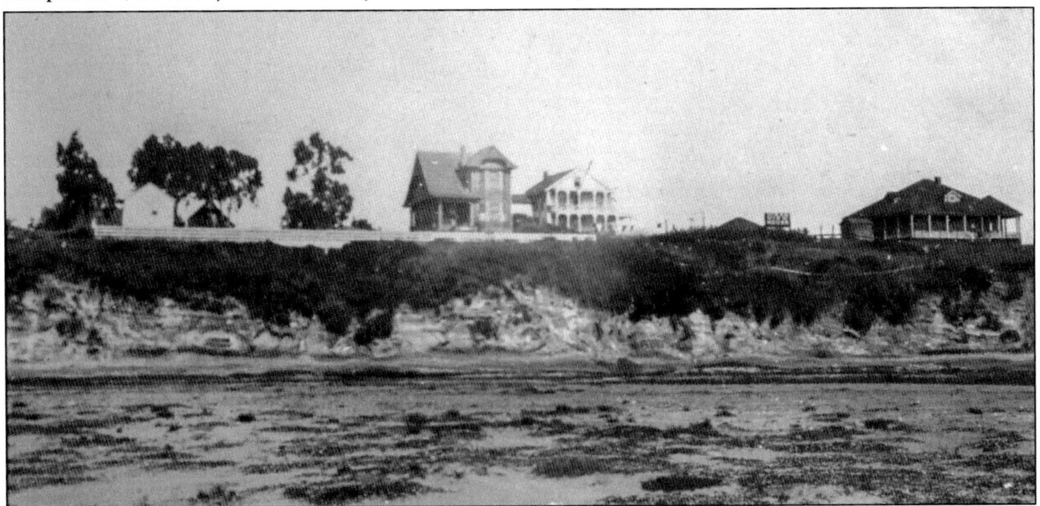

The houses on Newport Street overlooking the San Lorenzo River included the summer home of the Eschbachs of Stockton, center left, Lulu Green's Ocean View, and the McKendry home on the point. At far left is the Eschbachs' barn, one of several permitted in the Alhambra neighborhood. (Courtesy of the Joe Michalak collection.)

Two

Creating Community

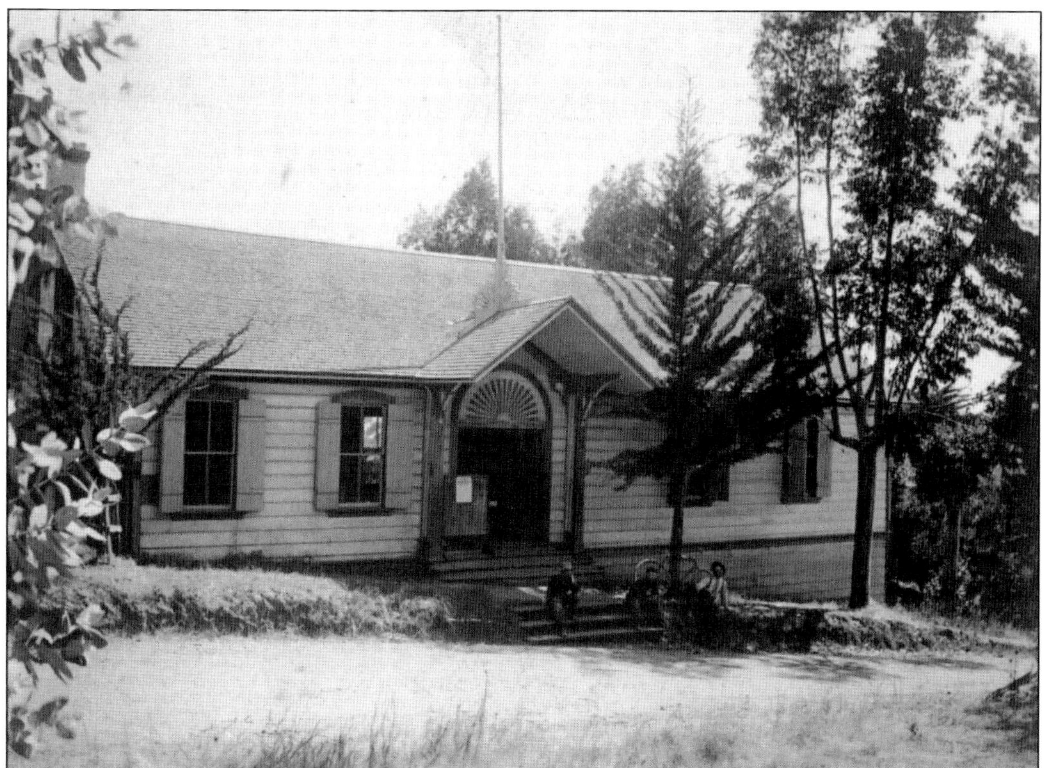

When Foster Mott built Seabright Hall, at the southeast corner of Forbes and Brook Streets, he included a large stone fireplace. With the aroma of burning driftwood, he helped make community gatherings warm and welcoming. Eager for a scenic roadway connecting the neighborhoods of Seabright with each other—and with Santa Cruz—Elizabeth Forbes, Lulu Green, and Nettie Murray used the hall for their fundraising effort with Mott's wholehearted support. Major donors included George Bliss, F.A. Hihn, and the Pilkington family. (Courtesy of MAH.)

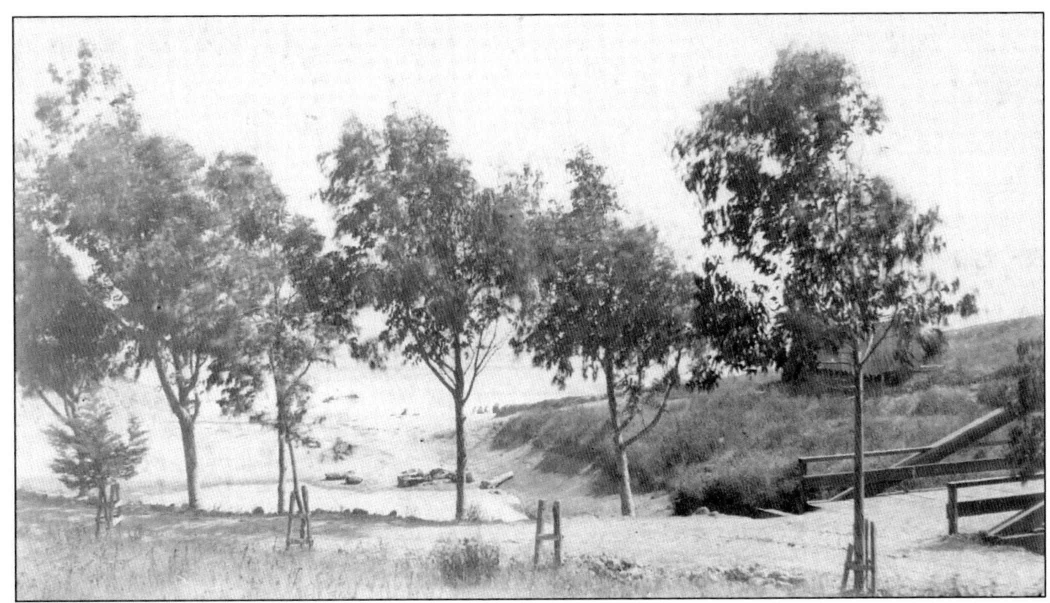

With the completion of East Cliff Drive in 1890, beautified with landscape trees, the former Alhambra campground was now separated from the beach, on the bay side of the bridge, above right. The three Pilkington children—Rebecca Gray, Thomas, and James—had already begun subdividing the area but continued to allow tent campers on their vacant lots. (Courtesy of SCMNH.)

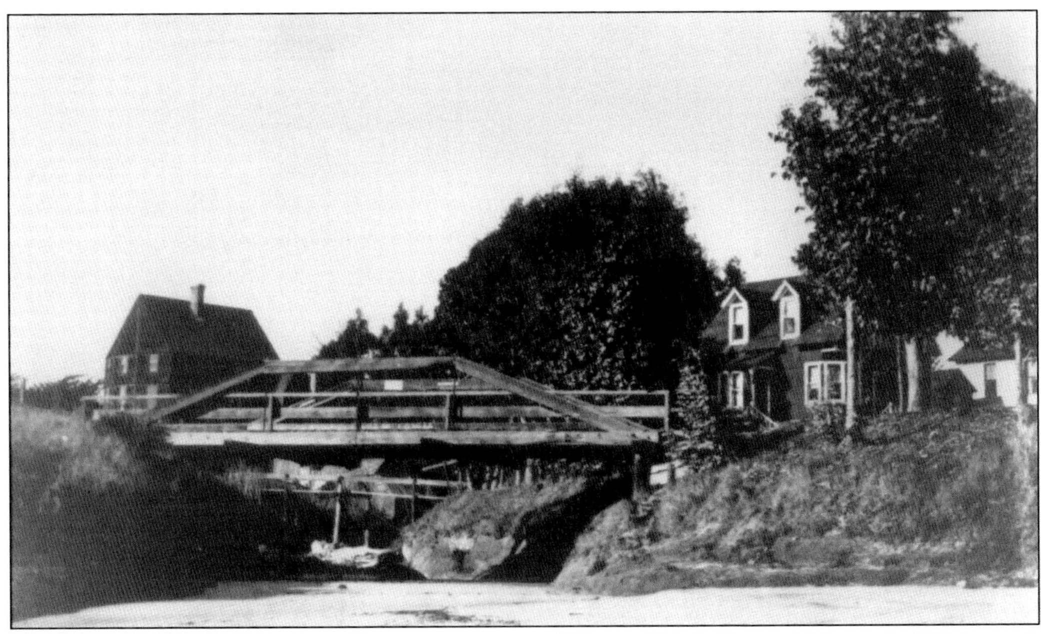

East Cliff Drive had two bridges. One span connected George Bliss's Ocean Villa to the Pilkington's Newport Street, today's East Cliff Drive. The other, pictured, connected Camp Alhambra with Foster Mott's development. To pay for this "necessity," property owners raised the total amount of $499.08. (Courtesy of SCMNH.)

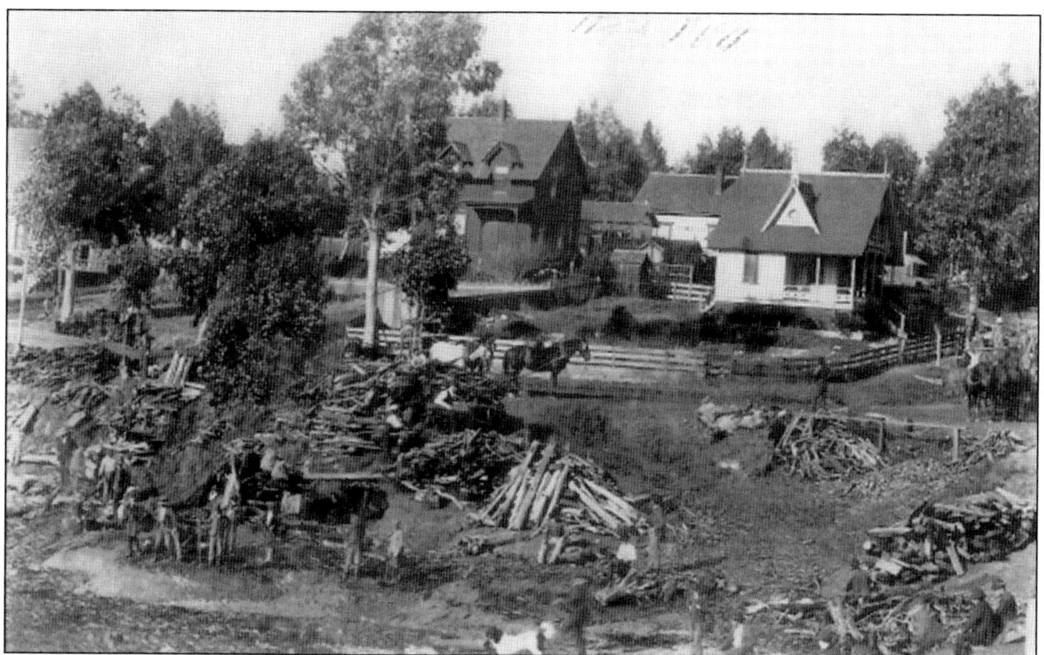

Winter storms left mounds of driftwood at the Cove, the name most used for the sheltered beach. Much of the wood, slow burning redwood, made its way down the San Lorenzo River from the many sawmills in its northern valley. Resourceful Seabrightans hauled away the lumber to heat their homes and cottages, a process made easier by bringing their wagons to East Cliff Drive, as seen here. (Courtesy of MAH.)

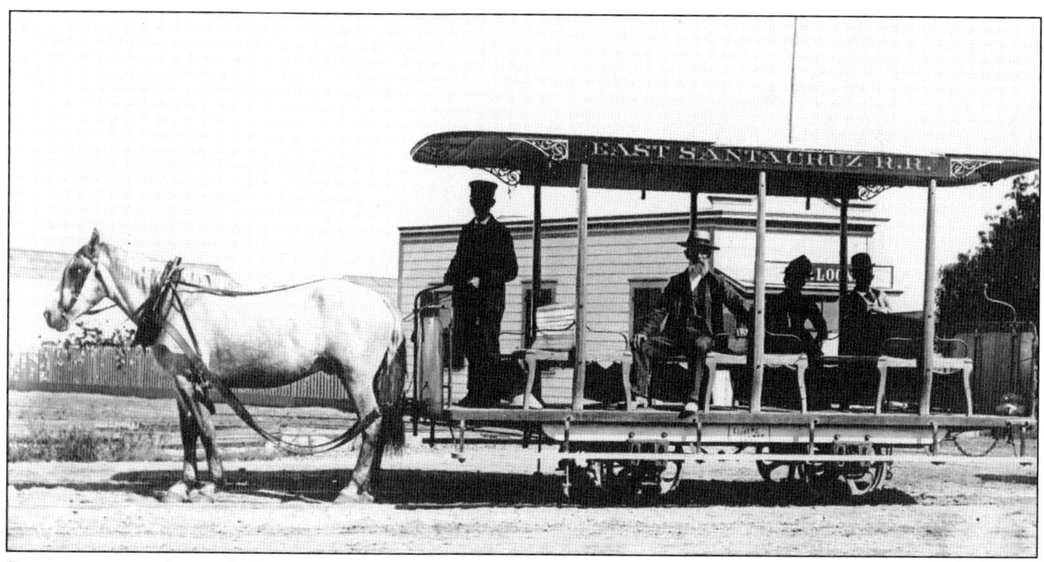

Passengers paid a nickel each to ride the horse-drawn cars of the East Santa Cruz Railroad when it opened in July 1890. The tracks ran from downtown Santa Cruz's Cooper Street, over the river and, by way of Cayuga Street, traveled Railroad Street to Seabright, bringing many visitors to the "lively little suburb." (Courtesy of MAH.)

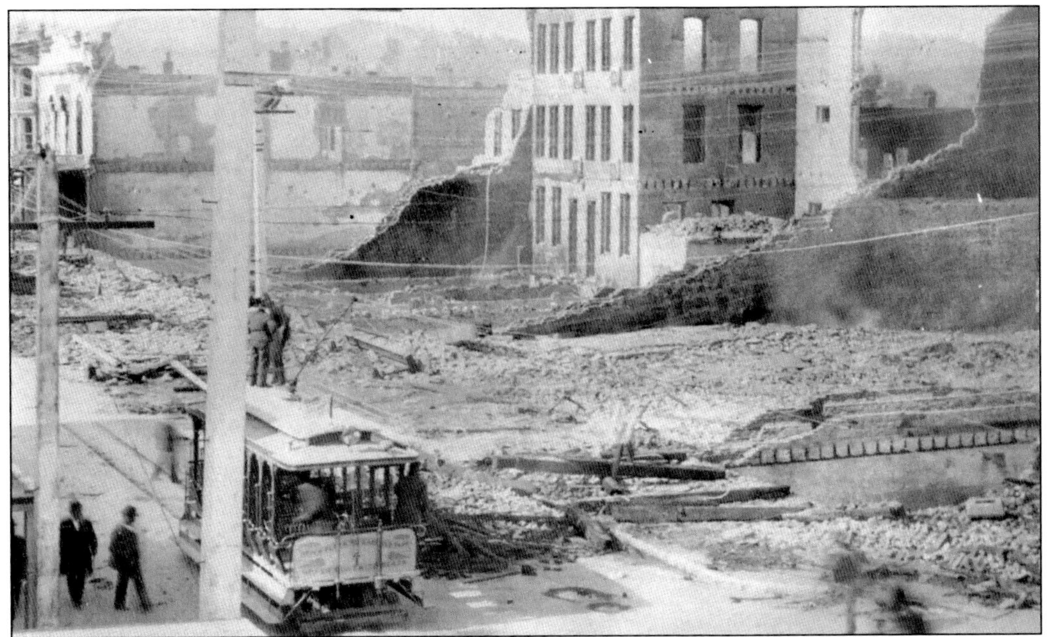

On the night of April 14, 1894, Seabrightans, gathered on the East Cliff, watched in horror as downtown Santa Cruz went up in flames. The city water system had been temporarily turned off for repairs, and the coincidence caused some to suspect arson. (Courtesy of MAH.)

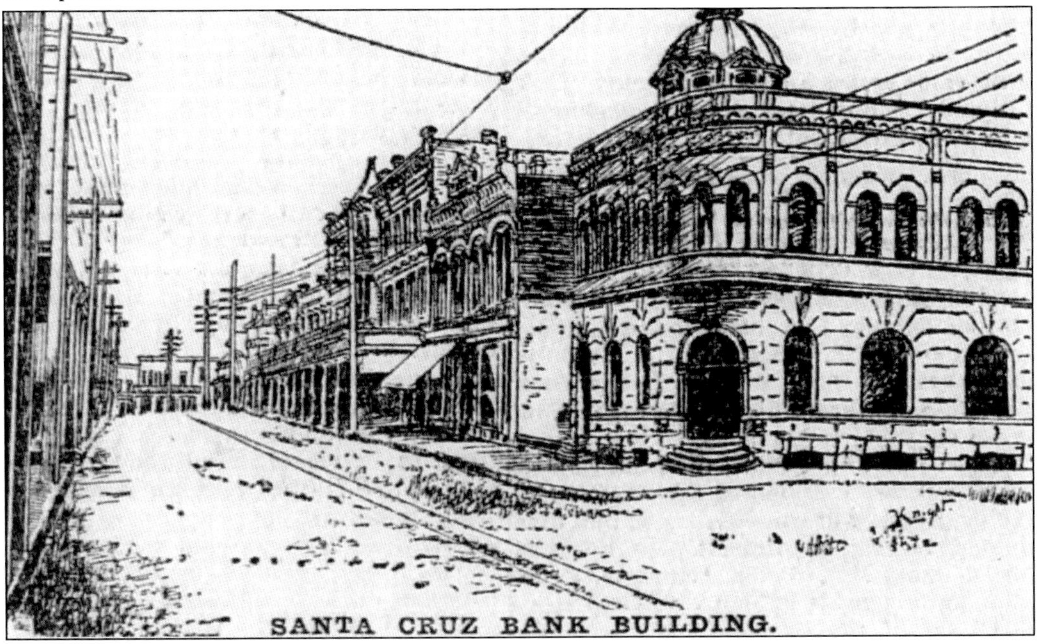

The *San Francisco Call* illustrated the rebirth of Santa Cruz in this 1895 engraving of the new County Bank. Buying land devastated by the fire, at the corner of Pacific Avenue and Cooper Street, bank president William T. Jeter "lost not a moment" hiring the architectural firm of Van Siclen and Haynes to provide an inspiring symbol of rebirth. The substantial Renaissance Revival building opened for business less than a year after the fire, and a motivated Seabright neighbor had already decided to expand upon the theme. (Courtesy of the Brown collection.)

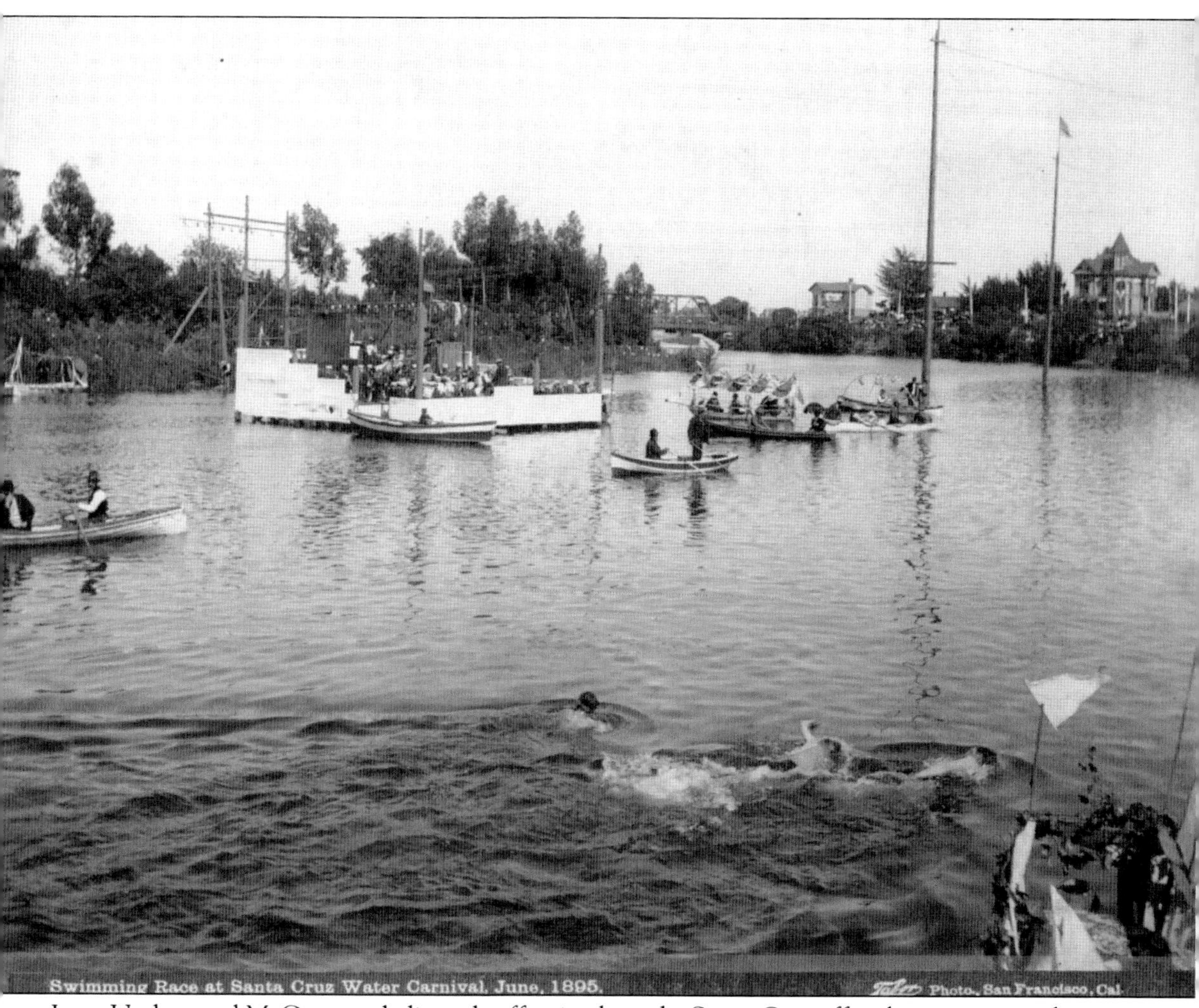

Lucy Underwood McCann, a dedicated suffragist, brought Santa Cruz officials an enticing idea to celebrate the city's renaissance. "Let's dam the river," she urged, "and paint the town red with fireworks." Embracing her plan, prominent citizens staged an elaborate Venetian water carnival in June 1895. Seabrightans helped build the carnival's temporary dam on the San Lorenzo River and designed a float depicting a woodsy camp complete with trees and a real bonfire. The ingenious design won first prize in the novelty category, and after the event, Samuel Hall used the craft for mussel-bakes, delighting tourists. The three-day program of carnival events included the swimming race pictured. (Courtesy of Nancy Campeau.)

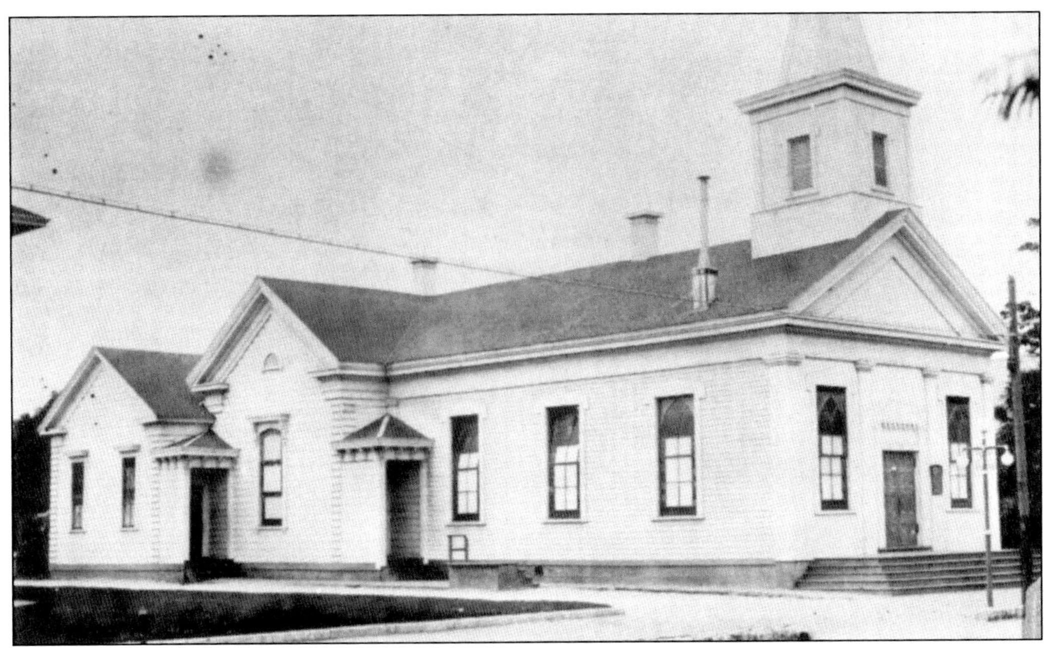

Seabright ladies were known for their activism. On May 18, 1896, a rally in favor of California's women's suffrage amendment convened at this Methodist church in downtown Santa Cruz. Lulu Green and fellow East Cliff resident Dr. Jennie Morgan participated as staunch supporters. Although Californians as a whole rejected the measure, a majority of Santa Cruzans voted in favor. (Courtesy of MAH.)

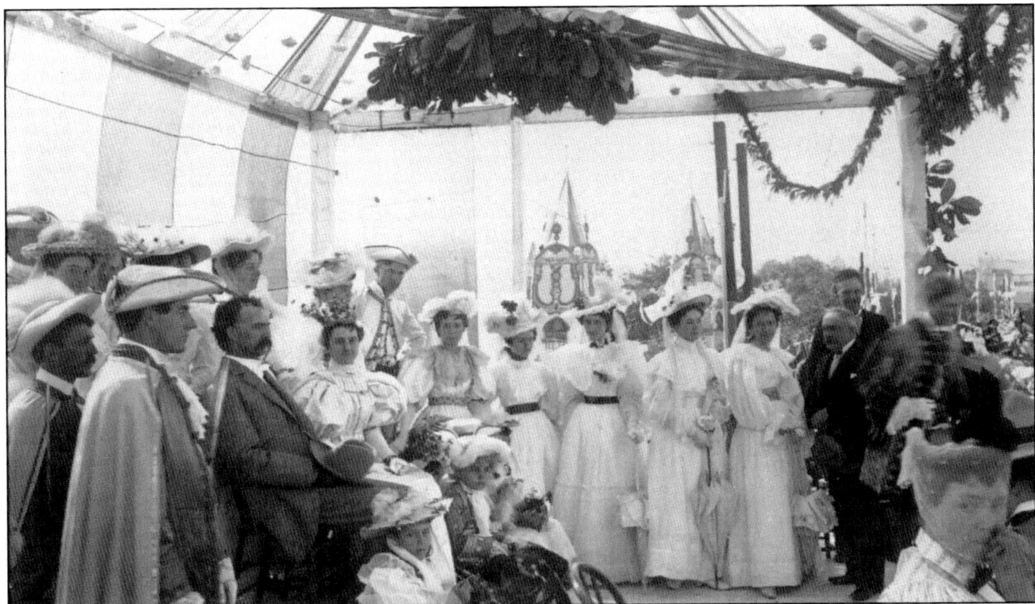

When Democrat William Jeter accepted appointment as lieutenant governor in 1895, he became the first Santa Cruzan to hold a statewide office. Serving as program chair for the second water carnival in 1896 and representing the governor, Jeter is shown here presiding over the festival with its queen, Josephine "Josie" Turcott. The local Chinese band entered a float in this carnival. (Courtesy of Covello & Covello.)

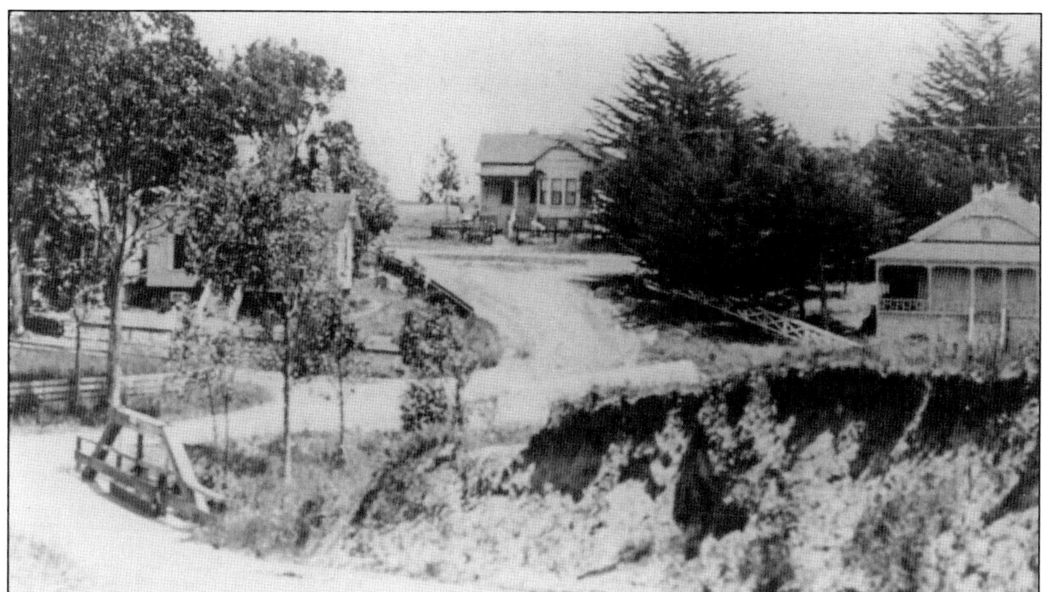

In this 1890s view, East Cliff Drive curves from Seabright Bridge along the edge of the Cove to Railroad Street past quaint cottages on the left. The Craftsman-style home of Robert and Marion Rice Kennedy, of Fresno, at right, became the first structure on the bay side of the new street, now 1580 East Cliff Drive. The Jorys, of Stockton, chose the more formal Eastlake style for their summer residence, at center top, which today is 122 Seabright Avenue. (Courtesy of Joan Kimble Miller-Prescott.)

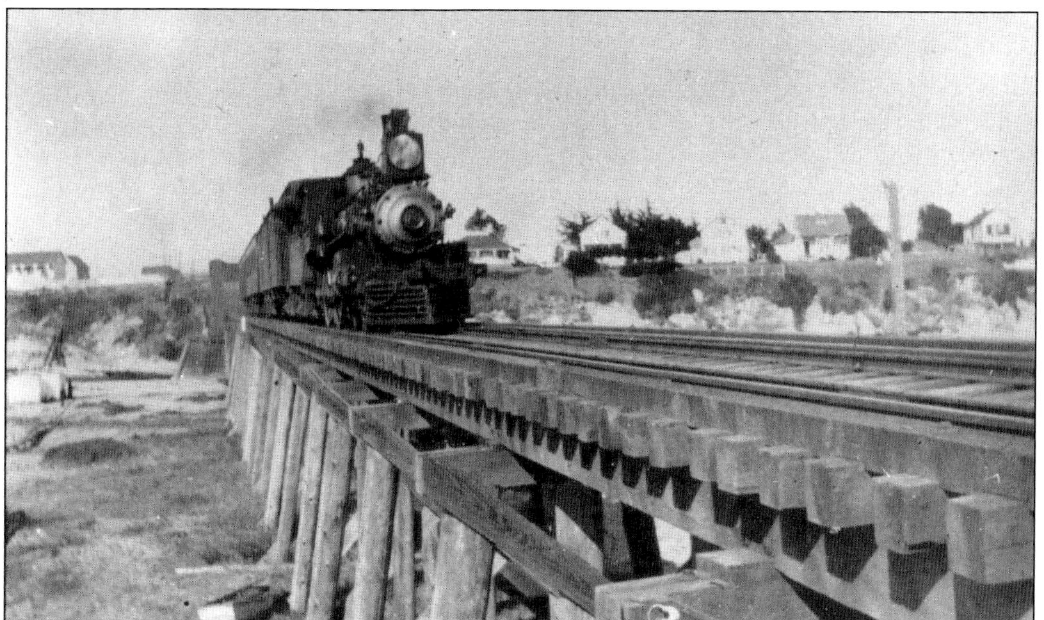

A Southern Pacific train, one of a dozen a day passing through Seabright, crosses the San Lorenzo River, with East Cliff homes in the background. Temporary footbridges across the river routinely washed out in the winter, tempting pedestrians to cross the trestle. After multiple injuries and at least one death, Seabrightans would create a better alternative within a decade. (Courtesy of MAH.)

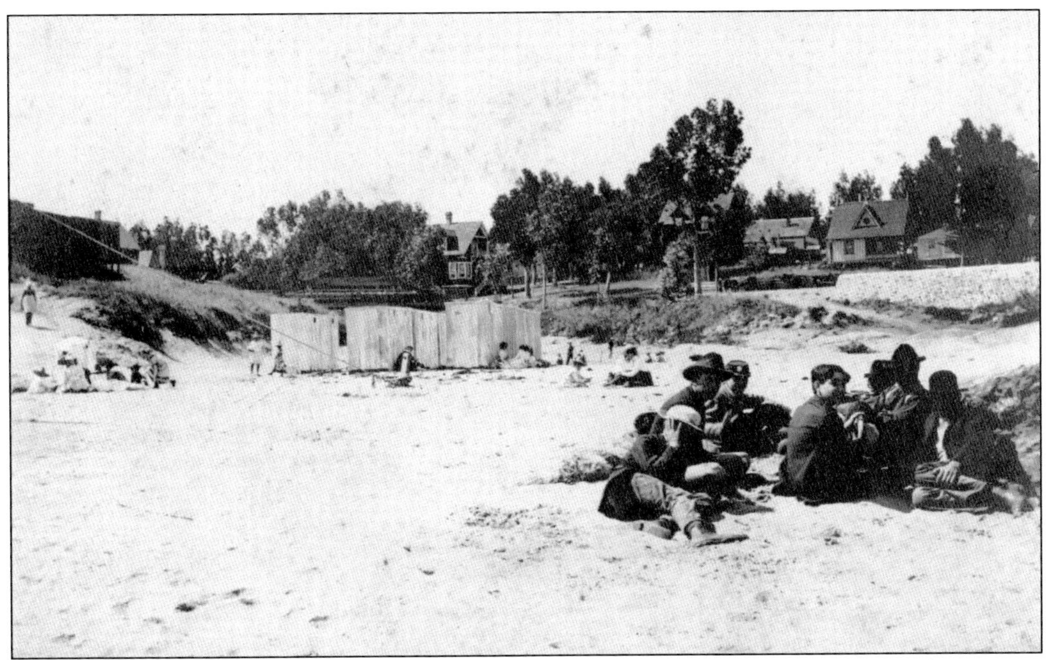

"Seabright is becoming quite a popular suburban resort," advised the *Santa Cruz Surf* in August 1900. "The beach is clean and timid bathers now have a rope on which to cling." That rope is visible in front of the boxy dressing room at left, and above right is the latest civic improvement—a stone retaining wall to protect against high tides. (Courtesy of MAH.)

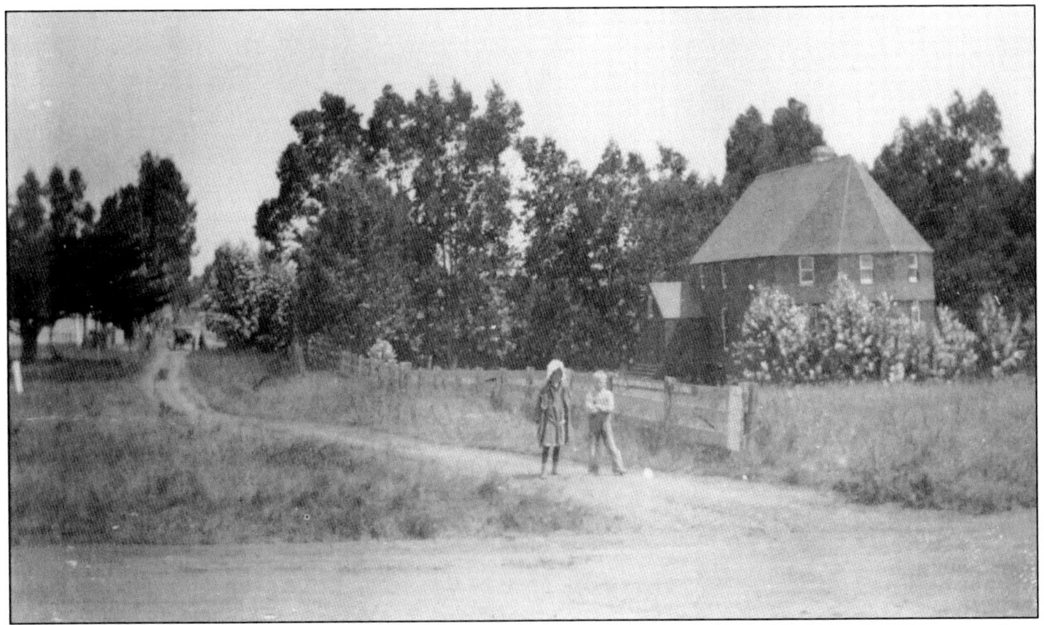

William Tyrrell, an elderly bachelor, purchased a lot on the former Alhambra campground in 1893. Creating his own architectural design, he made use of beach lumber foraged after winter floods. Tyrrell's three-story building at 114 Pilkington Avenue alarmed neighbors who feared he would convert it into a hotel. Meanwhile, the dirt bed of his bottom floor proved excellent for raising chickens. (Courtesy of MAH.)

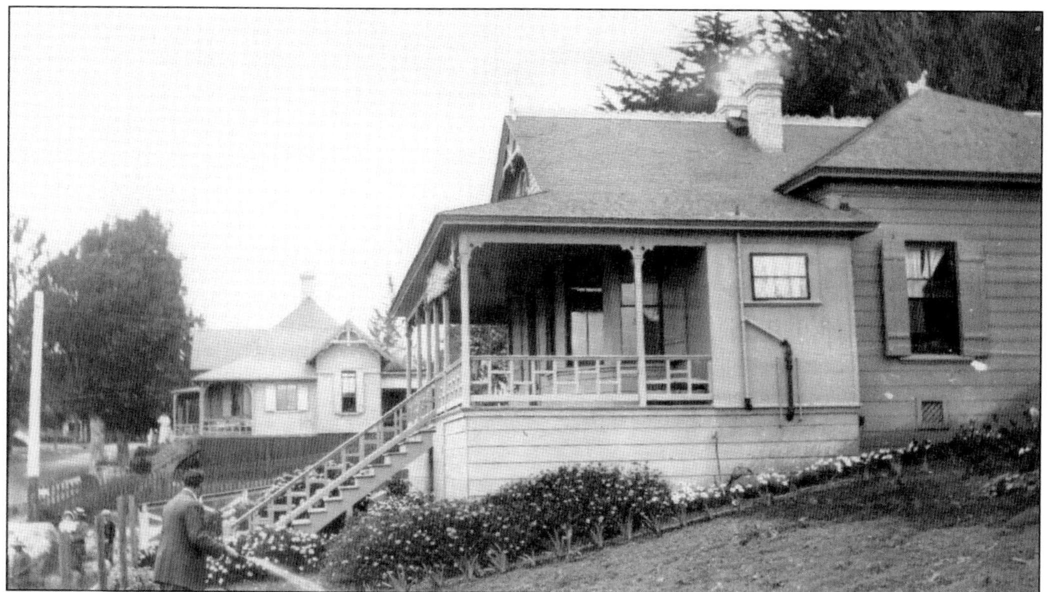

Each summer, the Kennedy family packed their baggage in a freight wagon and boarded their surrey for the three-day journey from Fresno to Seabright. The Crydenwises, of San José, owned the house across the street at 104 Cypress Avenue. After a storm in November 1903, the elder Mr. Crydenwise, trapped beneath a log, drowned while gathering driftwood. (Courtesy of Joan Kimble Miller-Prescott.)

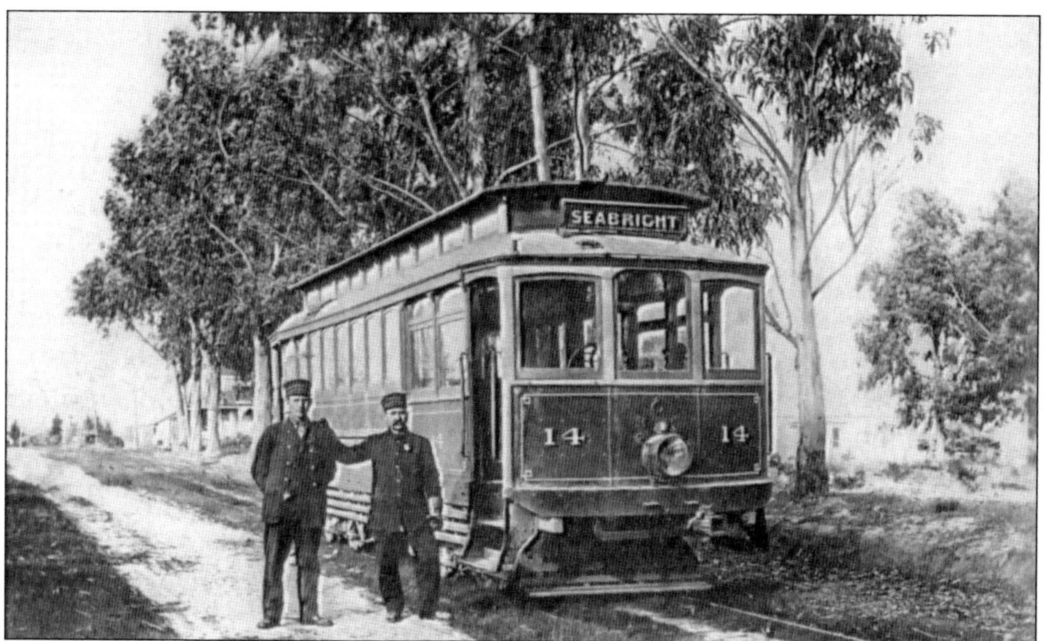

"Those who have spent their vacation at Santa Cruz, Seabright, or Capitola," proclaimed the *Santa Cruz Sentinel* in July 1903, "have witnessed the vast advantages of electric roads [i.e. trolleys] as builders of a community." Santa Cruzans attending the weekly dance at Seabright Hall boarded this electric trolley when the party ended. (Courtesy of MAH.)

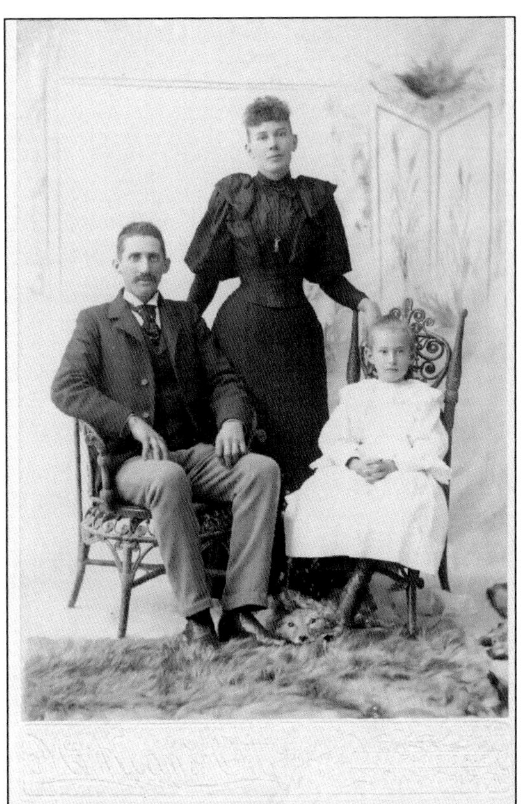

After the death of Thomas Pilkington in 1888, his son Thomas Jr. sold cottage lots and added Pilkington Avenue to the map. The younger son, James, seen here with his wife, Lillian, and daughter Maude, began building cottages on the cliff overlooking the bay. (Courtesy of Special Collections, University of California, Santa Cruz.)

In the spring of 1903, James Pilkington hurried to finish construction of his Seabright Hot Salt Water Baths. The spacious facility on the east side of the Cove would contain six steam-heated rooms, thirty dressing rooms for surf bathers, and even enough space to house the private Seabright Library. The grand opening in July featured a beach bonfire and taffy pull. The pole at right indicates that telephone service had recently reached the area. (Courtesy of MAH.)

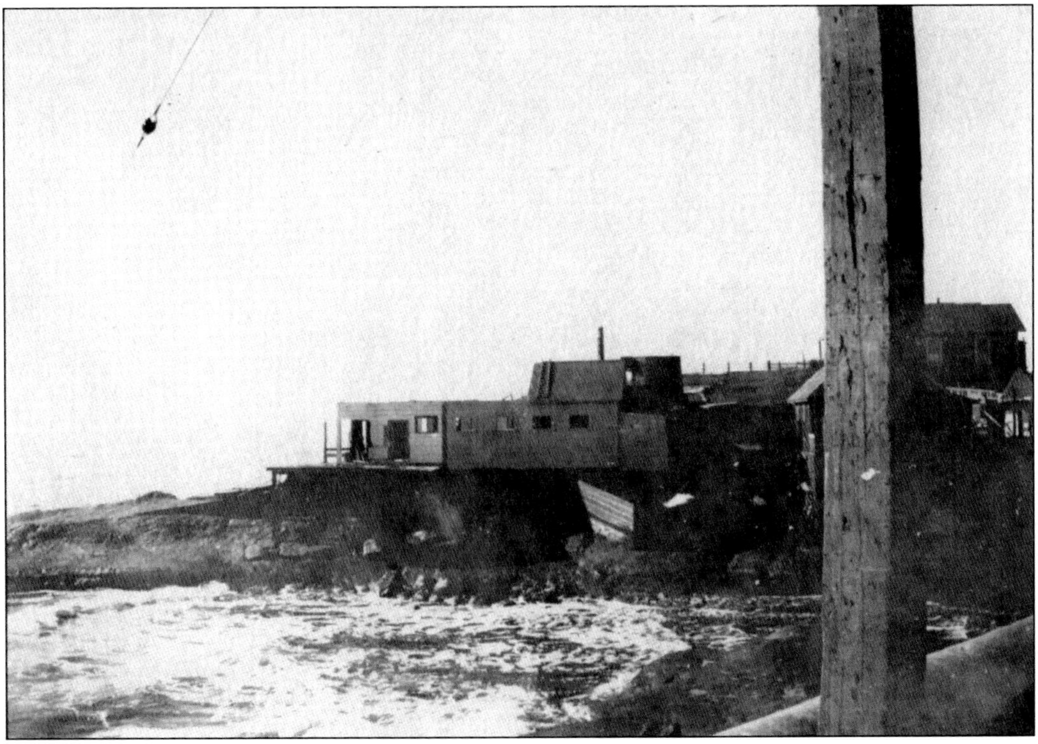

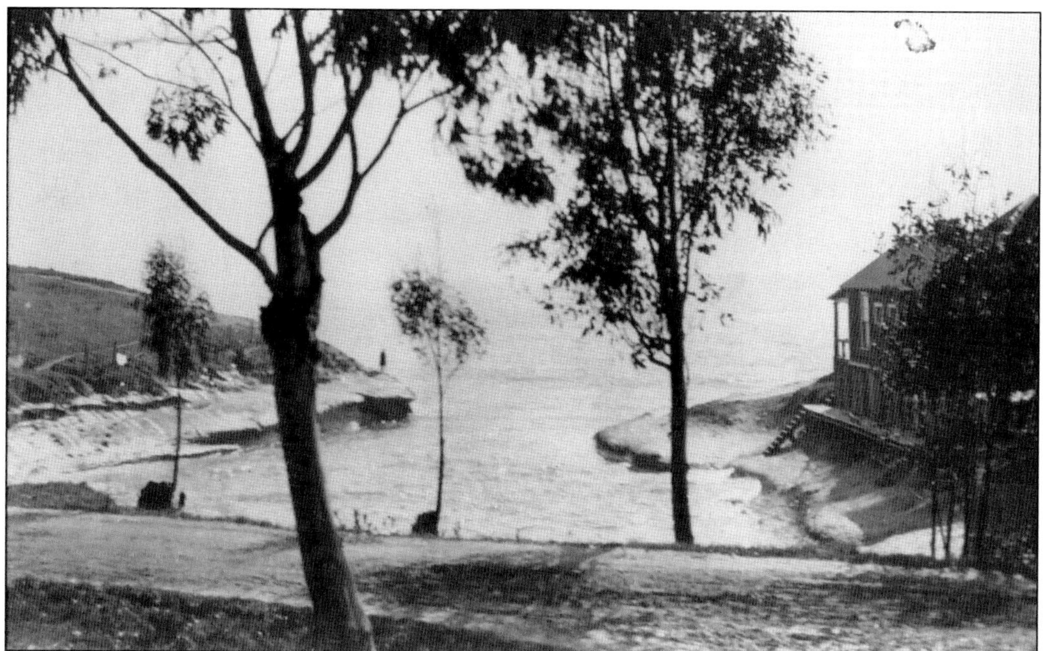

This scene typifies Seabright's winters as a high tide nearly reaches East Cliff Drive. As late as 1905, the vacant beachfront land at left had eluded developers. Nonetheless, James Pilkington's quaint bathhouse, on the other side of the Cove, Seabright Hot Salt Water Baths, compared favorably with the baths at Santa Cruz Main Beach. (Courtesy of MAH.)

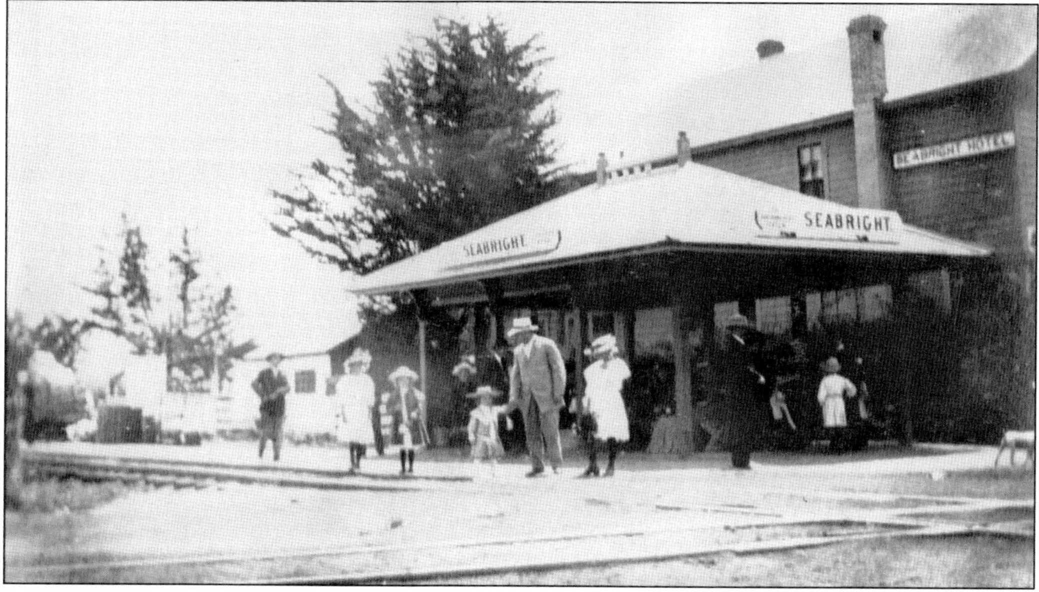

Opened in 1905, the Webber family's 20-room Seabright Hotel (right), located where today's Murray Street crosses Seabright Avenue, boomed with business. The local postmistress, Nettie Murray, had already spurred the development of Seabright's business district. She regularly met the Southern Pacific's mail trains and toted the pouches to her small office across from the station. Simultaneously managing the neighborhood's first store, Nettie used the post office window for dispensing groceries to patrons. (Courtesy of MAH.)

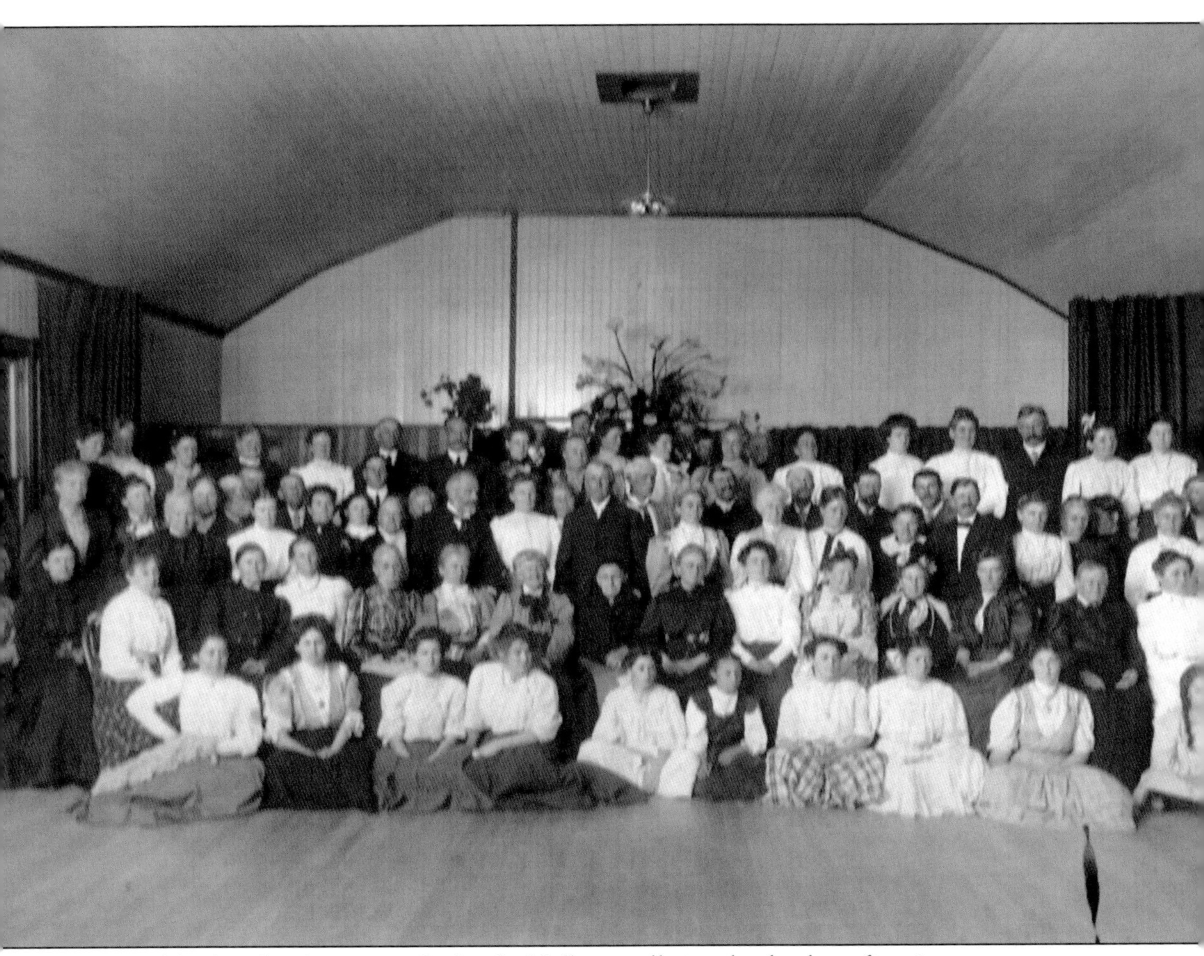

Neighborhood gatherings in Seabright Hall typically involved at least five times as many women as men. At the center of this social occasion are local leaders—Susan Tyrrell, in black, is in the middle of the second row, with Elizabeth Forbes seated to her immediate left. Maude Pilkington is second from left in the first row. Many local women, homeowners in their own right, used the Seabright Improvement Society for their collective voice. For example, society members, joined by James Pilkington, campaigned to have their village-like community annexed to Santa Cruz. On January 17, 1905, when voters approved the idea, the population of greater Santa Cruz increased from 7,000 to 10,000 in one day. At long last, all residents of the east and west sides of the San Lorenzo River united under one name and one municipal government. (Courtesy of SCMNH.)

Three

Public Works with Panache

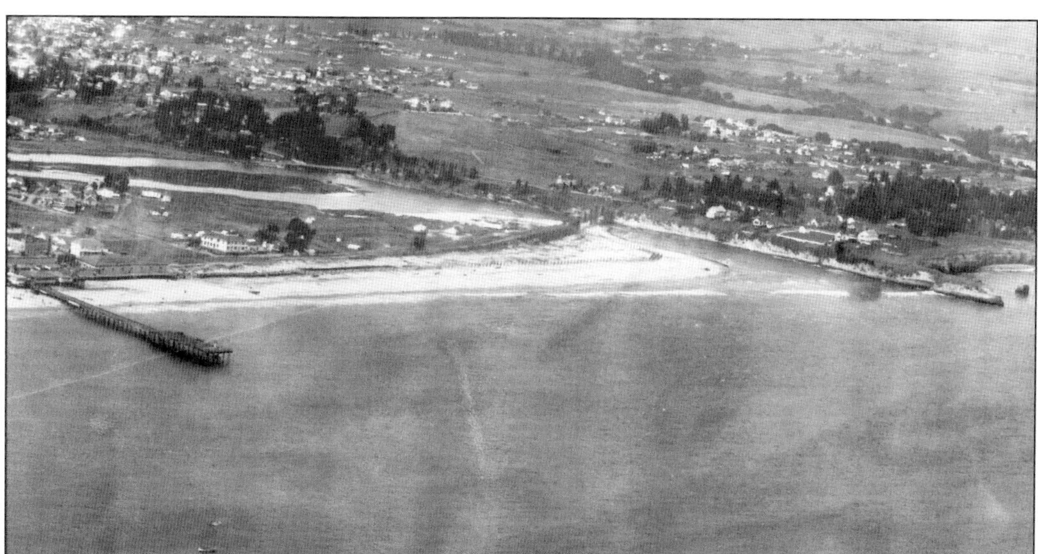

Renowned commercial photographer George R. Lawrence brought his balloon-mounted, panoramic camera to Santa Cruz in 1906. His aerial view shows Santa Cruz Main Beach from the Pleasure Pier to the San Lorenzo River. A new Southern Pacific bridge, at center, crosses the river. The East Cliff, well defined by whitish sandstone, has several houses and, on the other side of San Lorenzo Point, Pinnacle Rock stands out at far right. (Courtesy of the Library of Congress.)

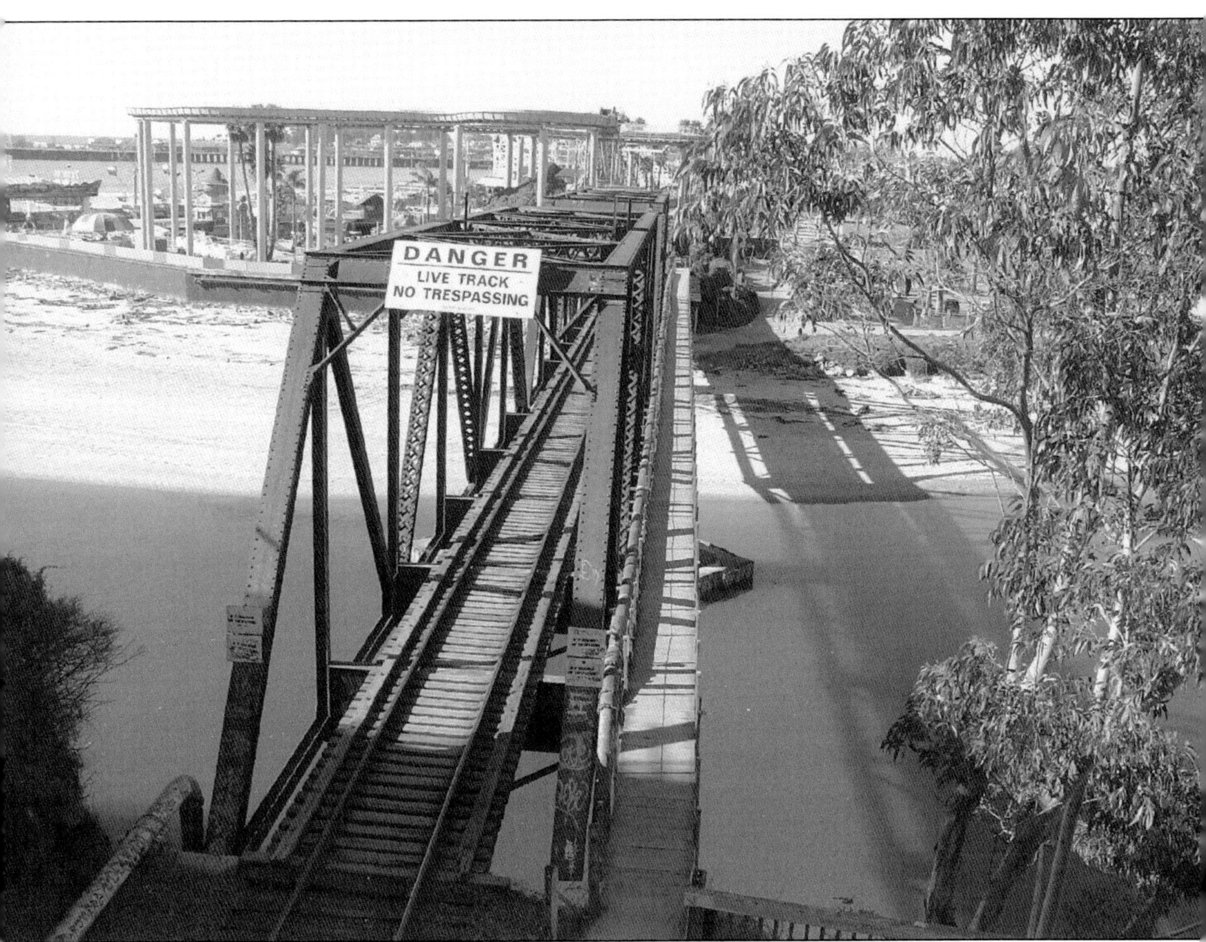

Soon after Seabright's annexation to Santa Cruz, the Seabright Improvement Society enjoyed another victory—this time providing residents with a more direct connection to their city. When the latest footbridge across the river washed out to sea in May 1905, locals sent a delegation to meet with city leaders, requesting that a permanent, steel pedestrian bridge be attached to the Southern Pacific Railroad trestle. James Pilkington led the successful campaign and Seabrightans raised 90 percent of the cost. Work was successfully completed in March 1906 and the Improvement Society sponsored a flight of stairs between the structure and East Cliff. The following year, the Santa Cruz Beach Boardwalk opened and tourists quickly made use of the walkway. This 2004 photograph provides the clearest extant illustration of the Seabright footbridge, much as it appeared a century earlier. (Courtesy of SNA.)

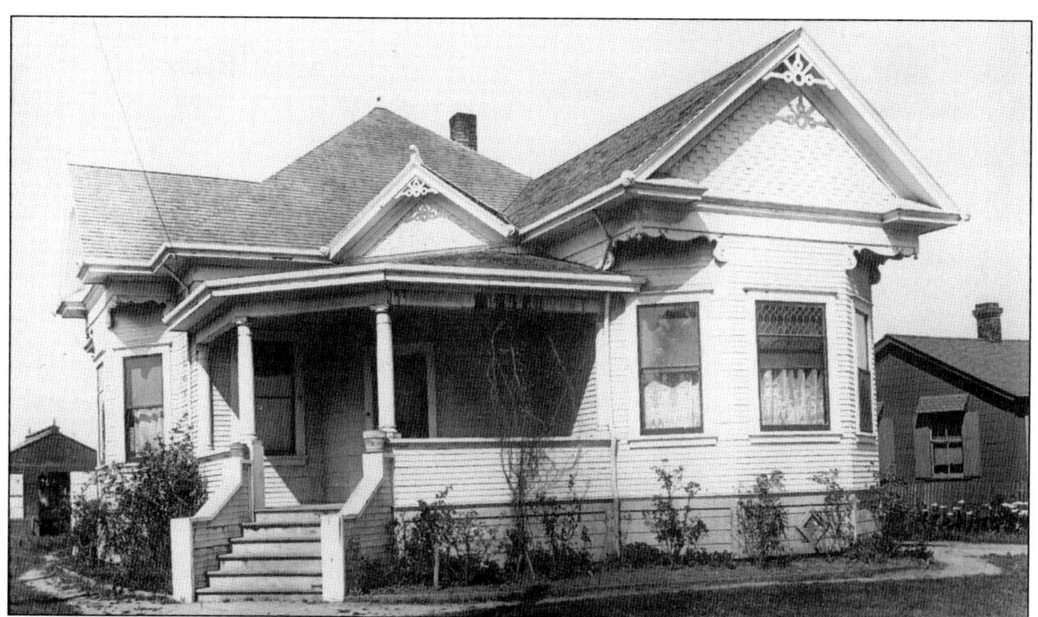

James Pilkington, having finished improvements to beach properties, focused on his additional land near the Seabright Station. He completed the family home on the northwest corner of Railroad and Laguna, now Seabright Avenue and Murray Street, which included the wonderful convenience of indoor plumbing. In June 1906, Pilkington became Santa Cruz's street superintendent—a true visionary promoting not just good roads but also bridges, sewers, and electric lights. A year later, Seabright elected him its first representative to the city council. Cooperating with the Improvement Society, Pilkington's tireless support for public works earned him the unofficial title of "Mayor of Seabright." (Courtesy of Special Collections, University of California, Santa Cruz.)

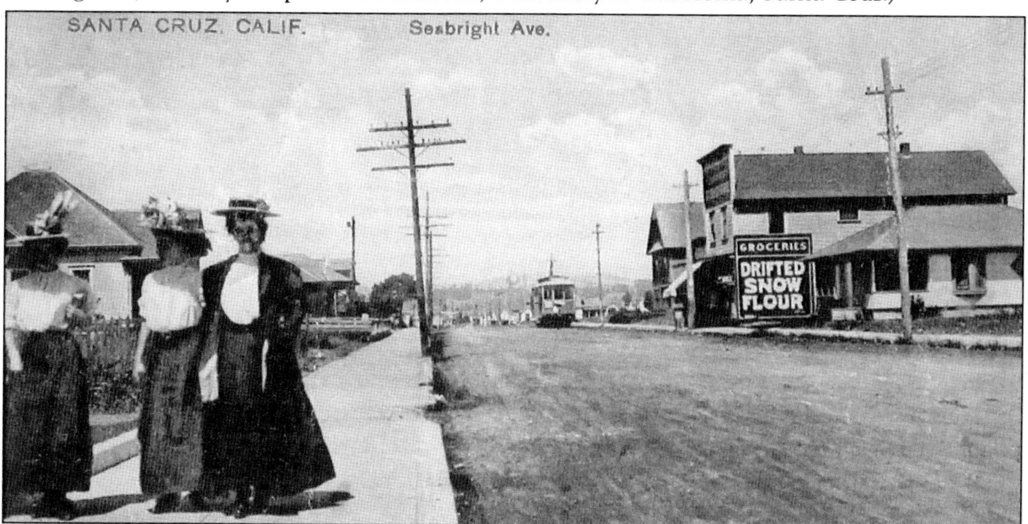

One of "Mayor" Pilkington's pet projects—concrete sidewalks—captured the enthusiasm of other local businessmen like Celesto P. Balzari of the Seabright Cash Store, the building with the "western" front, at right. Three ladies, at left, wear fashionable hats while strolling down the new walkway. The postcard's caption reflects another Pilkington-assisted development. Pilkington began his career as city councilman by voting to approve a name change for the major thoroughfare, and Railroad Street became Seabright Avenue in 1907. (Courtesy of SNA.)

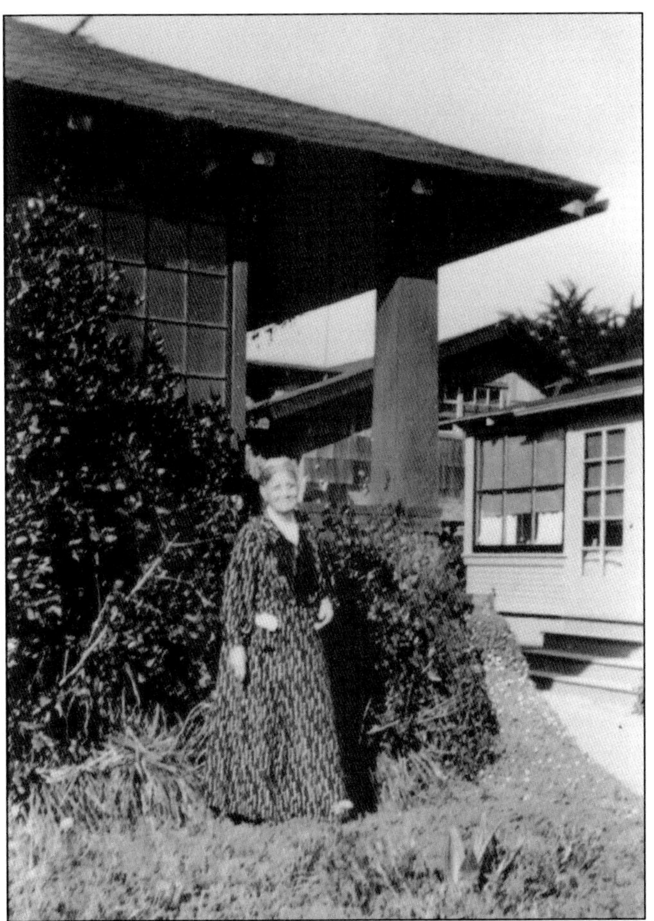

Ada Moulton, at left, served as one of the first schoolteachers in nearby Scotts Valley, beginning in the 1870s. In 1907, Maria B. Thompson, an architect and Seabright neighbor, designed a home for Moulton on Dashaway Street, now 1181 East Cliff Drive, seen below. A proponent of the simple bungalow style advocated by the magazine *Craftsman*, Thompson's "true California" homes featured large living rooms, numerous windows, and "buffet kitchens." Instead of painted interiors, the architect's designs used local redwood. Moulton enhanced her property by adding an octagonal cottage at the rear of the lot, bottom right, emulating the original one of her friend Elizabeth Forbes. (Both, courtesy of Michael Eck.)

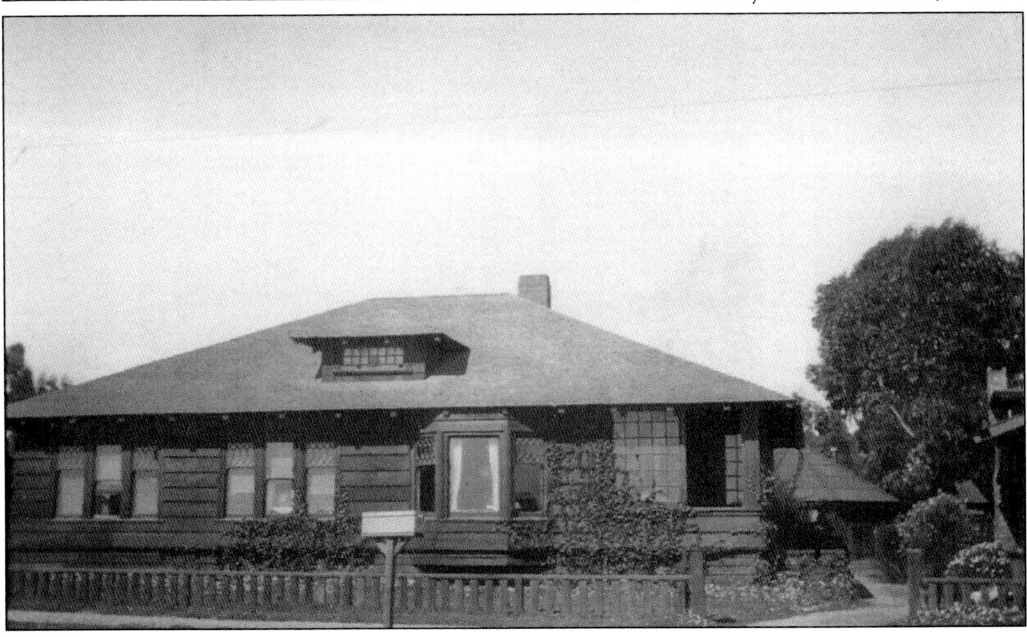

Susan Tyrrell and Elizabeth Forbes founded a private library that served the community for more than a decade. In the summer of 1907, a large canvas tent housed a temporary local branch of the Santa Cruz Free Library System, which was open three days a week and presided over by Irma Cole. (Courtesy of Santa Cruz Public Library.)

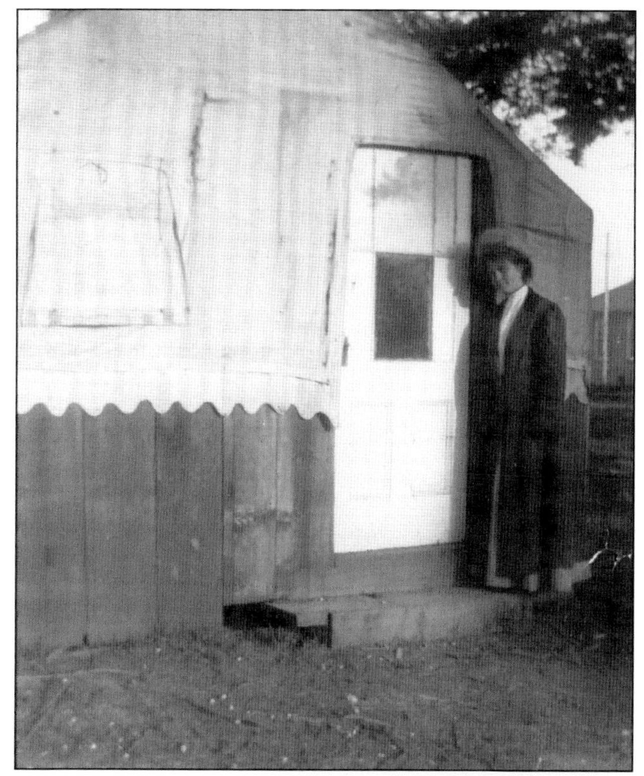

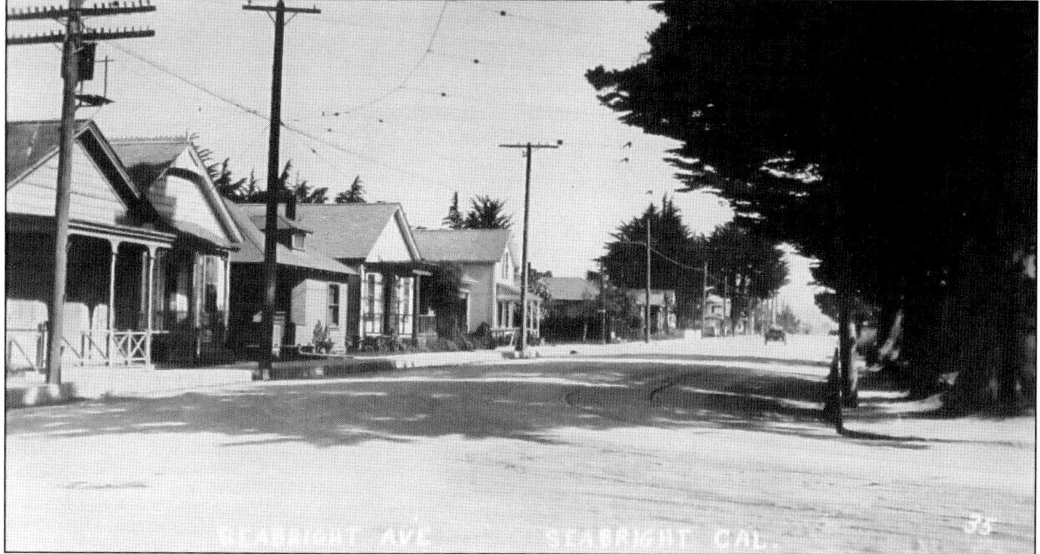

A row of vernacular beach cottages filled the first block of Seabright Avenue starting at the corner of Atlantic Avenue. Most were painted with a bright color, such as red, green, blue, or vermillion. The increasing concentration of dwellings provoked a campaign in favor of house numbers and distinctive street names. Frustrated merchants, attempting to make deliveries, objected to the overuse of common names like Second Street in Seabright, Second Street in Seabright Park, and Second Street in Santa Cruz but this problem did not get corrected until 1921, when a city ordinance changed most local street names. (Courtesy of the Ross Gibson collection.)

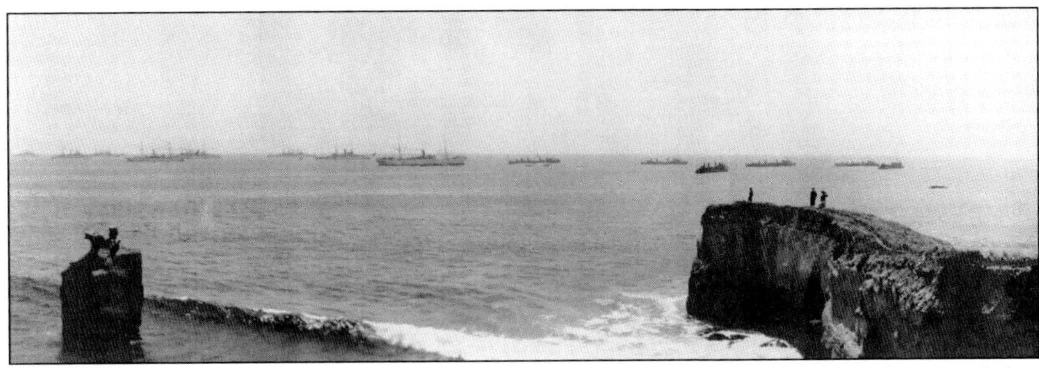

Pres. Theodore Roosevelt's Great White Fleet visited Santa Cruz on the final leg of its round-the-world trip. To fire salutes, the local Navy Reserve stationed a field gun on East Cliff. In this 1908 photograph, San Lorenzo Point provides onlookers a view of the historic moment. For the first time since its departure from Virginia, the entire fleet reunited in a single harbor, where Santa Cruzans wined and dined the sailors and officers for three days. The armada then embarked for San Francisco. (Courtesy of the Loewenstein family.)

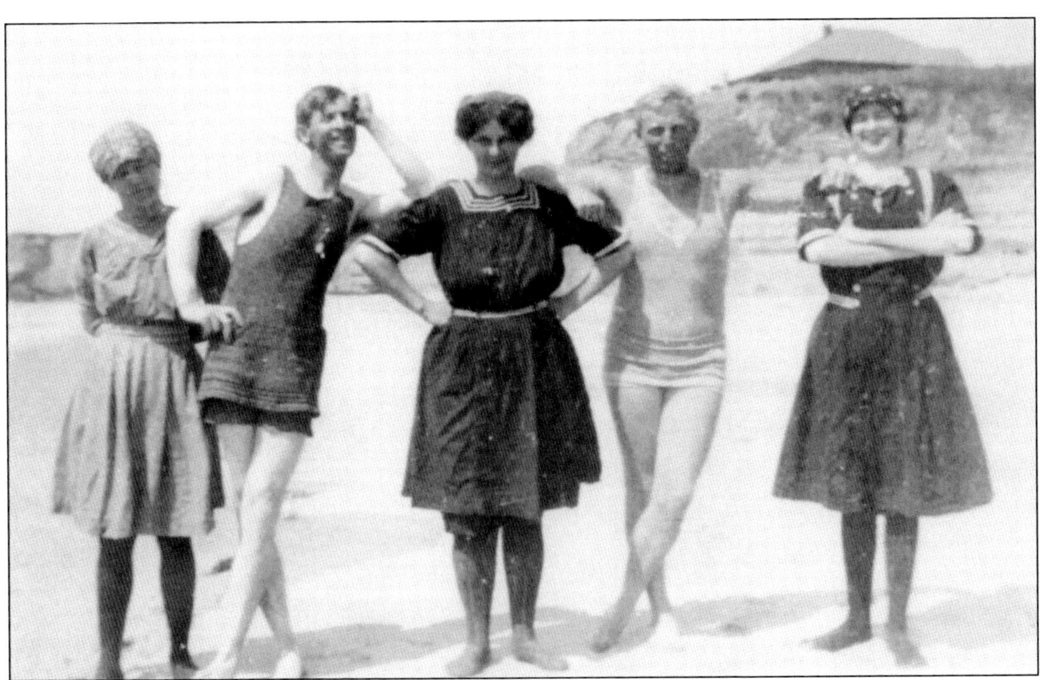

Seabright beachgoers model 1910 swimwear fashions, with ladies still covered from head to toe. At top right, perched on the edge of the cliff, is the home of Adriana Van Kaathoven, a Dutch-born widow. She enjoyed one of the neighborhood's best panoramic views, but cliff erosion by winter waves posed a threat to her peace of mind. (Courtesy of the Engfer family.)

As the population grew, merchants moved to Seabright Avenue, where the Balzari family opened the Seabright Cash Store in 1907. Initially, the building also contained the Seabright Post Office, but by 1910, burgeoning business at the store required the construction of an annex for the post office. Today, La Posta restaurant at 538 Seabright Avenue occupies this old building. Butcher John C. Hodges, the driver of the local meat wagon, established the business seen below in 1908 and successfully ran it into the 1920s. Modern Seabrightans will recognize the altered meat market as the home of Brady's Yacht Club at 413 Seabright Avenue. (Right, courtesy of SNA; below, courtesy of MAH.)

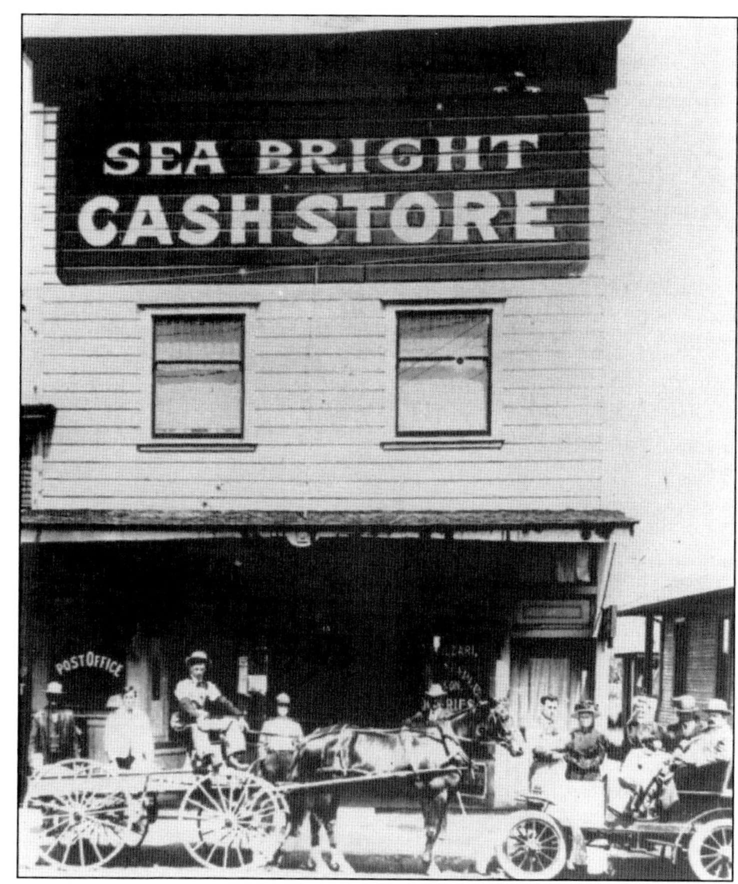

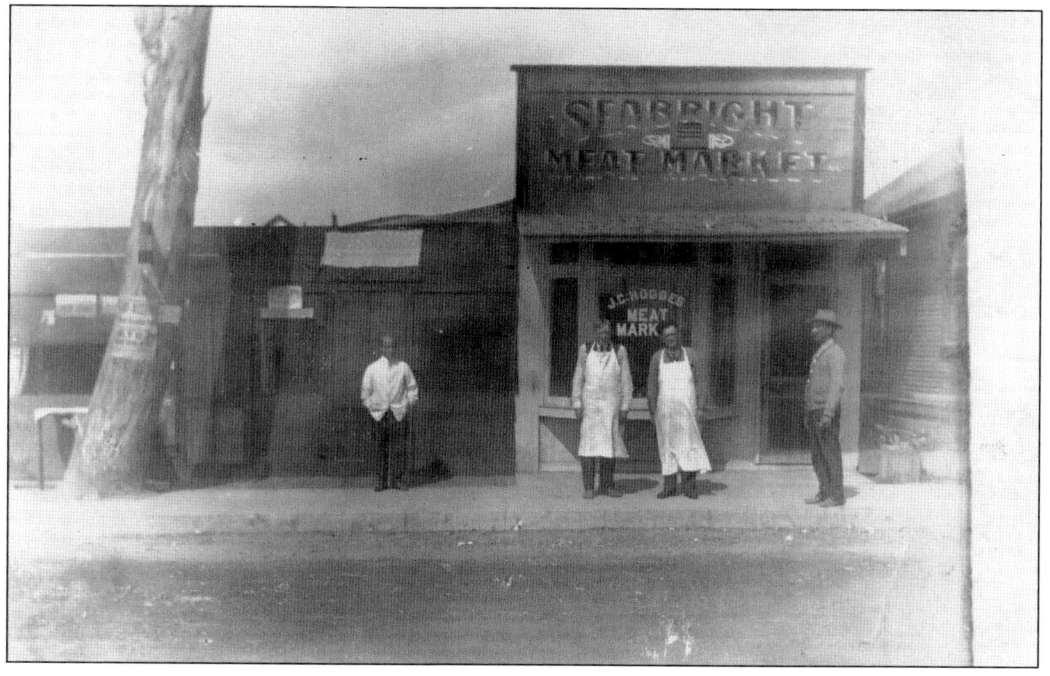

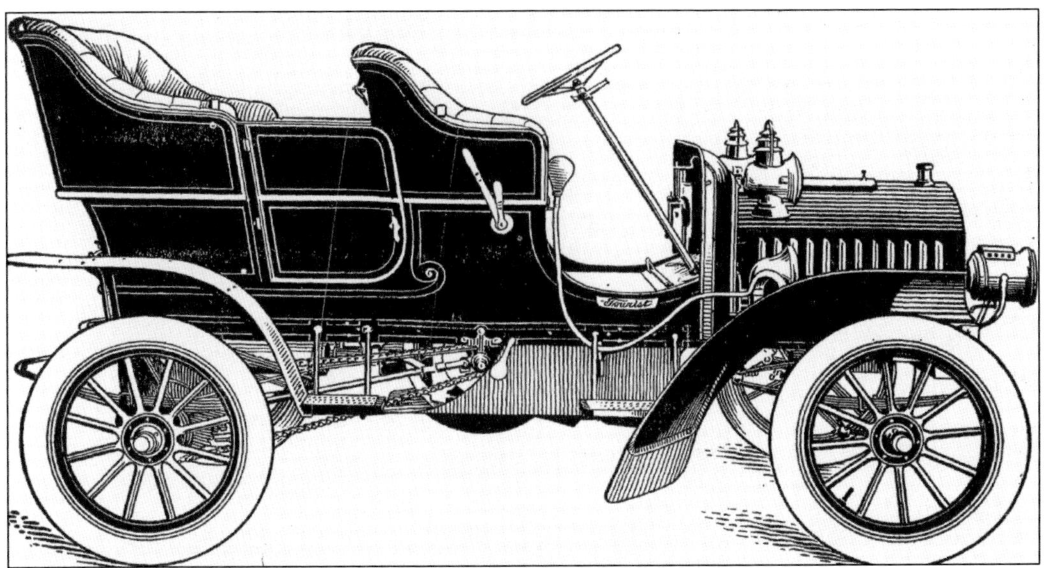

With the coming of the automobile, the area's undeveloped easternmost section became accessible. In 1908, Robert and Nan Scott Barton made the regular summer trip from Fresno in their new car, a Royal Tourist, the model depicted here. Nan devoted her vacation to mastering the art of driving. The couple's bungalow, completed in 1909, occupied a prime bay-view location at 1907 East Cliff Drive between Third and Fourth Avenues and remained in the family for several decades. (Courtesy of the Brown collection.)

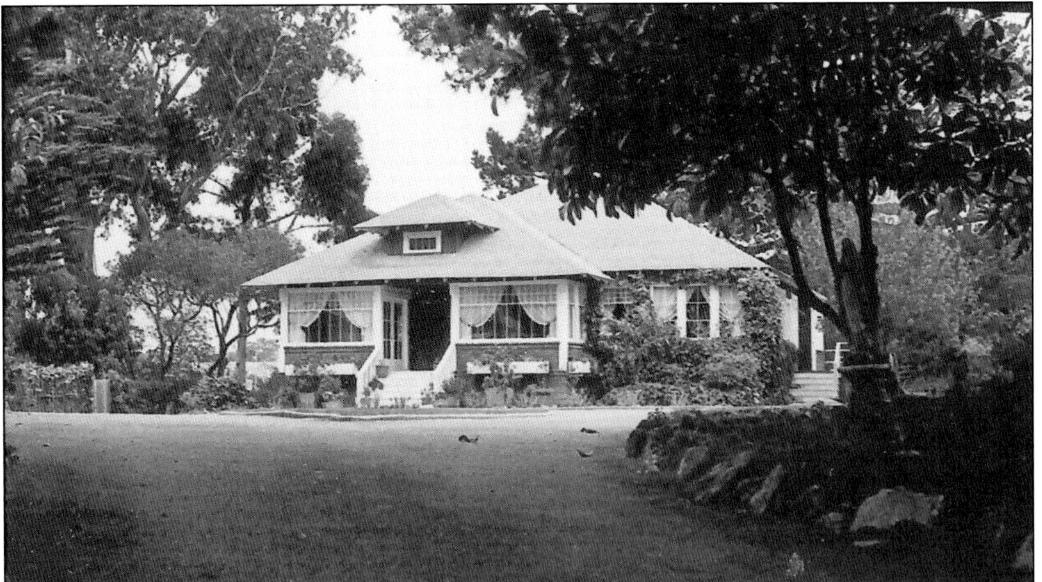

Following the Bartons' lead, other families built on nearby vacant lots. On the idyllic north corner of Fourth and Atlantic Avenues, Walter G. Willmore constructed a Craftsman-style cottage in 1910 and sold it to Robert Armstrong, a retired fruit grower from Davis, in 1913. Fresnans Arthur B. Tarpey and his wife, the former Hope Vickers, bought it in 1920 and named it Laguna Vista, listed in the *Santa Cruz Historic Building Survey, Vol. 1*. Hope hosted Old World garden parties on the lush grounds of 206 Fourth Avenue. One such event was the elegant wedding of Blanche Barton, daughter of Robert and Nan, to George O'Brien. (Courtesy of City of Santa Cruz.)

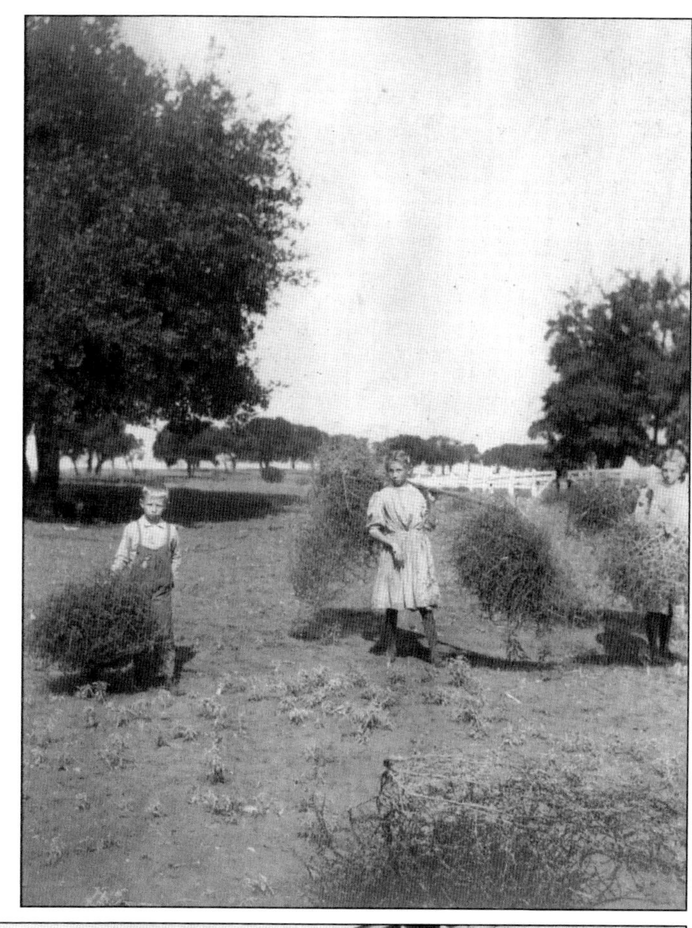

Adriana Van Kaathoven's grandchildren gather brush from the fields of the old Alhambra campground to prepare for a beach bonfire in 1909. Where they stand is the future site of Tyrrell Park, and a row of trees behind them marks East Cliff Drive. (Courtesy of MAH.)

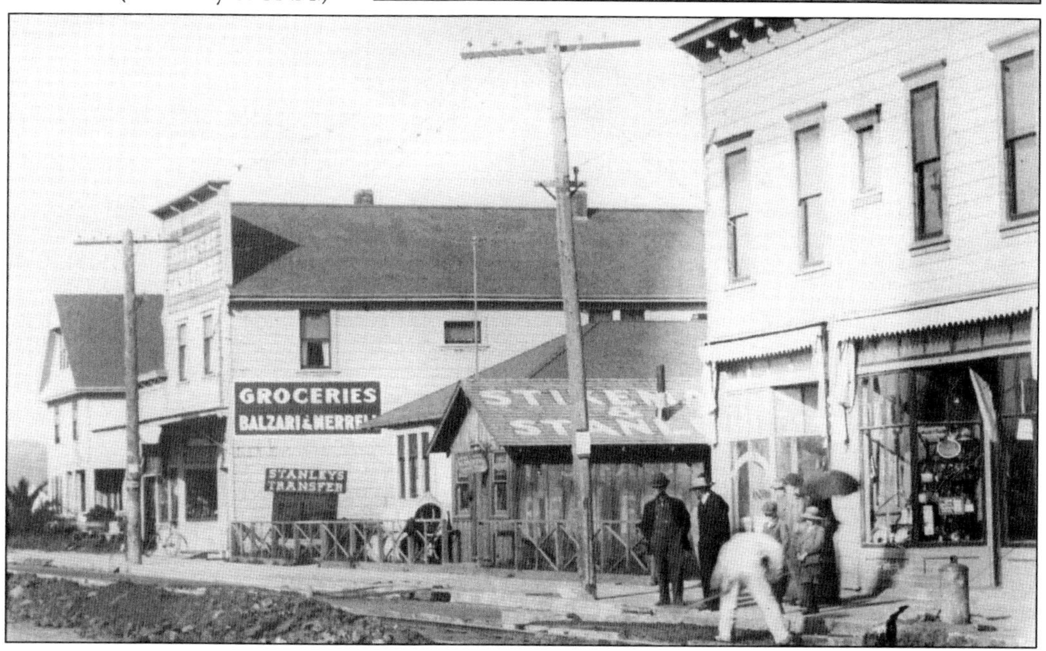

James Pilkington built the two-story business building seen to the right on Seabright Avenue, across the street from the Southern Pacific depot. His plumbing business occupied most of the lower floor, while the upper half housed summer tourists in rooms with electricity and hot water. Pilkington graciously opened his building for elections and other civic activities. (Courtesy of SNA.)

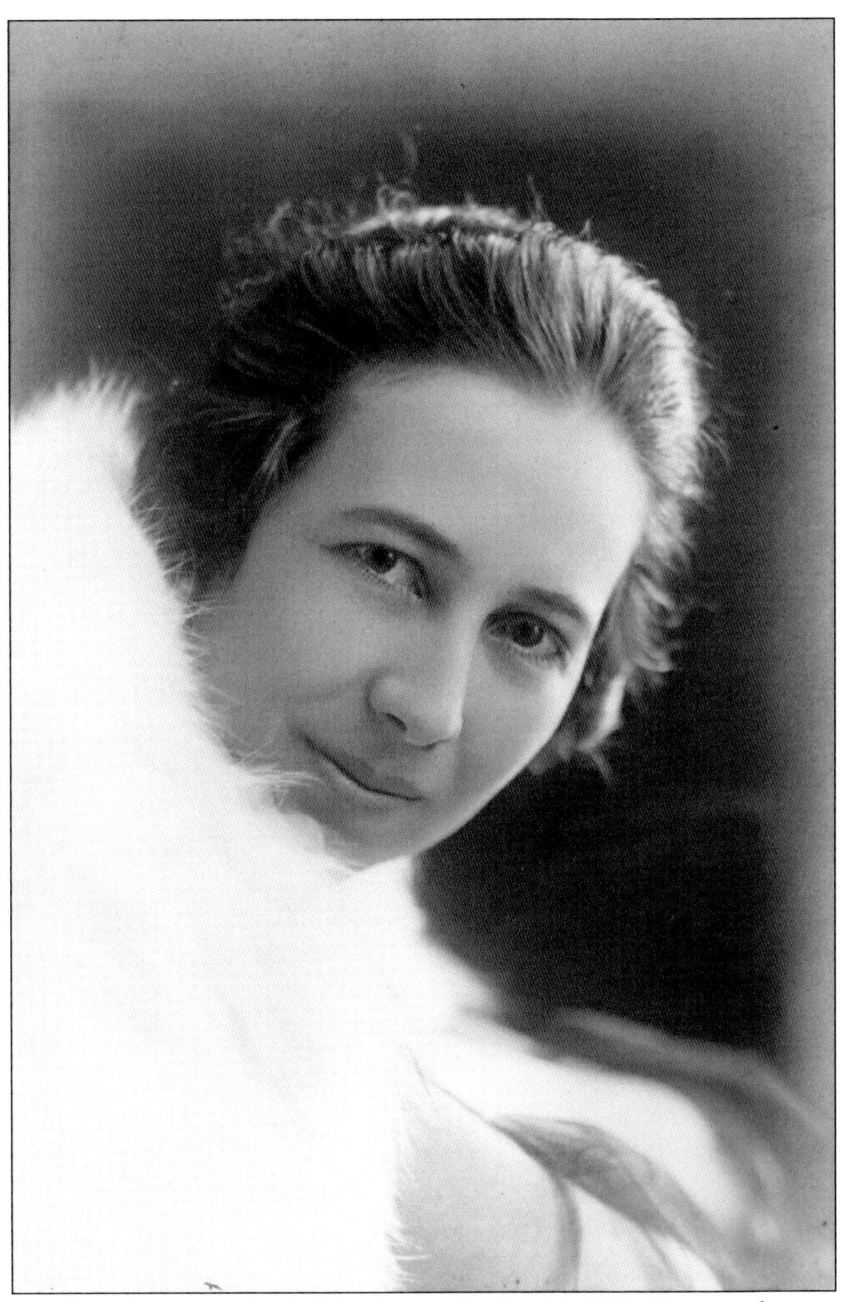

Women won the right to vote in California on October 10, 1911. Hearing the news, Maude Pilkington—in her early twenties and having grown up in the company of Seabright activists Lulu Greene, Susan Tyrrell, and Elizabeth Forbes—rushed to the county clerk's office to sign the roll. Since there would be no more elections that year, the clerk insisted that her request would waste paper, but "a short argument" ended in Maude's favor. A *Santa Cruz Evening News* writer thought that the historic certificate "should be framed and hung on the wall." Although Maude, the only daughter of James and Lily Pilkington, soon went to work for the *San Jose Mercury*, she regularly returned home to Seabright, especially on election days. (Courtesy of Special Collections, University of California, Santa Cruz.)

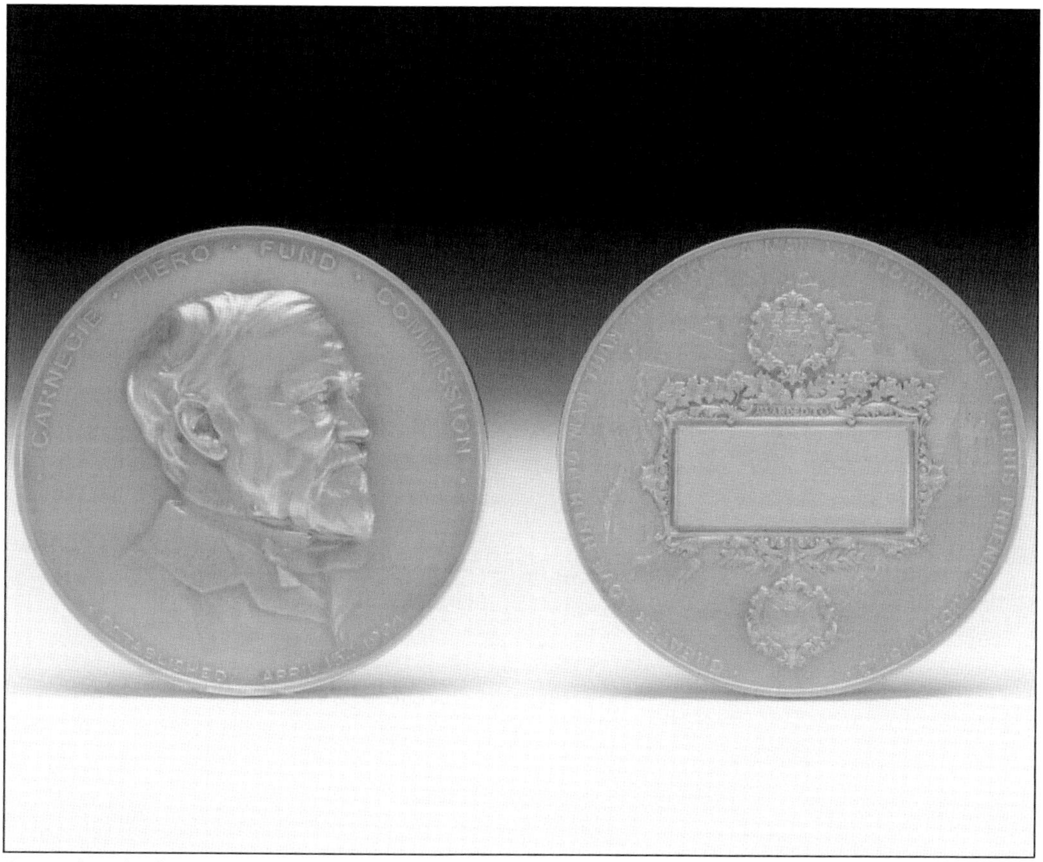

Conrad and Alice Gripenstraw Scholl (below left) settled near Seabright in the 1880s, where their son Louis grew up. A superb athlete at age 19, he, with the assistance of James Pilkington, saved Lue Quong from drowning. When the Chinese fisherman returned to offer Scholl his life savings, the rescuer kindly sent him home. Four years later, on July 9, 1911, when a canoe capsized in the waves of the river mouth, Scholl managed an arduous swim and pulled Ray Lanfear to Pinnacle Rock, where a boat picked them up. This feat earned Scholl (below right) a bronze Carnegie Hero Medal and $1,000 in 1913. (Above, courtesy of Carnegie Hero Commission; below, courtesy of Bart Gripenstraw.)

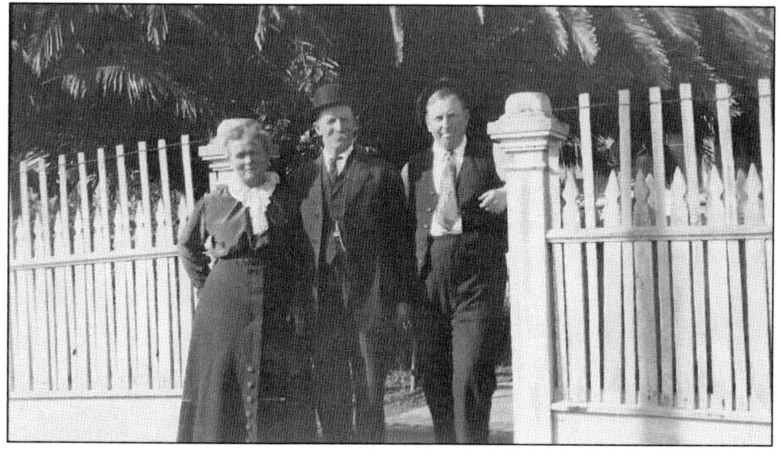

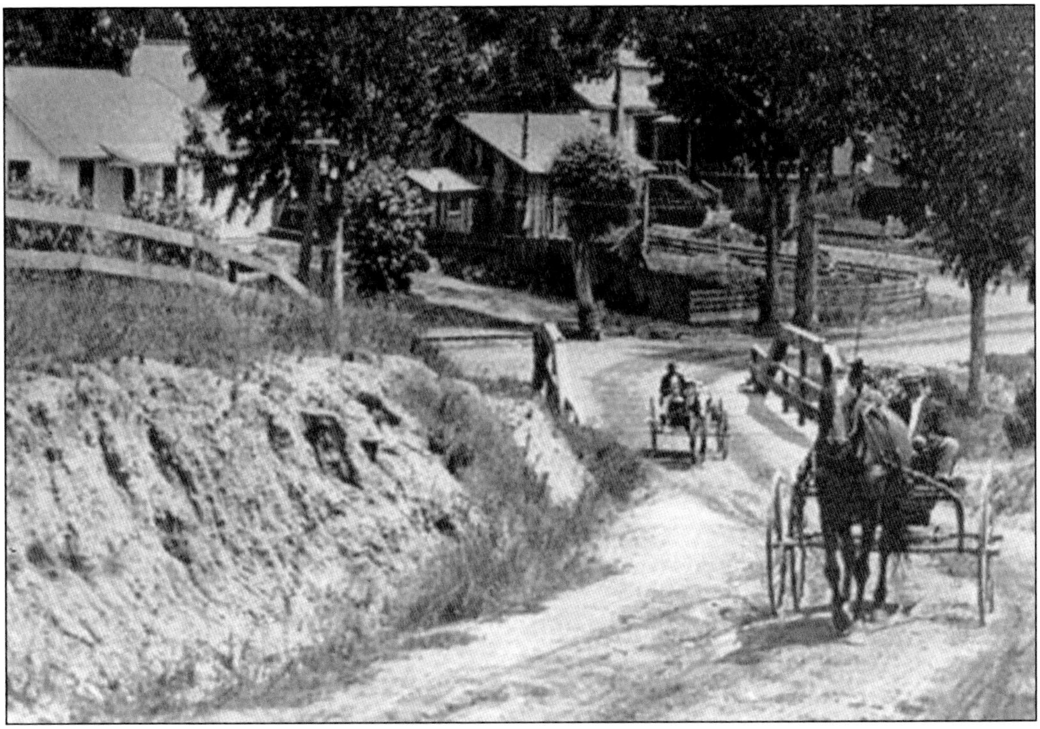

The older section of East Cliff Drive between San Lorenzo Point and the Cove, shown here in 1912, consisted of dust in summer and mud in winter, a steep grade, a rickety bridge, and no space for sidewalks. Residents urged the city council to fix these problems, which "contributed to a bad impression for summer visitors." The coming of the Carnegie library to East Cliff Drive a few years later galvanized the city into action. (Courtesy of Capitola Museum.)

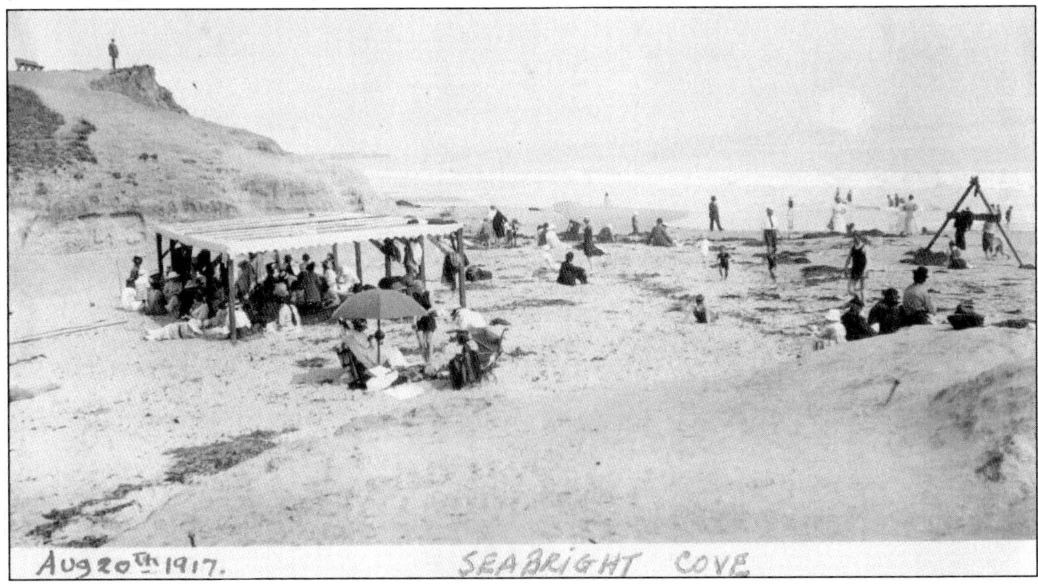

In this view of the Cove, some August beachgoers seek shade under a canopy. Additional amenities include the triangular structure at right—supporting a lifeline—and a bench atop the bluff at left, providing a convenient spot for watching the bay. (Courtesy of the Lionel T. Lenox collection.)

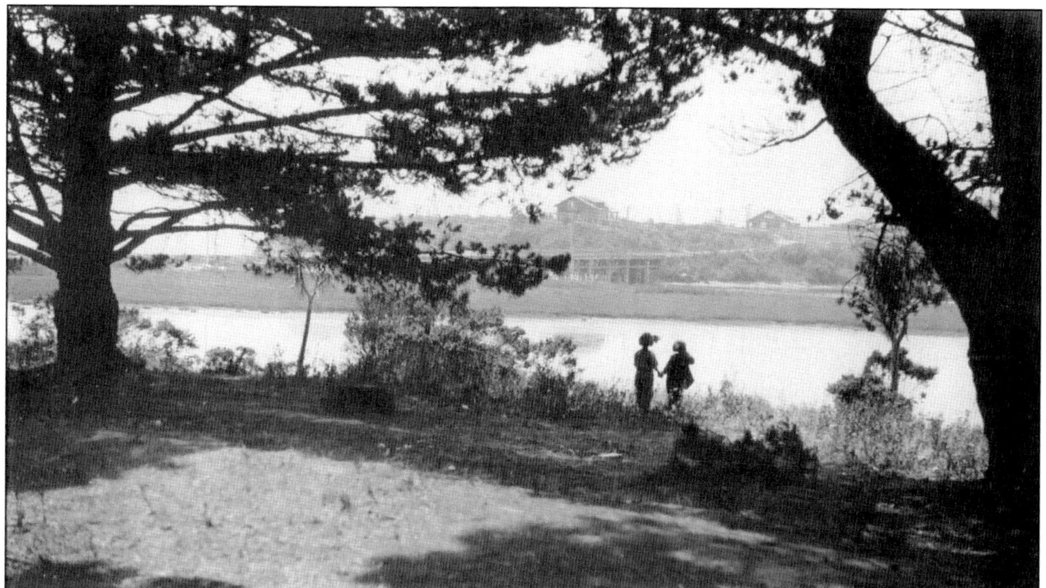

This bucolic scene, photographed from the Twin Lakes side of Woods Lagoon, at the edge of today's Small Craft Harbor, shows a few of the first homes on Seabright's easternmost boundary. Some of the earliest families attracted to the bluffs of Fourth Avenue were from the Bay Area and Fresno County. (Courtesy of the Lionel T. Lenox collection.)

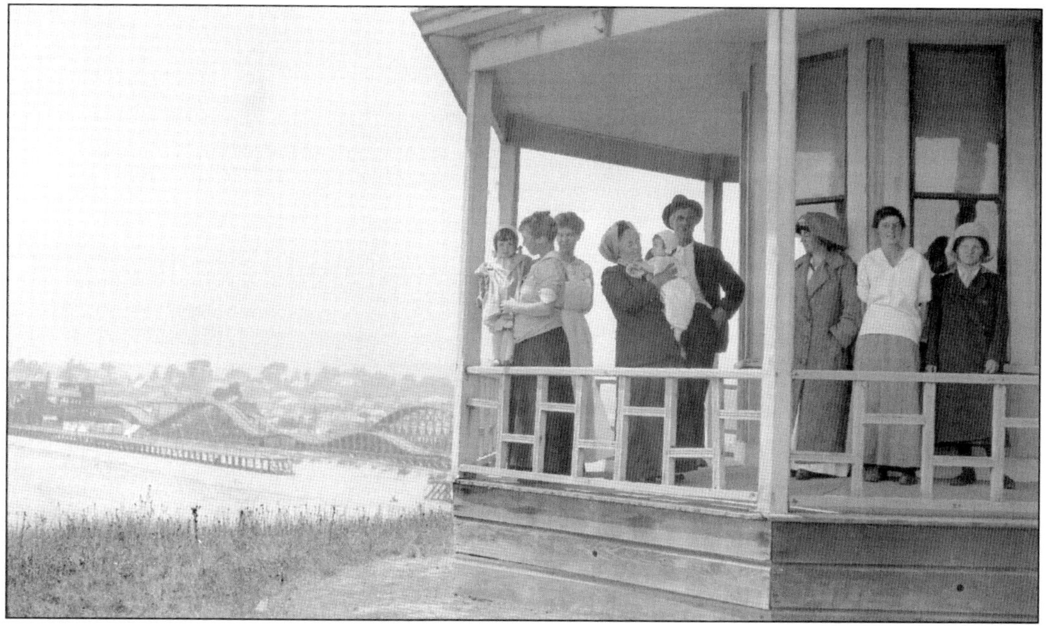

Three generations of the Lenox family gather in a popular summer rental, the McKendry house at San Lorenzo Point, in 1914. The porch looks out over Monterey Bay, the San Lorenzo River, Main Beach, the casino, and amusement park. The background shows the Thompson Scenic Railway, considered a type of roller coaster and predecessor to the 1924 Giant Dipper. (Courtesy of the Lionel T. Lenox collection.)

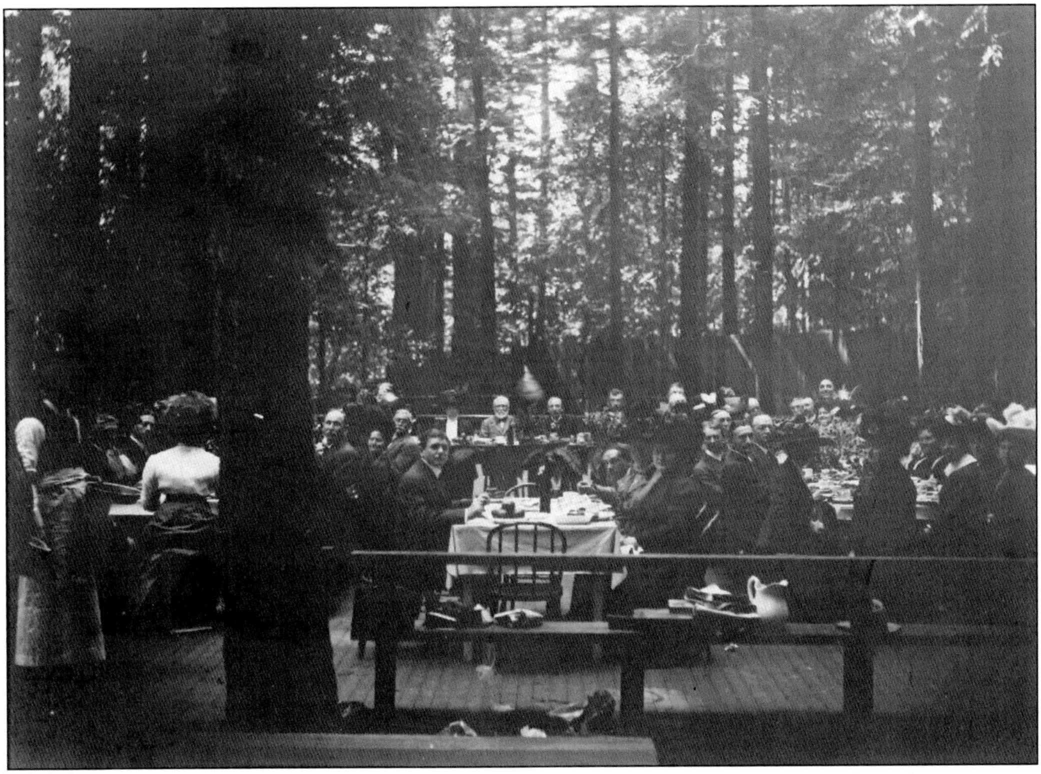

The Santa Cruz Free Library owed much to Andrew Carnegie, who funded its spacious downtown headquarters in 1904. On a visit to Santa Cruz County six years later, the multimillionaire philanthropist, back row with white beard, enjoyed a royal reception at this grand barbecue in the Big Trees near Felton. In the summer of 1913, library board president Dr. F.W. Bliss asked him for additional money to fund two branch libraries. Carnegie gave a conditional "yes" if the land for the buildings was donated and the cost per branch would not exceed $3,000. (Courtesy of Santa Cruz Public Library.)

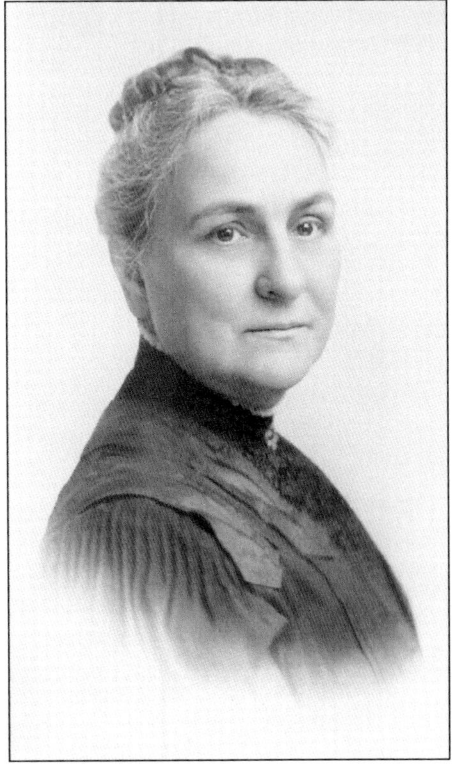

The Tyrrells, William and Susan, having settled in Seabright when it was no more than a village, were deeply committed to the community. Their brother John, a wealthy Chicago businessman, quietly provided for his eccentric siblings. John's daughter, Katherine Peck (left), spent summers in Seabright. When she heard that a donation of land could secure a first-class library, she quickly responded. Having inherited William's house and land in 1911, Peck offered the property's open space for a library and recreational purposes, to be known as Tyrrell Park. (Courtesy of SCMNH.)

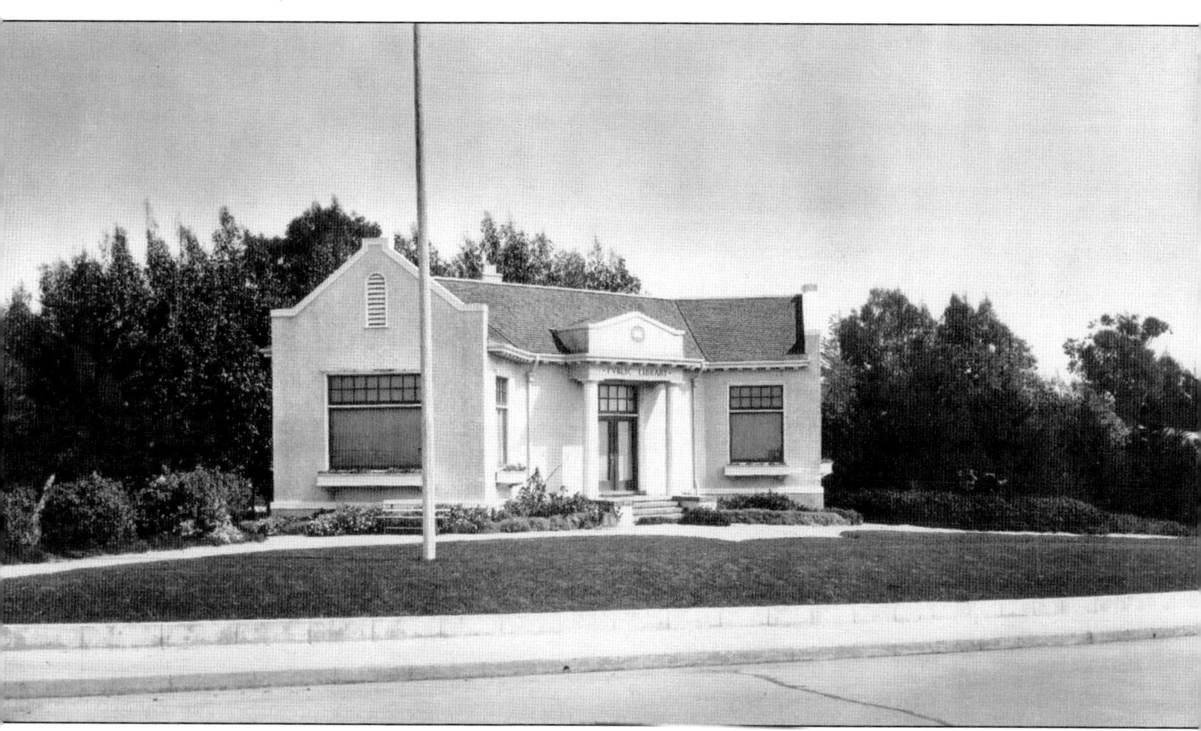

Renowned architect William Weeks drew up plans for the proposed Seabright branch library in 1914, but conditions had to be met before work could begin. The Improvement Society insisted on a permanent fix for the East Cliff Drive: landfill and a concrete culvert would replace the Seabright Bridge. As soon as the roadwork began, Kate Peck and the library trustees finalized her gift of Tyrrell Park. Hopes for speedy construction were curbed, however, when the Carnegie Corporation stipulated that the project must be accomplished within its $3,000 limit. Called to testify by the city council, library president Bliss convinced the officials; their subsequent resolution released $2,966, the amount necessary to pay for the building. The final cost, reported when the Tyrrell Park Library opened in early 1916, was $3,048. The Seabright Improvement Society cheerfully raised the additional $82. (Courtesy of SCMNH.)

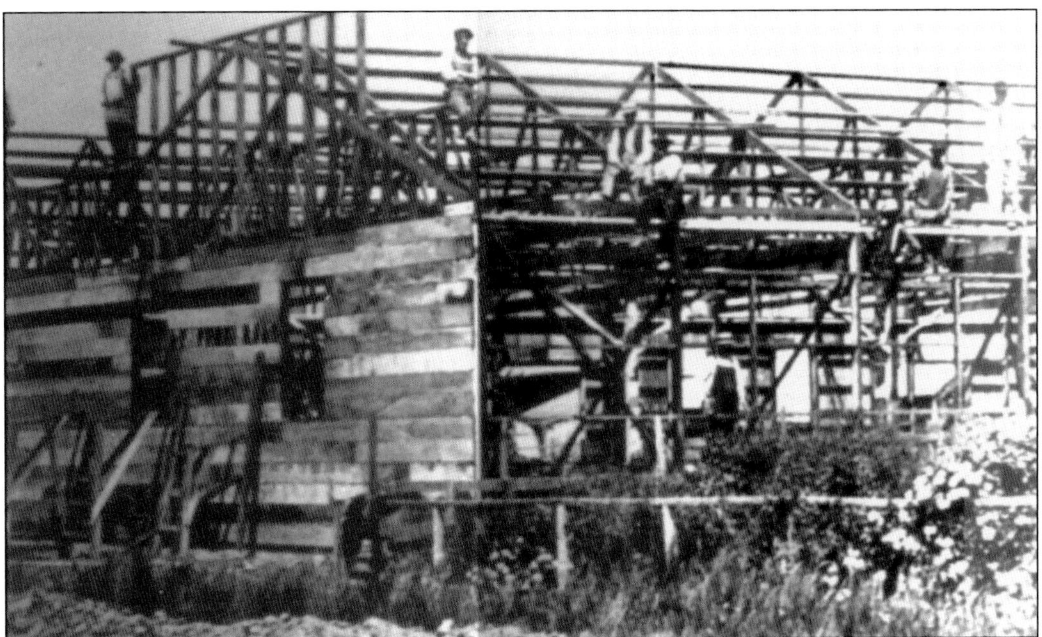

James Pilkington invited industry into the community. In 1914, the cannery of the Santa Cruz Fruit, Vegetable and Olive Corporation, partly owned by Pilkington, promised it would be a credit to the community—"thoroughly sanitary, non-odorous and non-objectionable." The plant opened at harvesttime, welcoming wagons bearing locally grown peas, pears, tomatoes, and loganberries for processing. When a shipment of pears went out to England, the local press celebrated the "First Freight from Santa Cruz to Pass Through the Panama Canal." (Courtesy of MAH.)

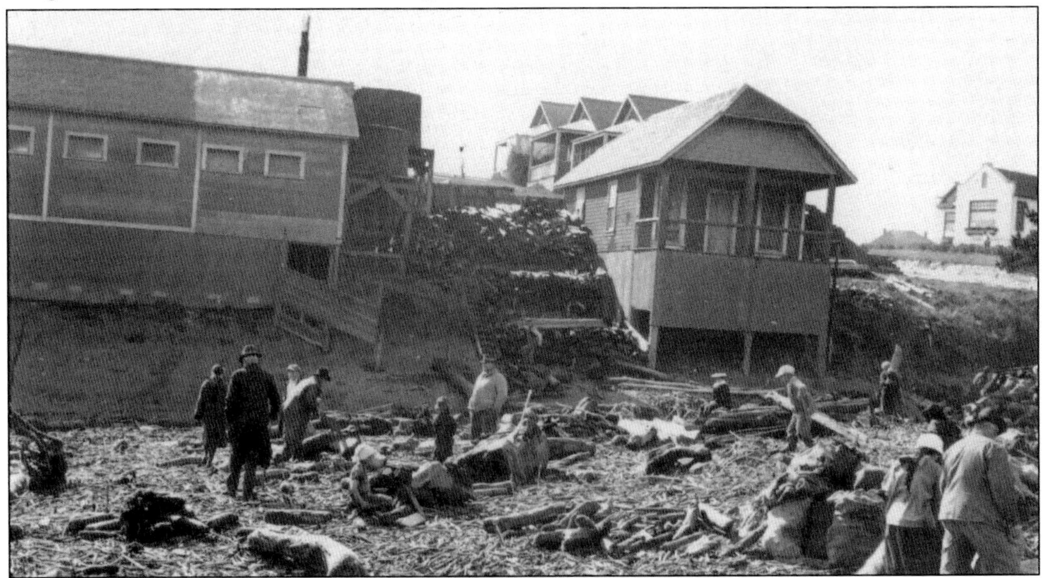

On a typical c. 1917 winter's day, almost all Seabrightans, young and old, made sure their heads were covered from the cold while searching for useable driftwood. James Pilkington developed this Cove resort with its bathhouse and prominent hot water tanks, left above, and a proprietor's home with three rental cottages in the rear, right above. The recently opened Carnegie library, at far right, became the pride of the community. (Courtesy of MAH.)

Entrepreneur and activist Elizabeth Forbes, at right with unidentified Seabright friends, earned mention in an *Overland Monthly* article titled "Business Women of California." She had managed a dairy, a chicken farm, and a tour business and also dabbled in real estate. In 1916, her longtime friends Susan Tyrrell and Lulu Green proposed a history of Seabright to which Forbes responded, "Who is going to write it?" The 40-page compilation of her articles, *Reminiscences of Seabright*, was reprinted by the Seabright Neighborhood Association at activist Dorothy Miller's urging. It remains a local classic. (Courtesy of SCMNH.)

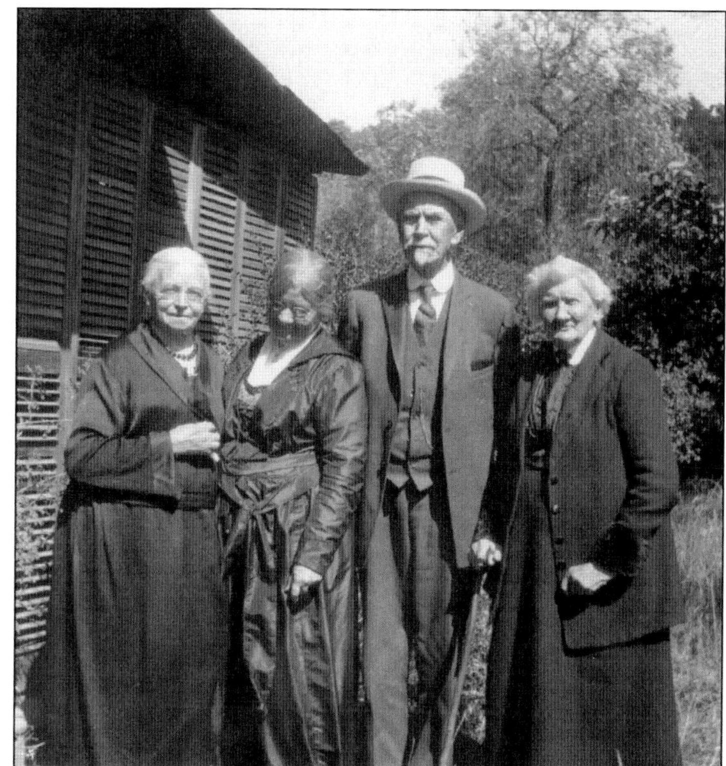

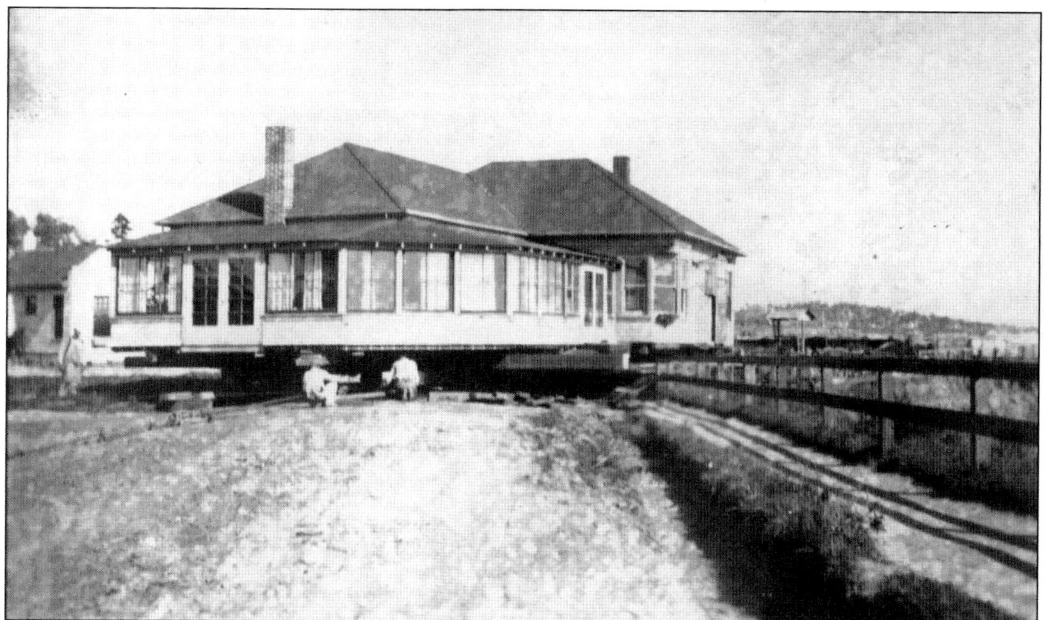

Adriana Van Kaathoven's East Cliff Drive property resisted the attacks of waves and storms for nearly a decade. After investing hundreds of dollars in a concrete seawall and similar reinforcements, she finally conceded defeat. In this 1916 photograph, the house is halfway across Dashaway Street, now East Cliff Drive, on its way to the corner of Alhambra Avenue, where it still stands with an added story. (Courtesy of MAH)

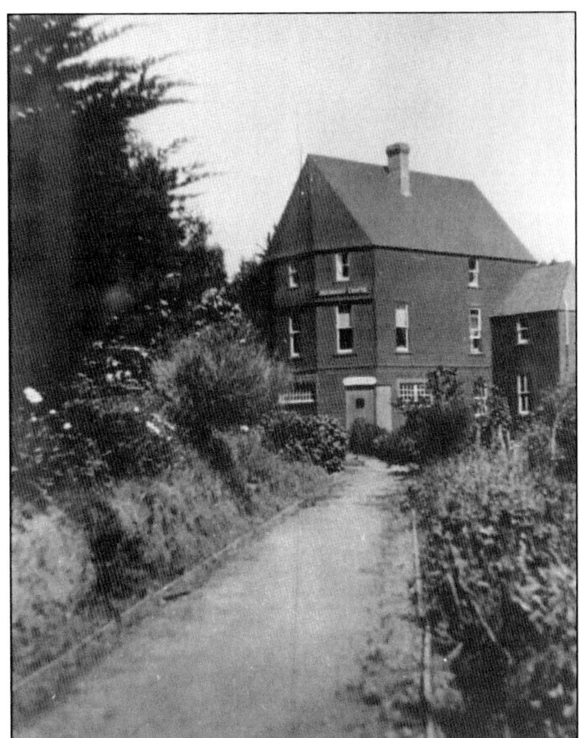

At age 90, Susan Tyrrell supervised the creation of the Seabright Crafts Society. In 1915, the industrious group made its headquarters in William Tyrrell's vacant house behind the library and began offering classes in sewing, basketry, china painting, and rug weaving. One of the first members of the Seabright Crafts Society, seascape artist Margaret Rogers envisioned the unused basement of the Tyrrell Building as a gallery. Working with landscape painter and teacher Frank Heath, she organized the Santa Cruz Art League, which moved into the basement in 1919. By then, Seabright's west side had become a cultural hub, complete with facilities for arts and crafts and literature. (Courtesy of SCMNH.)

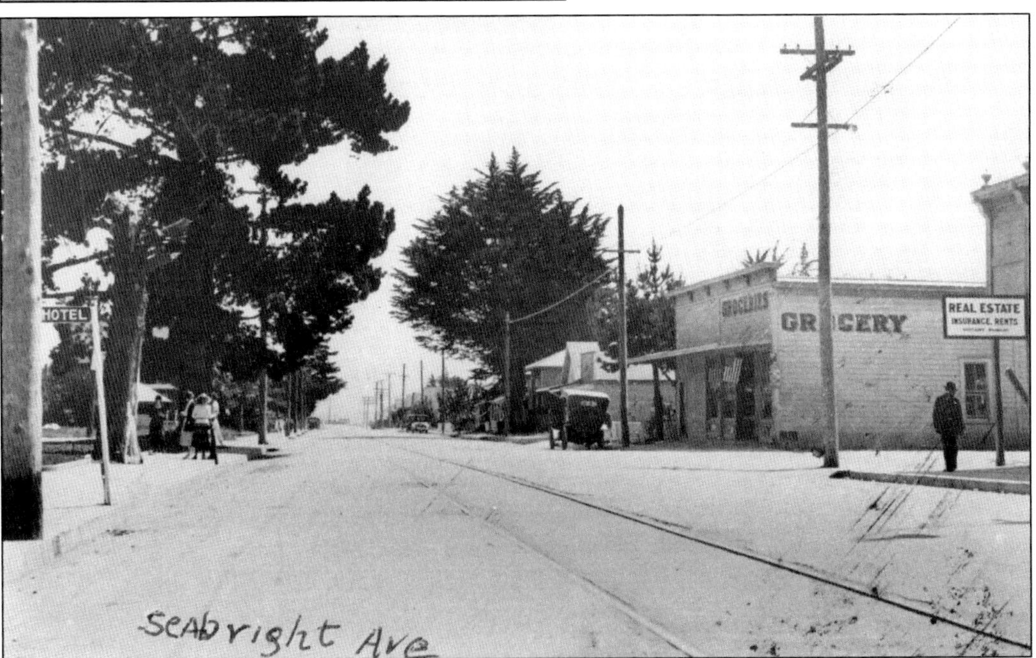

Crowding into Santa Cruz City Hall, locals demanded that Seabright Avenue be paved the entire mile from Seabright Beach to Soquel Avenue. It finally happened when James Pilkington became commissioner of streets and parks, ensuring the project's completion, as shown in this 1920 view. The real estate office of W.H. Cureton, at right, is today the site of Betty's Burgers. (Courtesy of MAH.)

Four

When Seabright Roared

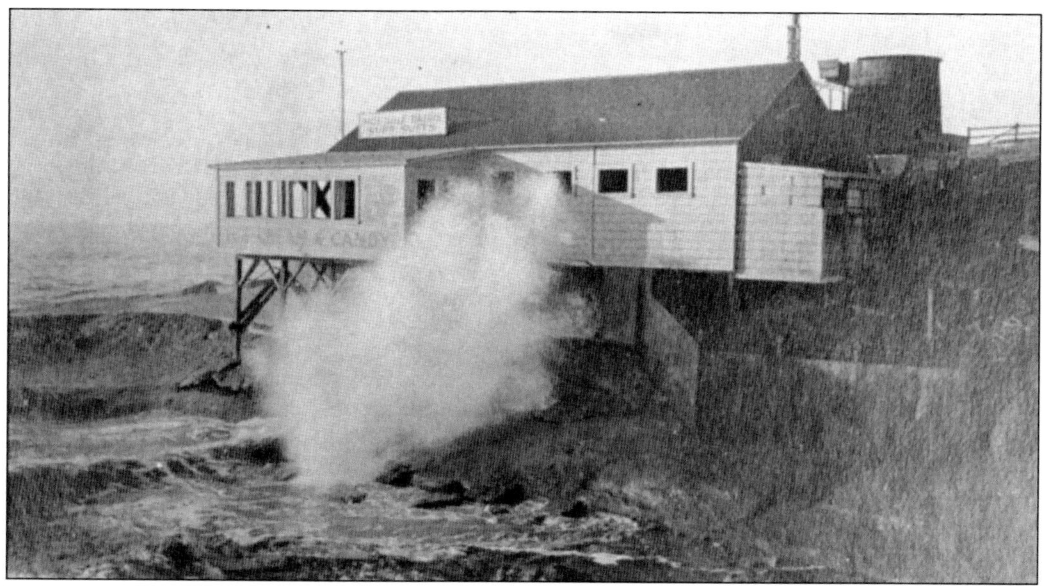

In January 1920, Louis Scholl purchased the Cove and bathhouse and immediately expanded his business to include an ice cream and candy store. His next decision—to put the building on stilts—proved disastrous. The sea raged during a 1921 storm, undermining the bathhouse. Undaunted, Scholl, an accomplished carpenter, remodeled and soon expanded his property to include cottages on the bluff. During the rest of the decade, he experimented with structures capable of withstanding the heavy winter weather while graciously catering to the needs of summer beachgoers. (Courtesy of MAH.)

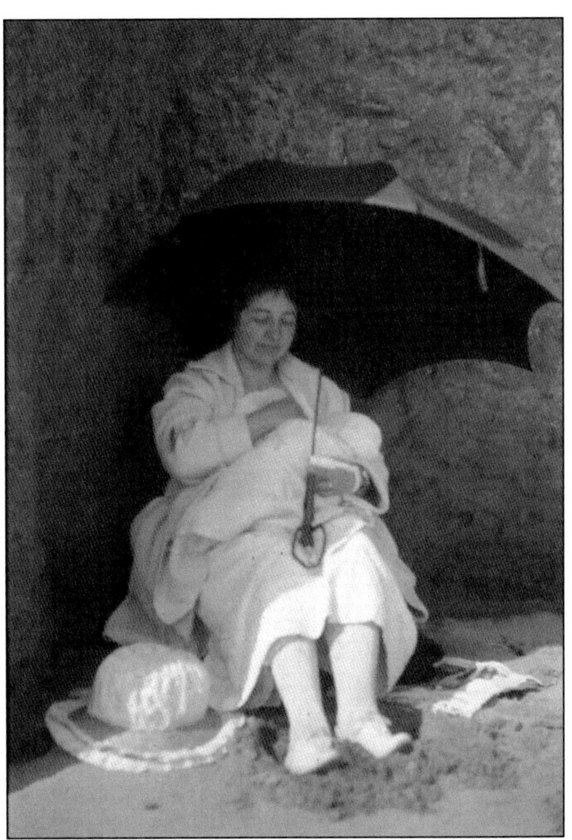

In the cool privacy of a partially hollowed cliff, Alice Jackson Lenox, of Campbell, nurses baby Marion. The cliff carving, above right, reveals a frequent tourist behavior, which is to leave one's mark. (Courtesy of the Lionel T. Lenox collection.)

Would Twin Lakes and Seabright "attract thousands and thousands of people"? That was the prediction of John Norton, who established Twin Lakes Lumber in 1921 and built the family home at 121 Fourth Avenue the following year. Convinced of the area's unique beauty, Norton made an unsuccessful offer on Mary Ellen Miller Eakle's extensive property, which included all of Woods Lagoon as shown on the map below. (Courtesy of the Ronnie Trubek collection.)

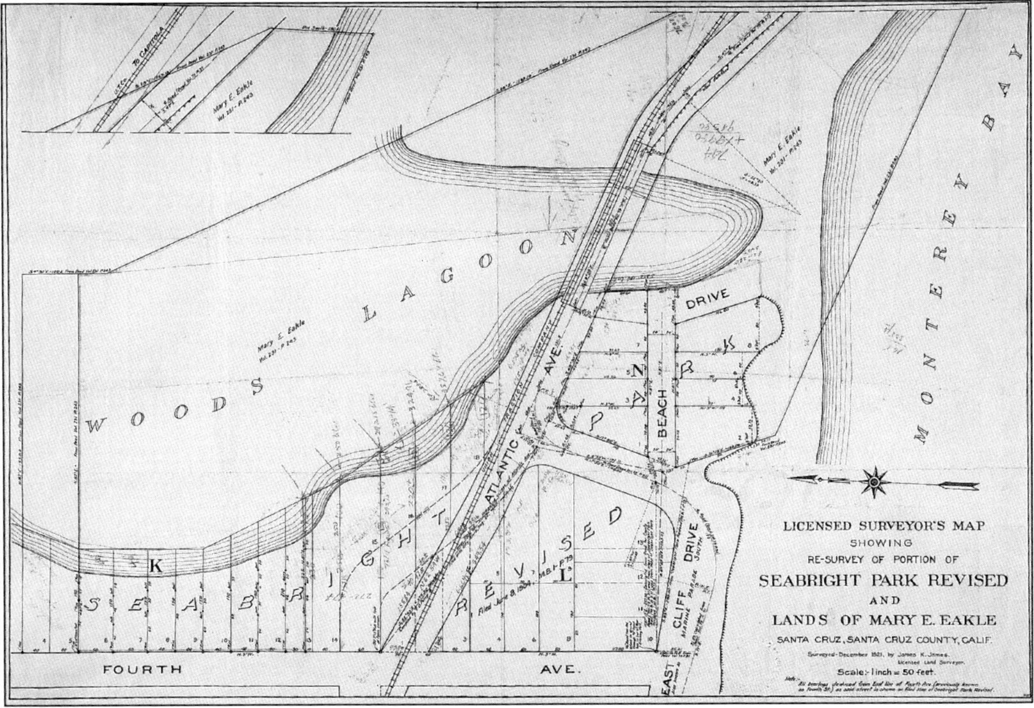

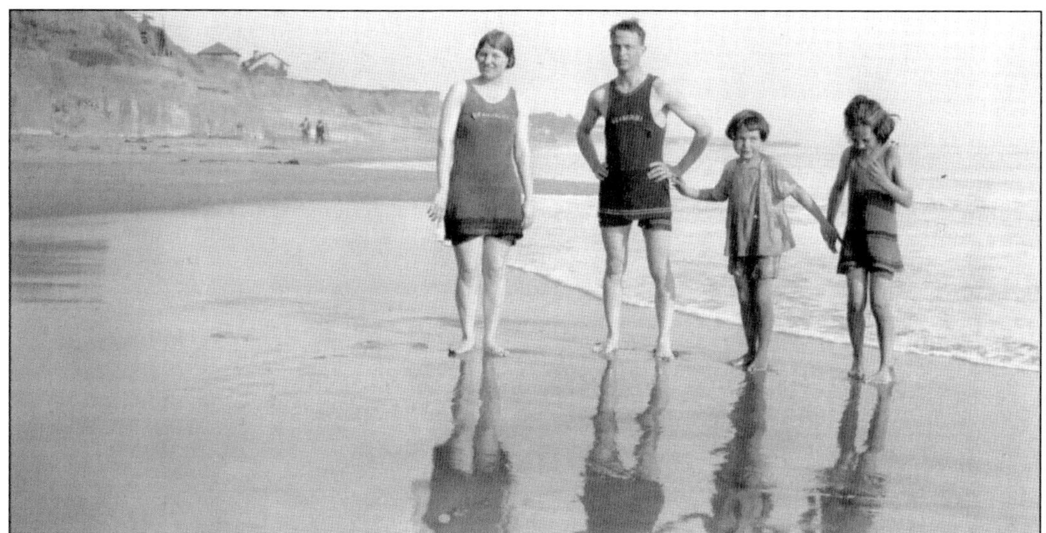

The Lenox sisters, as seen on the cover, catch their breath after frolicking down the beach. The white house in the distance belonged to Santa Cruz native Louis Pioda and his wife, Estelle. In 1914, the honeymooning couple stayed in Seabright to watch the construction of their summer home, designed by architect Lila Sweet Martin. (Courtesy of the Lionel T. Lenox collection.)

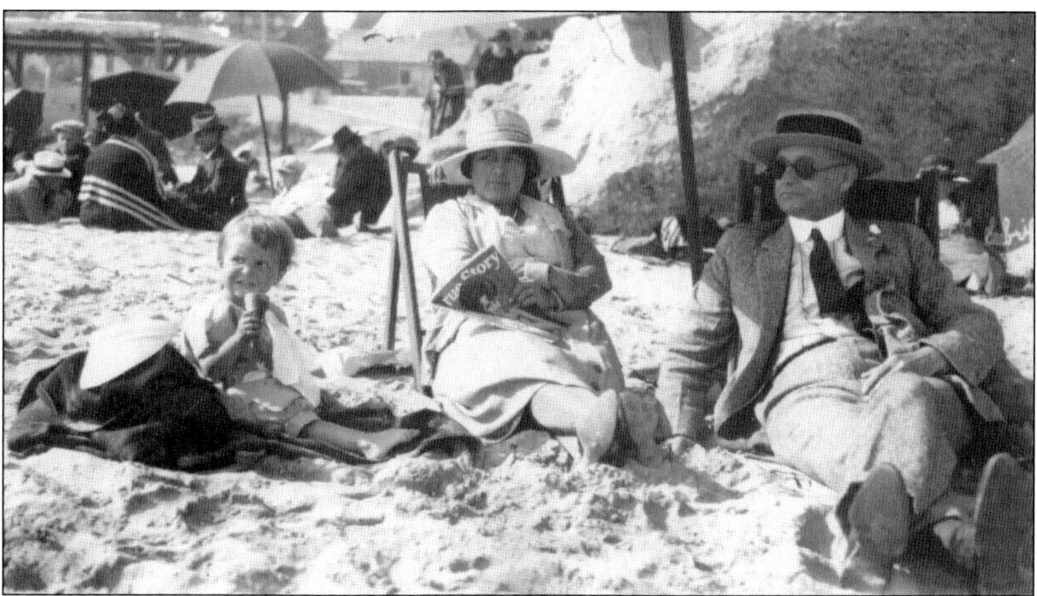

Valley visitors to Seabright Beach often remained fully clothed, delighted to be out of the summer heat. Lionel R. Lenox, right, a chemistry professor at Stanford for more than 30 years, relaxes next to daughter-in-law Alice Lenox, who reads *True Story* magazine. Alice's daughter Marion is the only one with her shoes off. After several years as renters on Seabright Avenue, the Lenox family built a summer home in Twin Lakes, overlooking Woods Lagoon. (Courtesy of the Lionel T. Lenox collection.)

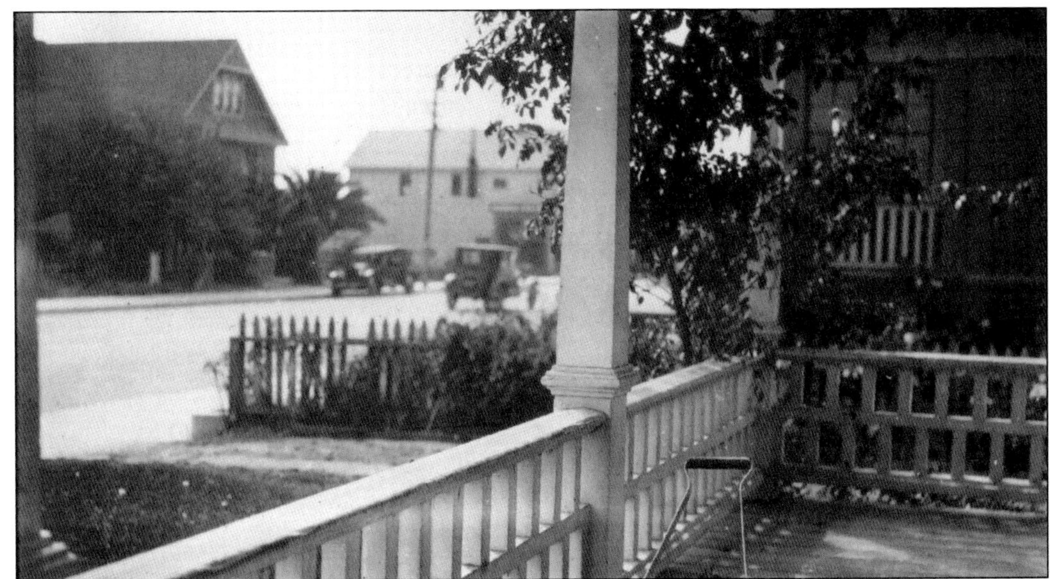

From the covered porch of a spacious summer rental on the west side of Seabright Avenue, one can see the whitewashed Seabright Cash Store in the center of the business district as it looked in 1924. Rentals such as this, on the north side of the railroad tracks, usually consisted of two-story homes for large families, while rentals on the south side of the tracks were single-story beach bungalows. (Courtesy of the Lionel T. Lenox collection.)

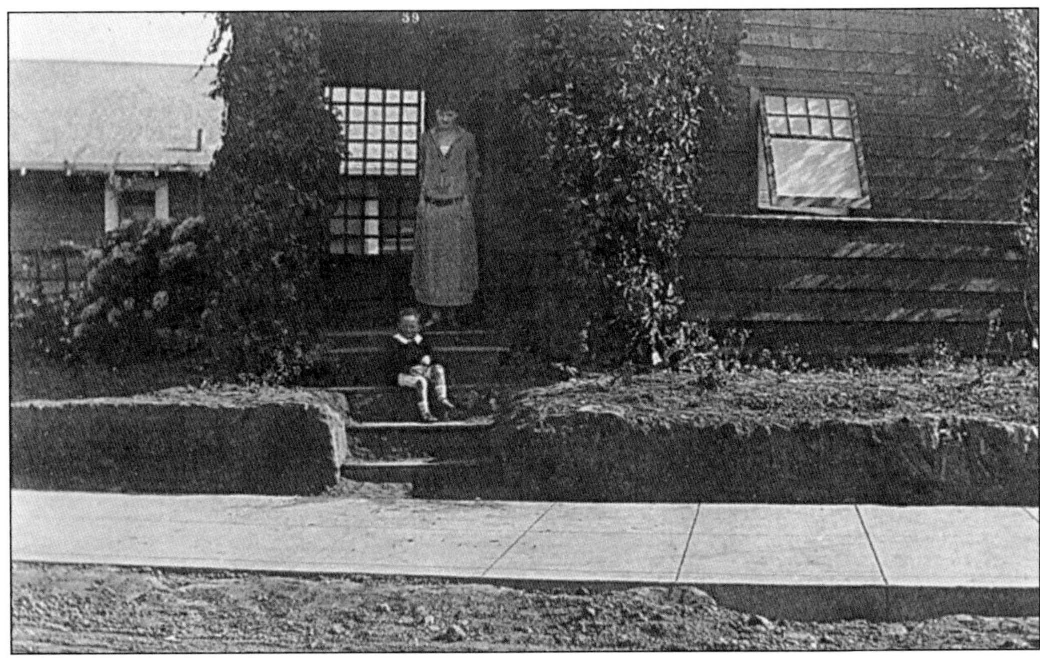

Meanwhile, the "Avenues" of Seabright Park attracted families seeking second homes. Lydia Hyde Pagen and son Jack, age five, pose in the doorway of the Hydes' summer cottage in the mid-1920s. Lydia's father, Henry Hyde, of Martinez, bought the land at 416 Atlantic Avenue from the Union Traction Co. in 1908. (Courtesy of the Pagen family.)

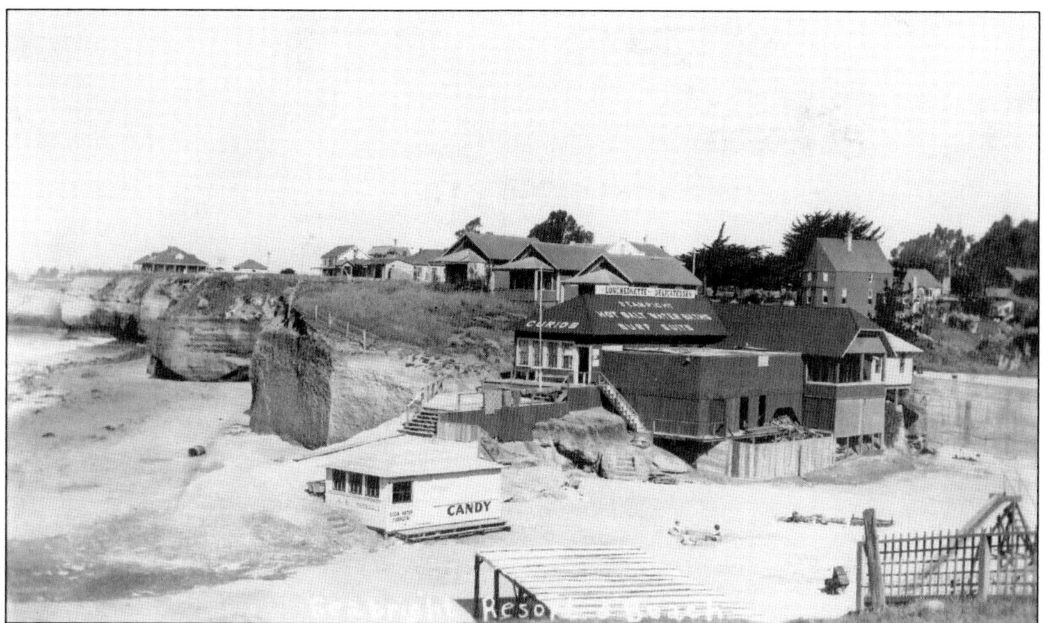

By the mid-1920s, Louis Scholl had a compound of several concessions, including a luncheonette run by Margaret Halliday, a family friend. The candy store in the foreground rests on a pallet, allowing Scholl to remove it in the off-season, avoiding a battering by winter waves. William Tyrrell's former home, upper right, housed Seabright Crafts Society and the Santa Cruz Art League. (Courtesy of the Ronnie Trubek collection.)

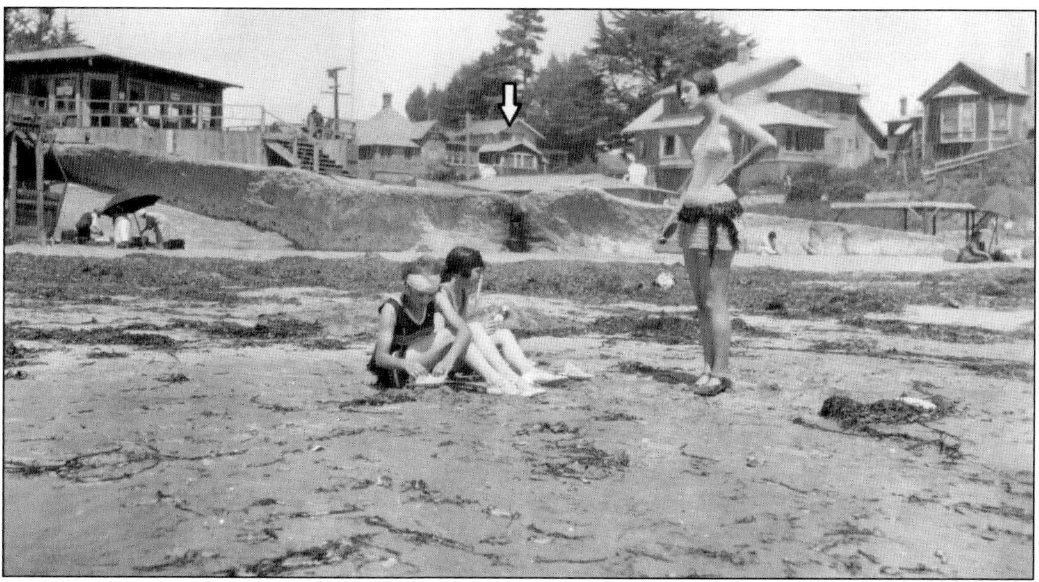

Beachgoers often found the Cove covered with seaweed floating ashore from dense offshore beds. Here, a tourist accessorizes her 1920s outfit with a seaweed belt. In the background, two adjacent homes on the north corner of East Cliff Drive and Seabright Avenue, upper center, had recently been purchased by Dr. Edward Cureton and his wife, Annie McKelvie, of Stockton. (Courtesy of the Lionel T. Lenox collection.)

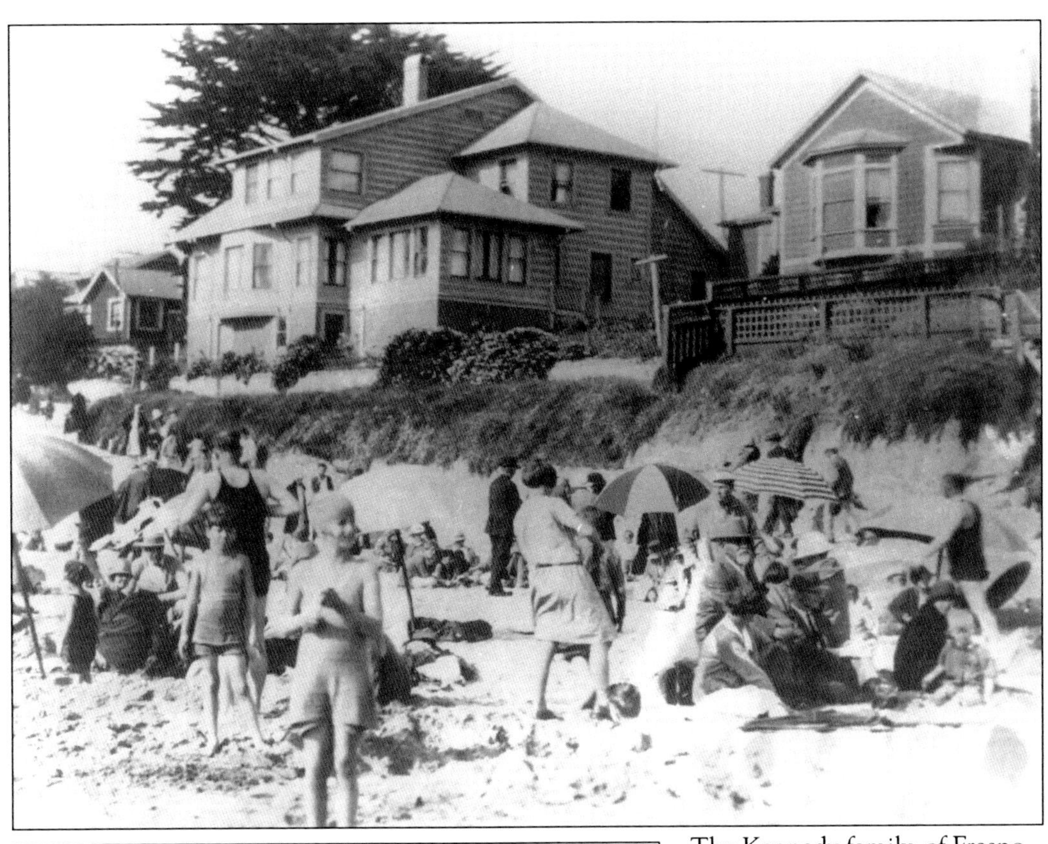

SEABRIGHT BEACH

The Family's Playground

Catering to Mothers and Children

Seabright beach has no drop off but is a gradual slope. There is a life line, life boats and buoy and always some one on the watch.

HOT SALT BATHS

Surf Suits and Dressing Rooms

Sand Buckets and Shovels — Beach Umbrellas to Rent

Ice Cream, Candies, Cold Drinks and Smokes
Lunches—Delicatessen
Hot Dog and Hamburger Sandwiches A Specialty

The Kennedy family, of Fresno, first came to Seabright in the early 1890s, building their home directly above the Cove, today 1580 East Cliff Drive. When their three daughters brought husbands and children to Seabright, Robert and Marian Rice Kennedy added a smaller building to their lot, at center. As the third generation—Cutters, Minturns, and Prescotts—began to marry, the grandparents planned ahead by replacing their original house with a two-story structure, at left. Patriarch Robert Kennedy, at bottom right with white beard, celebrates with his extended family, including great-grandchildren, in the summer of 1924. (Above, courtesy of Joan Kimble Miller-Prescot; left, courtesy of the Brown collection.)

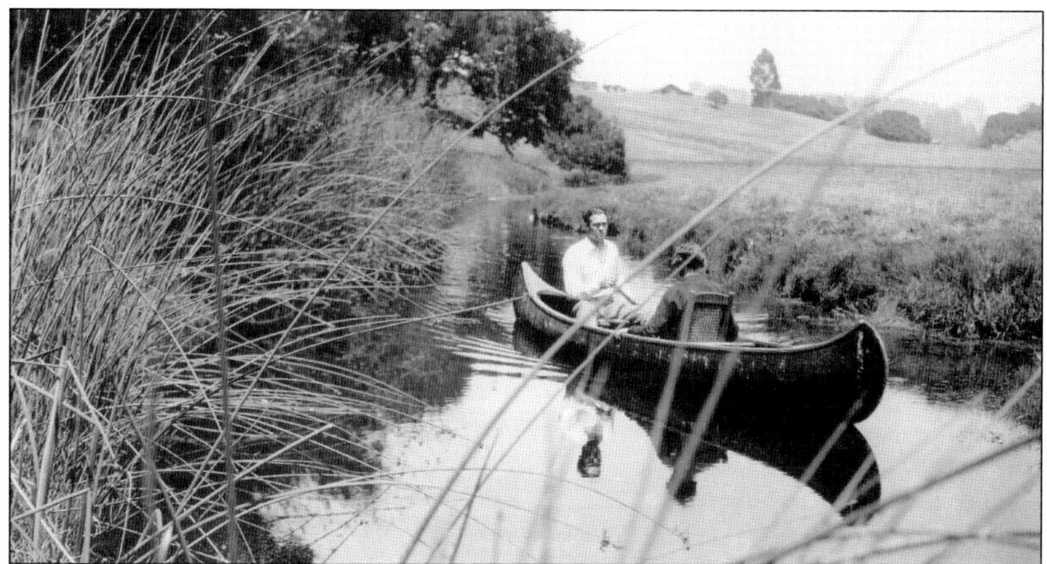

From June to September, exuberance and gaiety filled Seabright, yet one could still find tranquility. Summer residents enjoy a canoe ride at the pristine Woods Lagoon (pictured). During duck season, hunters stalked their abundant prey beside the quiet water. (Courtesy of the Lionel T. Lenox collection.)

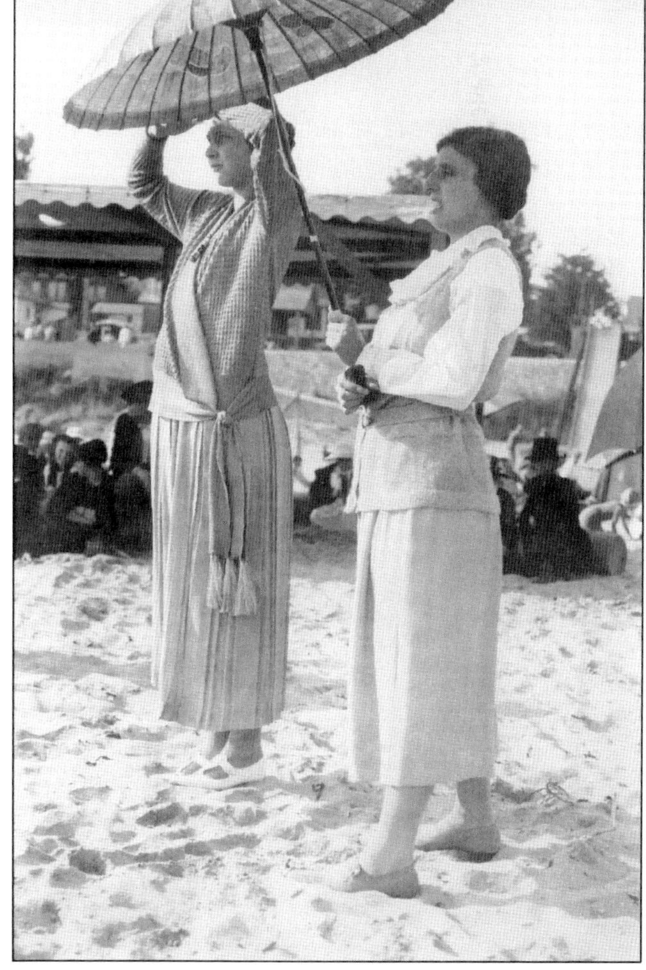

Japanese parasols, very much in vogue in the 1920s, were often seen at the Cove. Here, a tourist sports one of those colorful sunshades, undeterred by the impracticality of a paper fashion accessory so near to wind and water. During the decades that followed, motley umbrellas of all sizes remained a staple at local beaches and those rented by Louis Scholl included a large rendering of the word "Seabright." (Courtesy of the Lionel T. Lenox collection.)

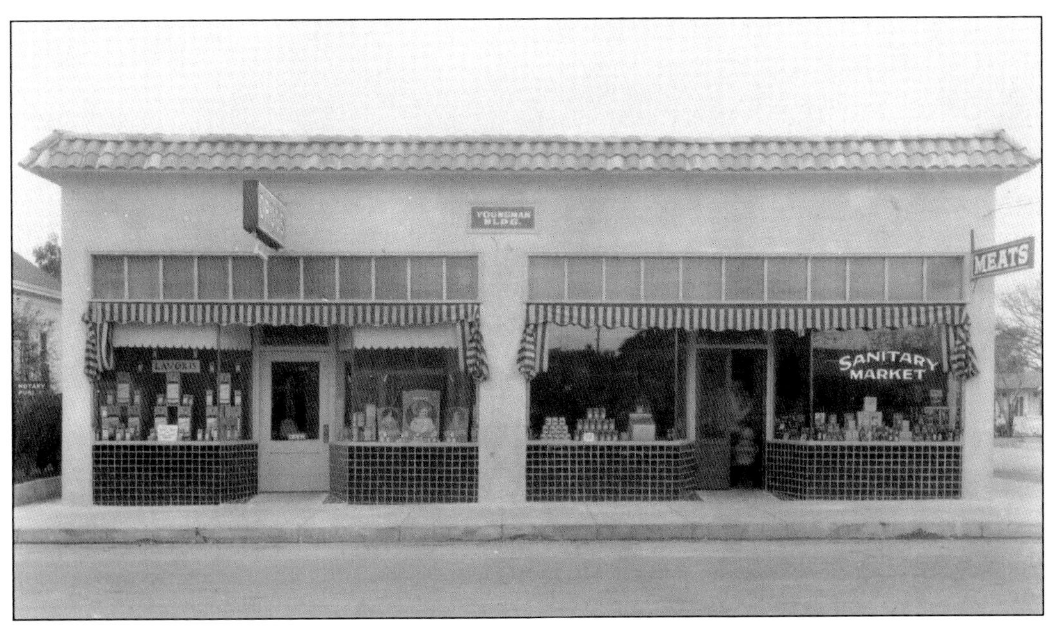

Summer resident Franklin Youngman, a pharmacist, moved his family to Seabright from Sacramento in 1926 and opened a drugstore near the railroad station. During Prohibition, alcohol could be prescribed as medicine, perhaps contributing to the pharmacy's considerable success. In early 1927, Youngman joined his son-in-law, Joseph Yoho, a contractor, to form the Seabright Construction Company. A year later, the Youngman Building at 541 Seabright Avenue (above) won praise as "artistic and substantial," according to the *Santa Cruz Historic Building Survey, Vol. 3.* The structure's left half became the pharmacy's new location, while the Sanitary Market next door, a butcher shop owned by Tony Day, quickly grew into a "groceteria." Youngman added another three stores in an adjacent building (at left below) in 1929. (Above, courtesy of Traci Bliss; below, courtesy of the Ronnie Trubek collection.)

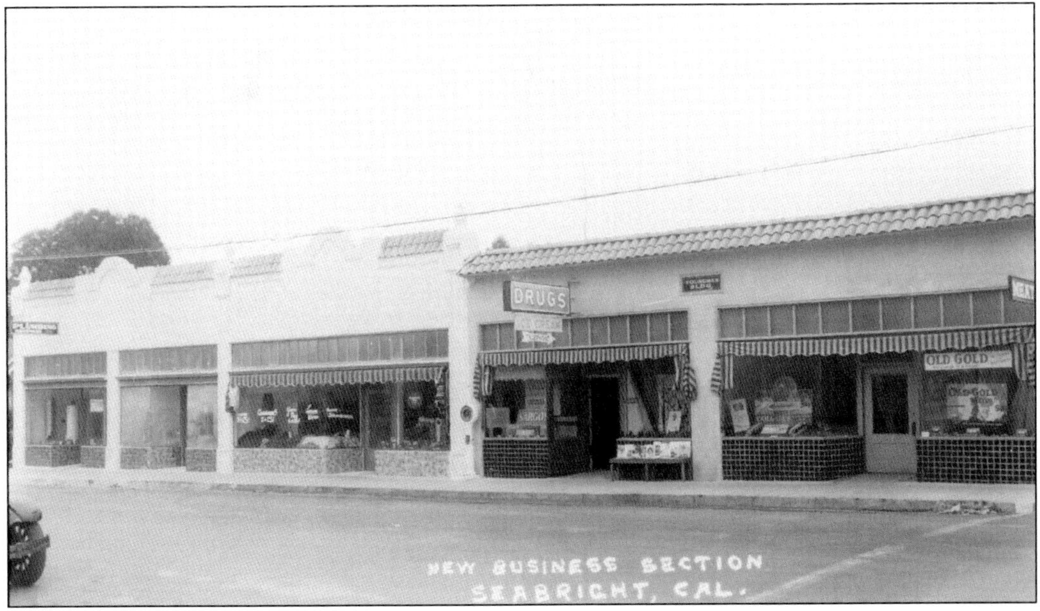

The strip of beach known as Seabright extended from San Lorenzo Point to the bluff at the base of Fourth Avenue. This easternmost section, then called Pioda Beach, got its name from the family whose home overlooked it (see page 57). In the foreground, Lionel T. Lenox balances his daughter Virginia. Behind them, the sandstone outcropping creates a fun challenge for swimmers: how to safely navigate to Twin Lakes Beach just beyond the Santa Cruz city limit. (Courtesy of the Lionel T. Lenox collection.)

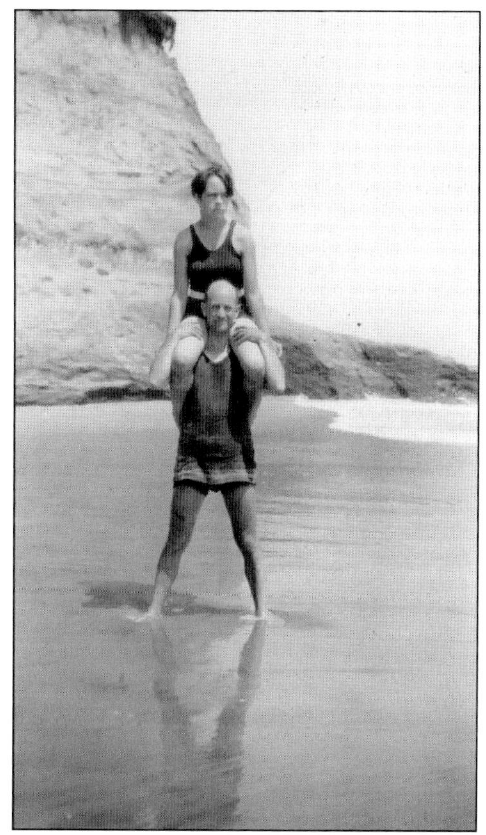

The diligent efforts of the Seabright Improvement Society provided the neighborhood with first-class concrete roads just in time for the automobile boom of the 1920s. Before the end of the decade, passenger train service declined and trolley tracks were demolished. Above the Cove, cars fill all the parking spaces on East Cliff Drive. (Courtesy of SNA.)

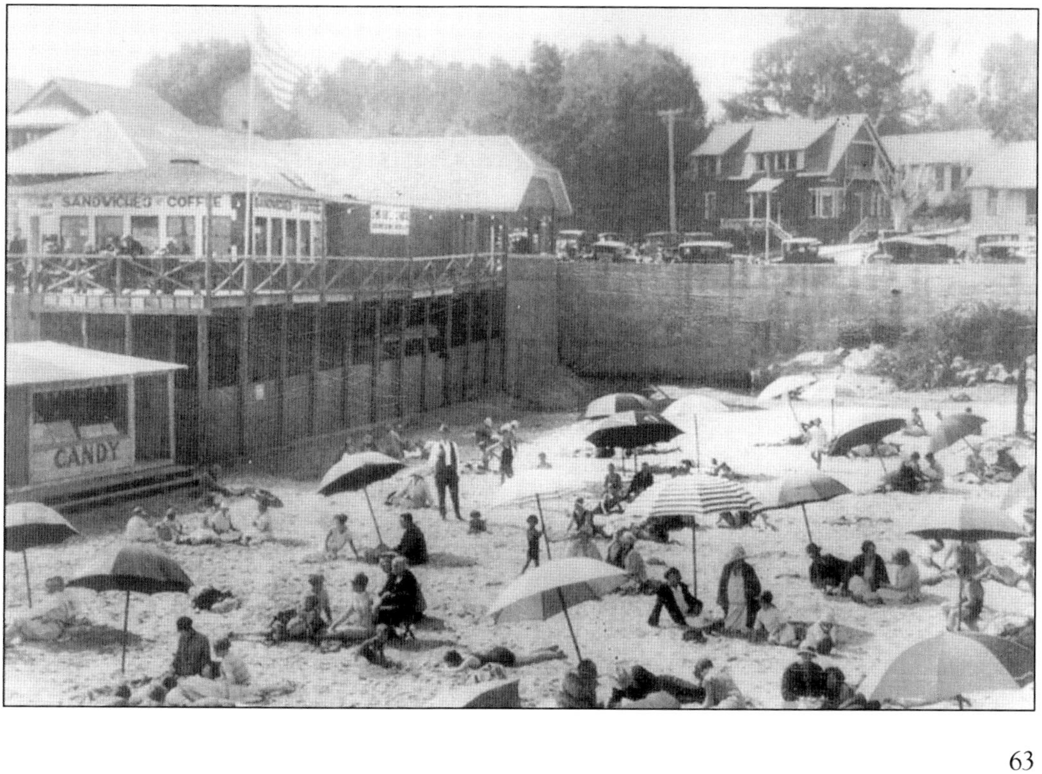

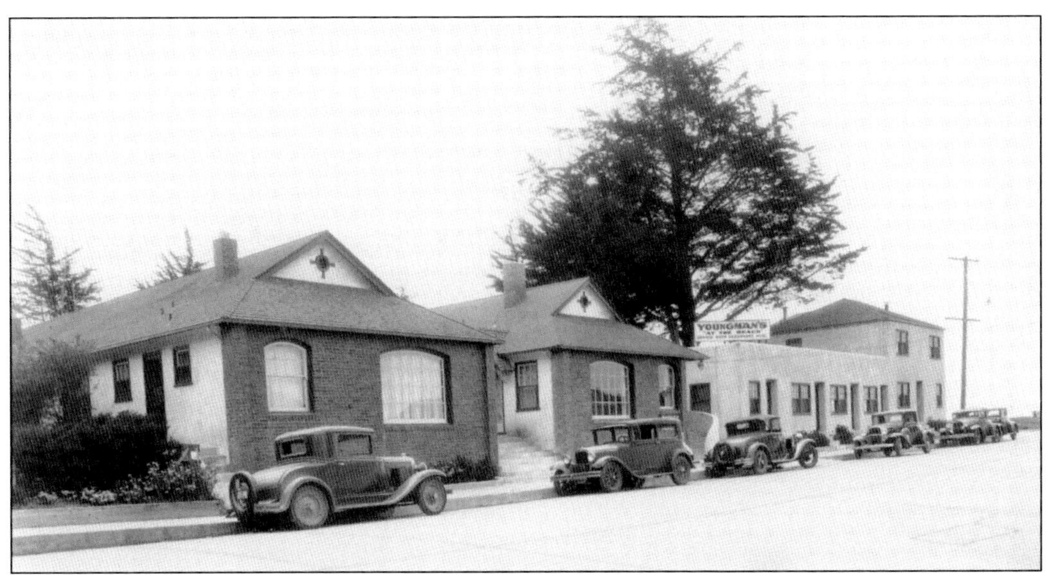

Franklin Youngman built numerous cottages and a complex of affordable rental apartments at 108 Seabright Avenue, above. Eager to accommodate the summer throngs, he began construction of a huge freestanding garage in the center of the complex. After neighbors complained, police arrested the entrepreneur for violating a city zoning ordinance. While a judge considered the matter, armed guards deterred further work, but ultimately Youngman won the case, and the completed structure, Youngman's at the Beach, is seen below. (Above, courtesy of the Ronnie Trubek collection; below, courtesy of SCMNH.)

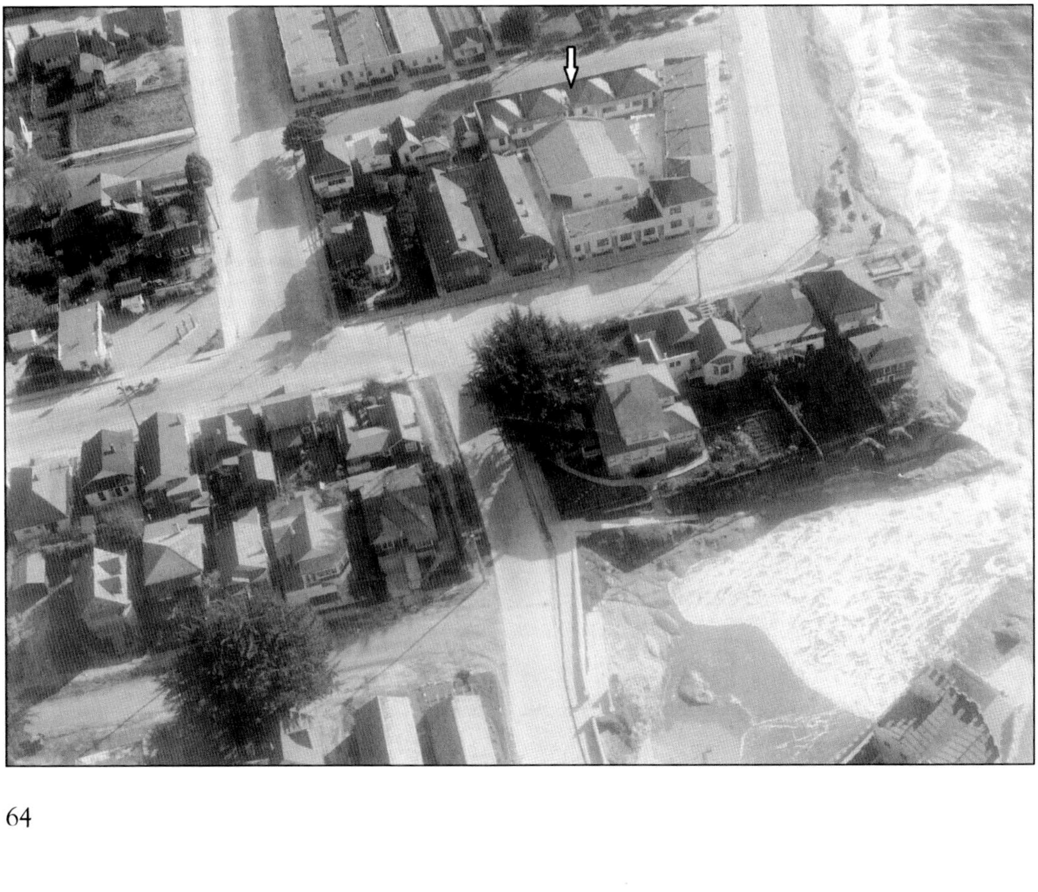

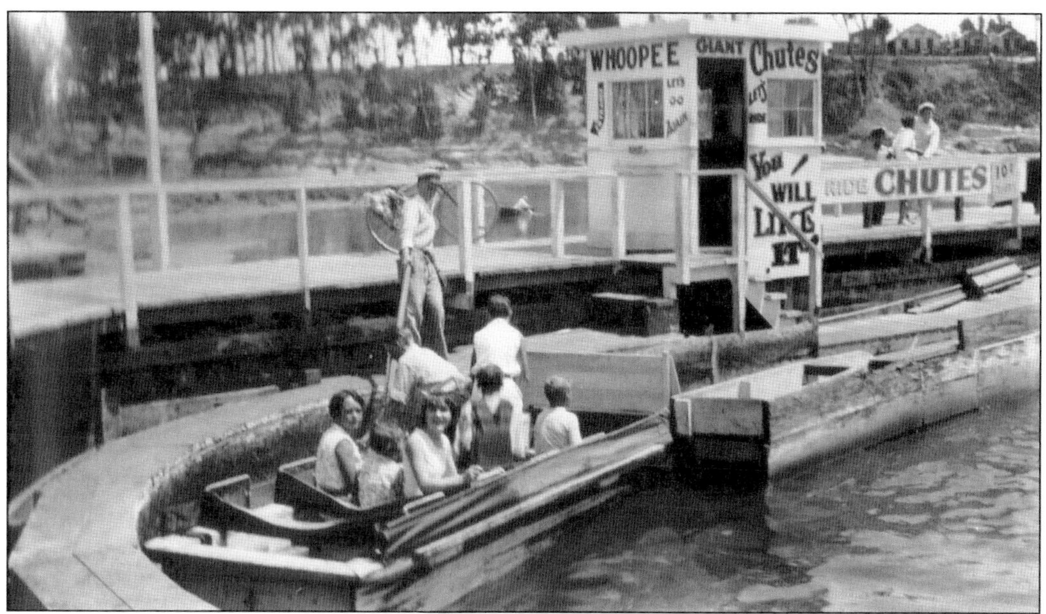

In 1928, a revival of the water carnival tradition featured a large waterslide located on the west bank of the San Lorenzo River at the end of the Boardwalk. The next year, fascinated Seabright residents watched as the Shoot the Chutes rose to a height of 85 feet, almost twice as high as the previous year. From the top of the chutes, boats plunged down the incline at an advertised speed of a mile a minute before "striking the water with a tremendous splash." Due to an injury and resulting lawsuit, the thrilling ride closed after two seasons. (Both, courtesy of the Lionel T. Lenox collection.)

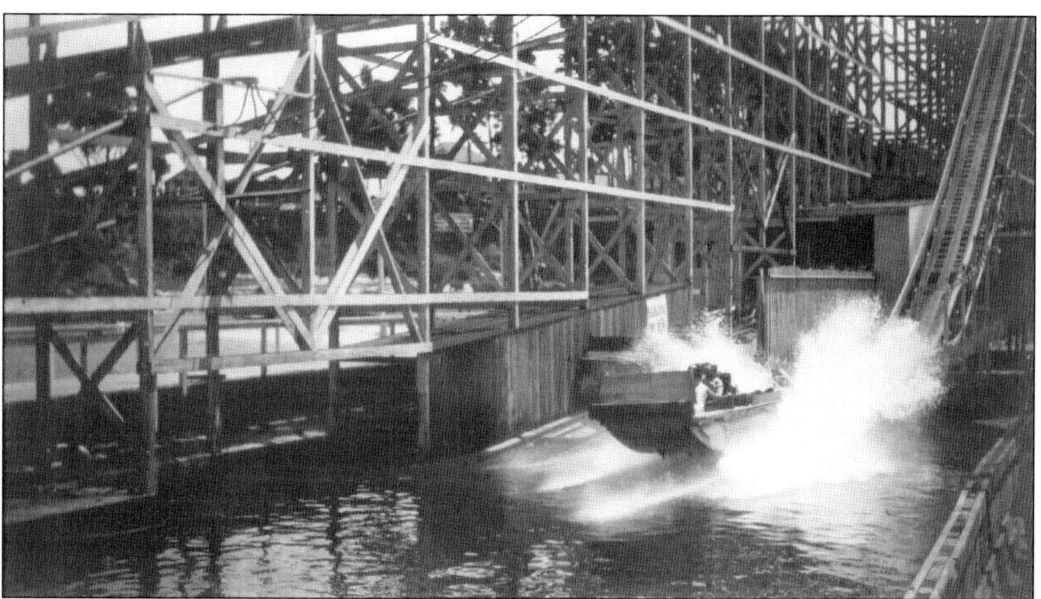

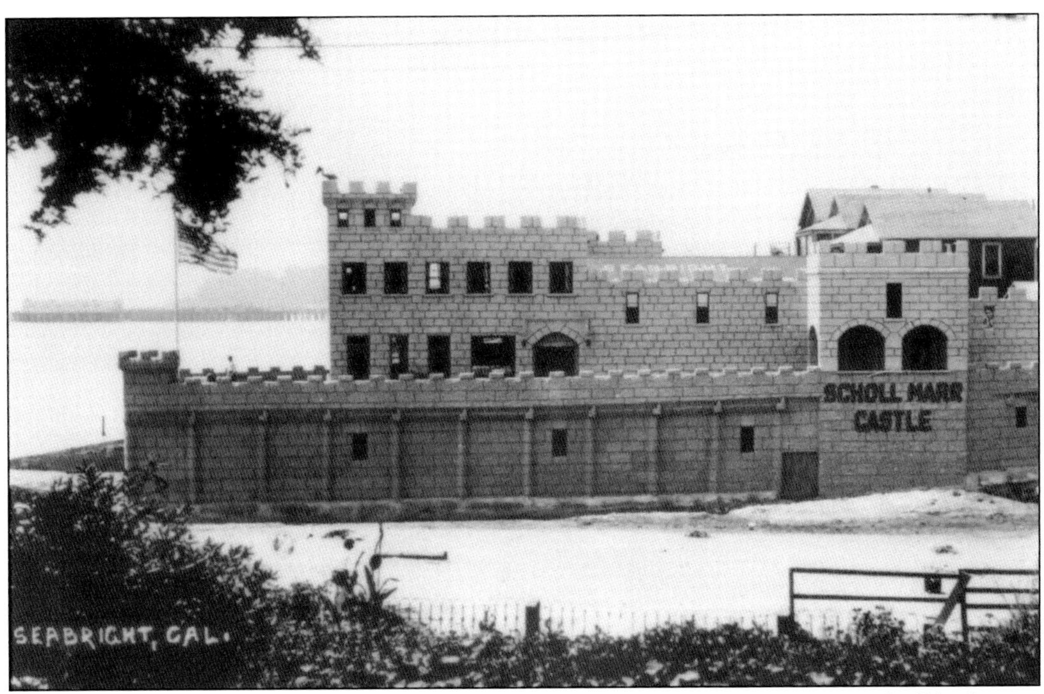

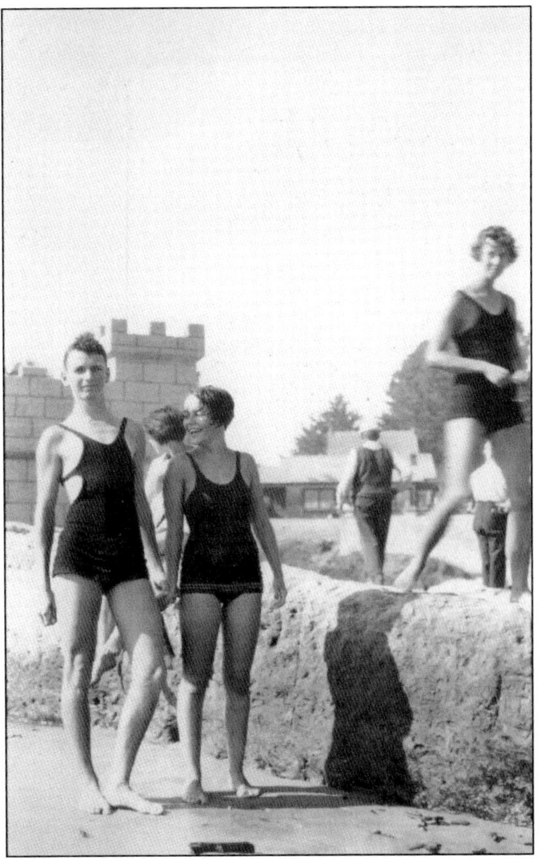

In the era of excess, Louis Scholl had a grand vision that would not disappoint. When his Scholl Marr Castle opened in June 1929, the *Sentinel* reported, "In fact, many persons who have traveled to all parts of the world claim it has no equal." The Scholl Marr Castle left no doubt that the charming village of yesteryear had become a stylish beachfront resort. Built on a jagged rock with five lookout towers, the Moorish-looking structure conjured up romantic images of chivalrous deeds. The main floor housed more than 100 dressing rooms, 10 saltwater baths and candy, ice cream, and cigar concessions. The addition of a second floor provided bay-view dining and ample space to "Charleston the night away." (Courtesy of MAH.)

Among the first visitors to the newly opened Castle were sweethearts Louie Gripenstraw, a cousin of Louis Scholl, and regular summer resident Virginia Lenox, of Campbell. By August 1929, the former Cove became known as Castle Beach. Long-term Santa Cruzans still use that name today, despite the Castle's demise half a century ago. (Courtesy of the Lionel T. Lenox collection.)

Five

Challenging Times

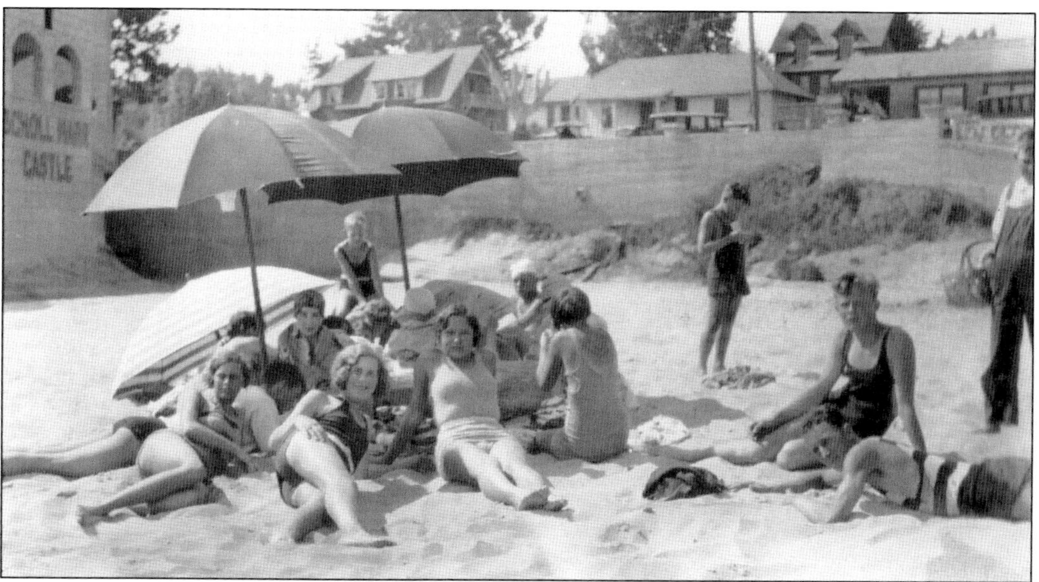

Showing off the current trend in bathing suits, ladies display their entire legs at the Castle. In April 1932, Mayor Fred Swanton led the city council in addressing the problem of diminishing body coverage for both men and women. The city attorney urged a crackdown: "I do not care to have my children frequent the beach, which is becoming positively indecent," and advocated for a law governing modesty standards on the beaches. Ultimately, city leaders opted to leave decisions concerning indecent exposure to the police department. (Courtesy of the Lionel T. Lenox collection.)

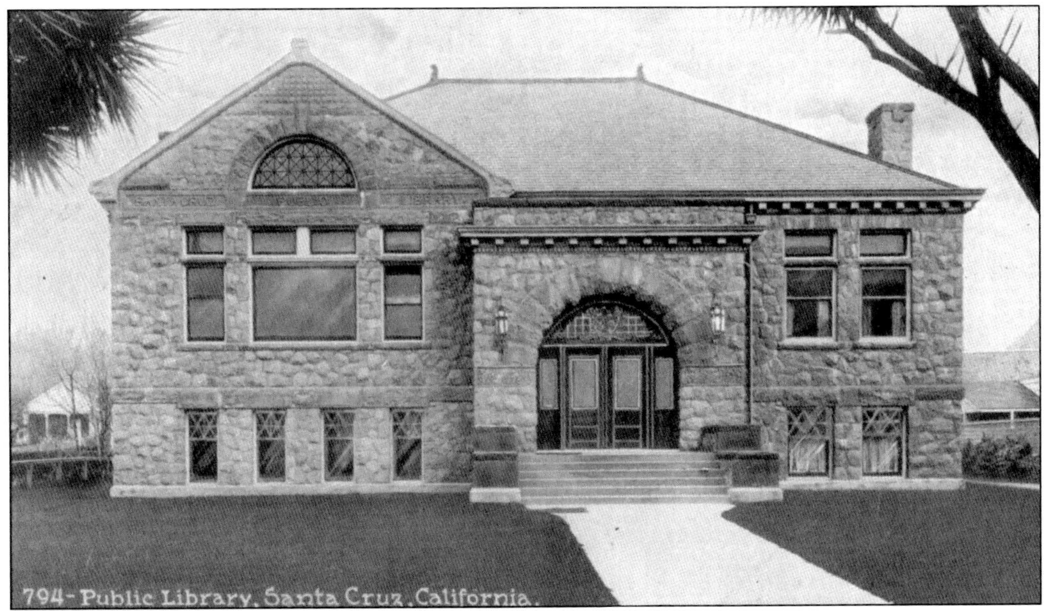

Architect William Weeks used sandstone from the Santa Cruz Mountains in his design for the downtown public library. Within a year of the 1904 opening, thanks to longtime lighthouse keeper Laura Hecox, the city's first public museum occupied a room in the basement. The donation of her natural history collection, consisting of flora, fauna, geological, and anthropological specimens, and a rich assortment of marine artifacts formed the nucleus of the museum. But a decade later, the library reclaimed the space, sending the Hecox exhibits to Santa Cruz High School "for educational purposes." (Courtesy of the Brown collection.)

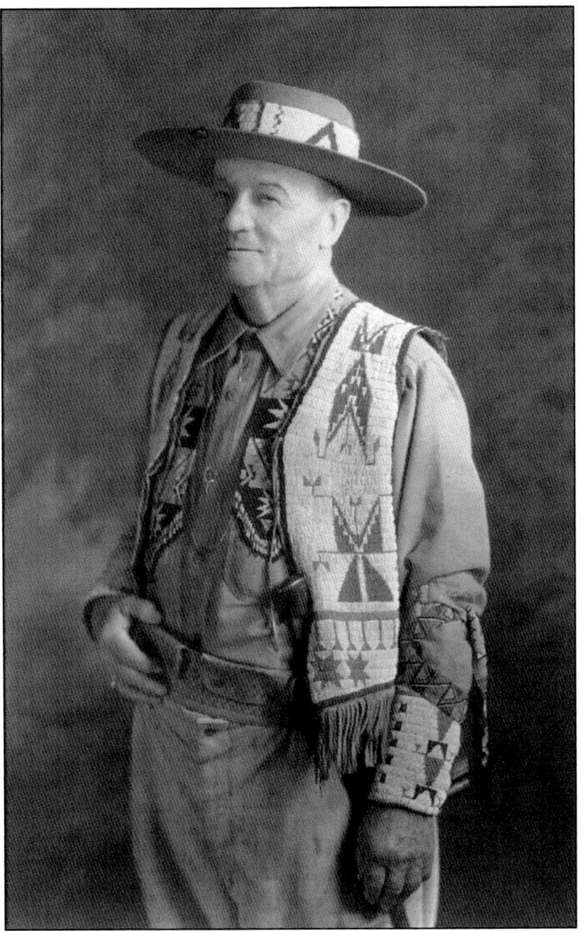

Jed Scott (pictured), a Seabright realtor, orchestrated a campaign to find a local home for the extensive collection of Native American artifacts bequeathed to the city by James Pilkington's cousin Humphrey in 1929. The timing seemed perfect. Under the leadership of Adriana Van Kaathoven, the Seabright Crafts Society offered to move out of its two stories at Tyrrell Park to make space for a proper Santa Cruz Museum. (Courtesy of SCMNH.)

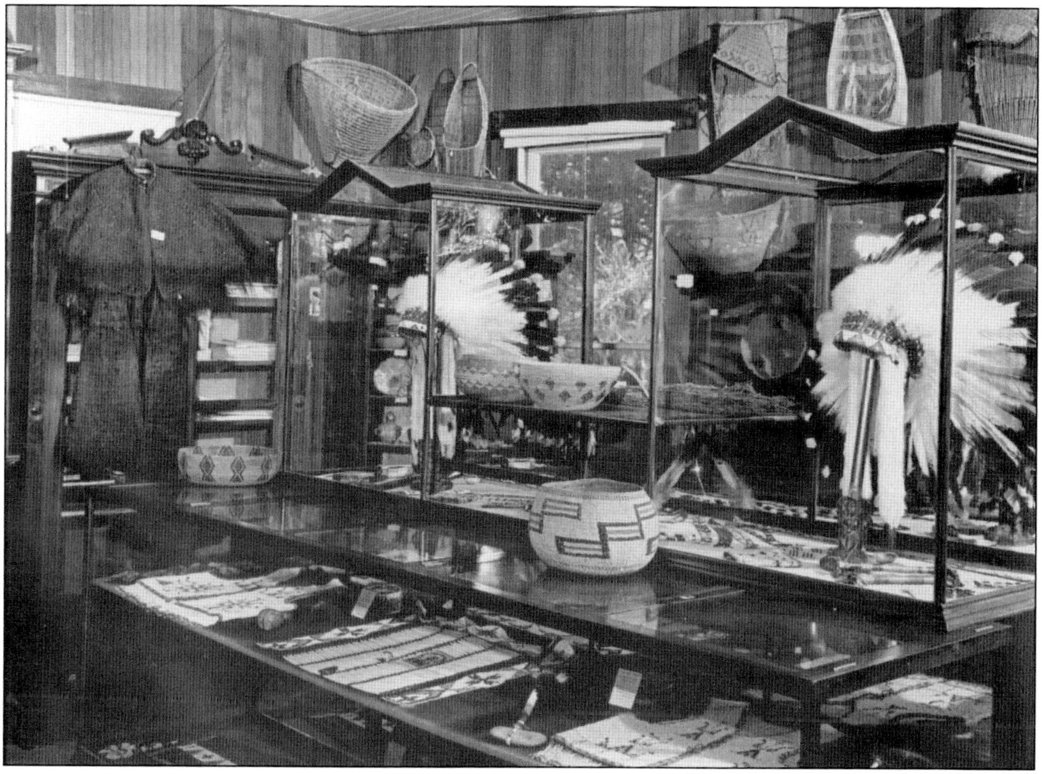

As curator of the Pilkington collection at the William Tyrrell House, Jed Scott contributed many of his own artifacts. As seen here, one entire floor of the museum practically overflowed with Native American items. (Courtesy of SCMNH.)

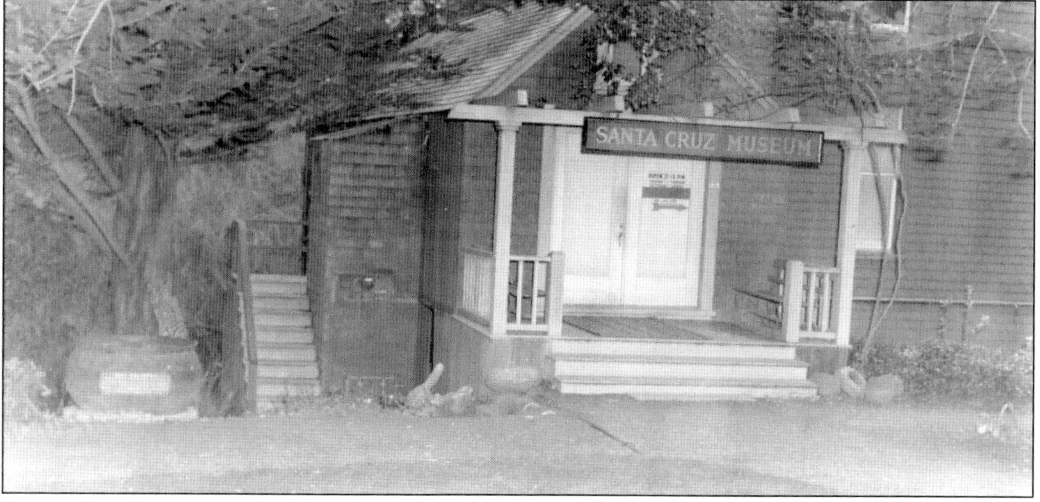

Soon after the museum's opening in 1930, board members campaigned to acquire the treasures gifted by naturalist Laura Hecox, which were languishing at the high school. Mayor Swanton and the city council voted to send "the collection of bugs, moths, beetles, birds, rocks, and other relics" to Seabright "where they will be properly cared for." Today, the combined collections have been joined by many additional collections to form a very diverse set of holdings. (Courtesy of MAH.)

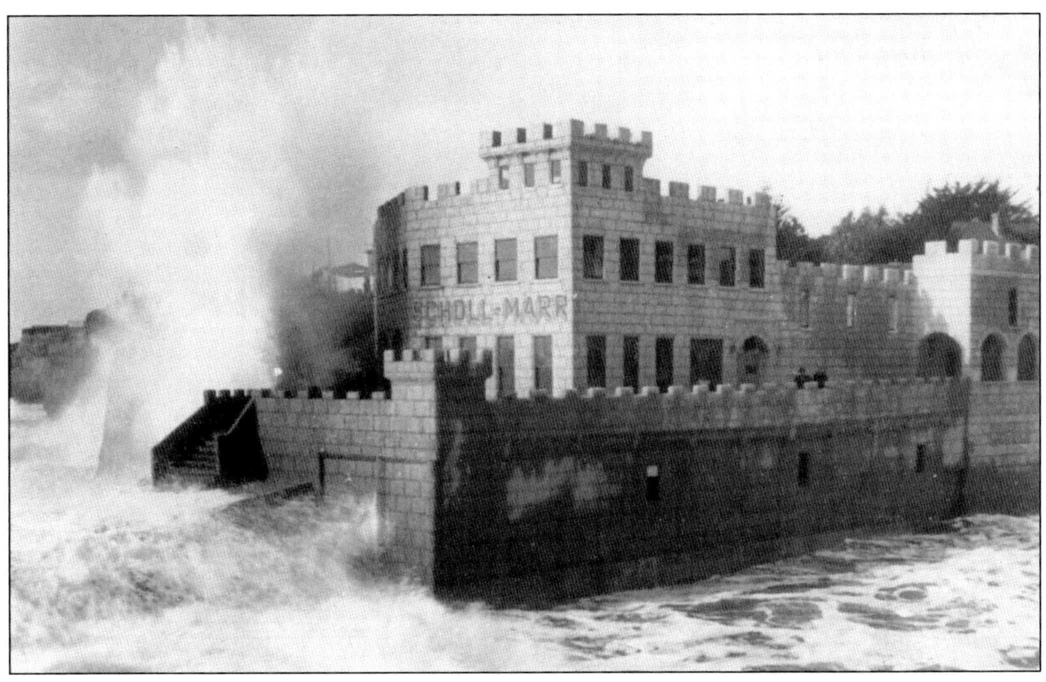

When the first winter storm endured by the Scholl Marr Castle broke most of the windows, Louis Scholl constructed a concrete seawall to deflect attacking waves. His fortifications proved successful against the record-breaking rain of December 1931—a storm that flooded much of Santa Cruz. Once again, piles of logs and lumber washed up on the Cove, enabling Scholl to gather enough wood to fuel his hot baths for the upcoming summer. (Above, courtesy of the Geisreiter collection; below, courtesy of MAH.)

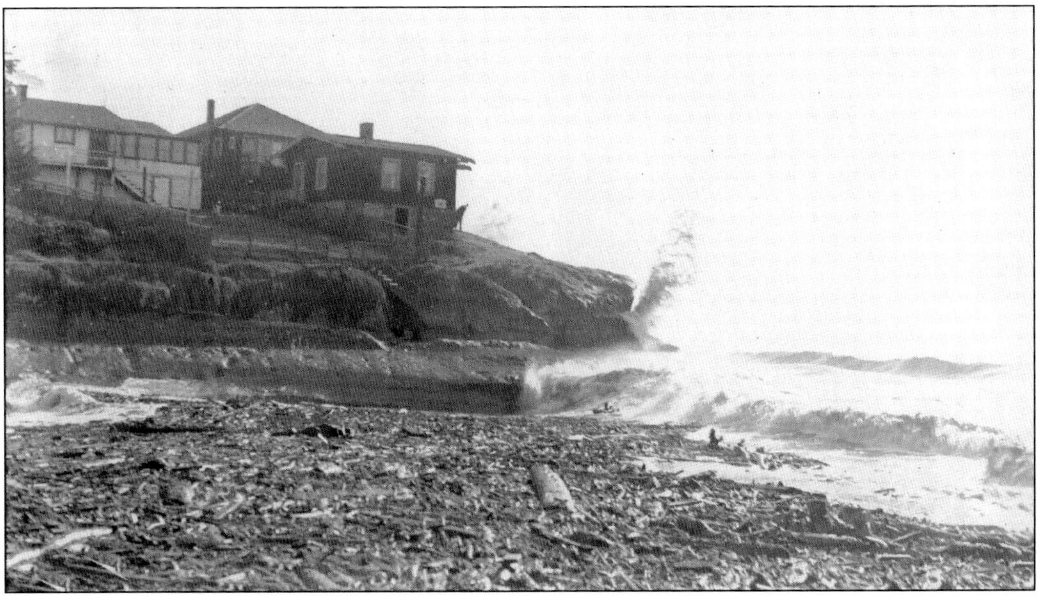

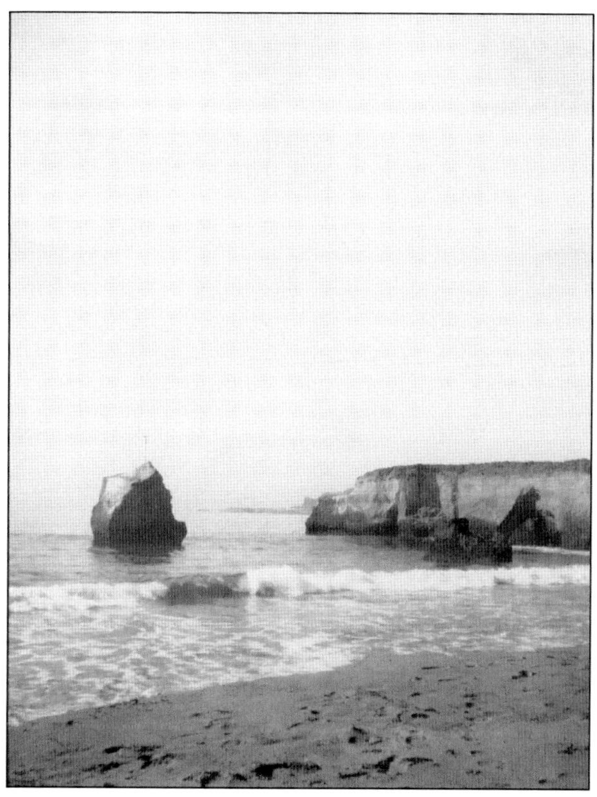

The sandstone formation known as San Lorenzo Point had a tunnel near its midpoint, connecting the river and the ocean, often a danger for unwary swimmers. In September 1932, an undertow sucked a woman and two children out of the river and into the crevasse. Hearing calls for help, two Seabrightans, Harold Stewart and a friend, rushed to the rescue but were only able to save one child. Arriving too late, Louis Scholl urged authorities to eliminate the deadly gap. Stewart's deed earned him a job as a city lifeguard, but he lost his life a few years later trying to rescue a stranded ocean swimmer. (Courtesy of SNA.)

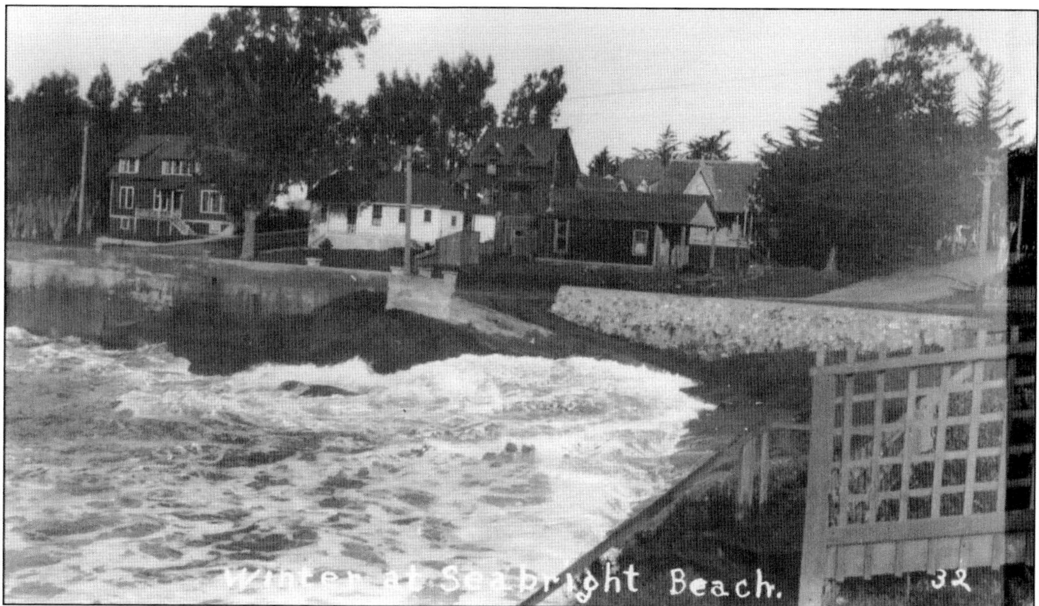

The tallest structure pictured here, 110 Mott Avenue, was originally built by local activist Susan Tyrrell in 1889, and she lived there until her death in 1918. The Dunhams, of Fresno, bought it as their permanent home in 1930 along with the single-story white cottage in front. Their son Dick, who was nine years old at the time, became Santa Cruz High School's student body president and football star in 1939. (Courtesy of Joan Kimble Miller-Prescott.)

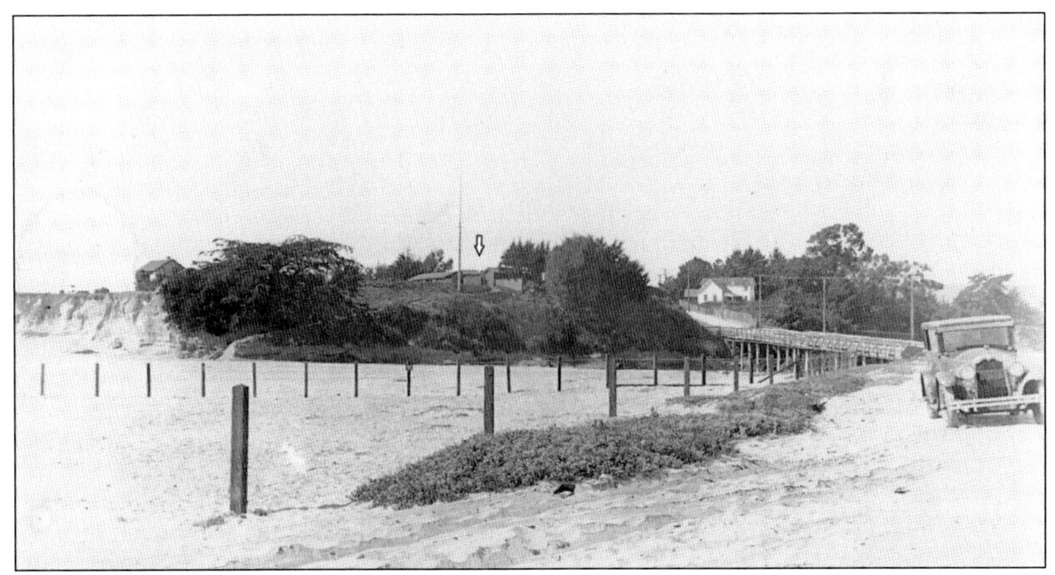

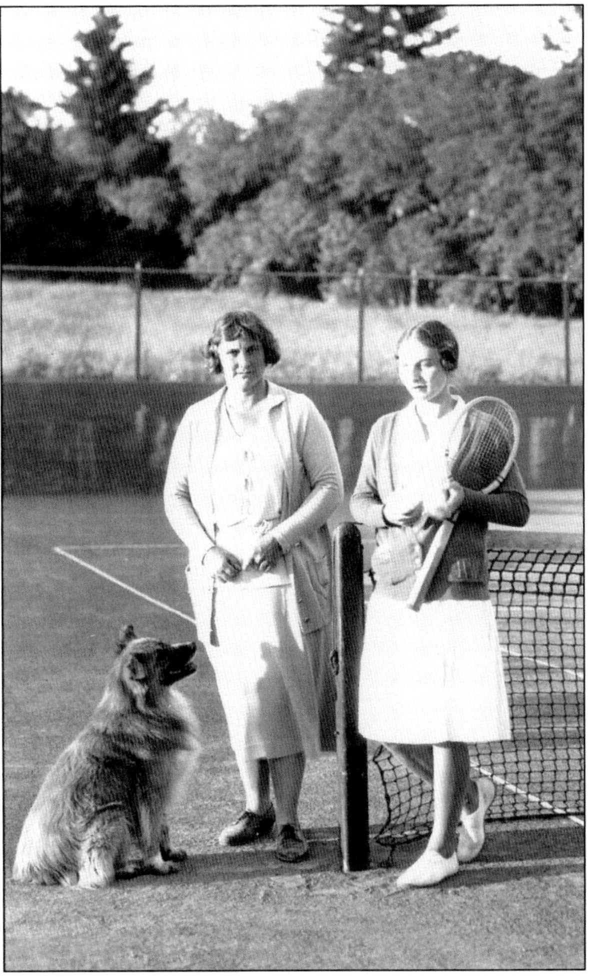

At the boundary of Seabright, poverty coexisted with glamour in the early 1930s. The Woods Lagoon Bridge, far right above, provided shelter for a colony of unemployed "knights of the road." Meanwhile, famed golfer Marion Hollins, having established her Pasatiempo Golf Club, added the Pasatiempo Beach Club (above center). She remodeled the former estate of a lumber baron, creating a volleyball court, cabanas, and patios for posh parties and welcoming celebrities like tennis star Helen Wills Moody to both locations. Pictured with Hollins's dog Carlos, Hollins and Moody enjoy the Pasatiempo tennis courts. Some in Santa Cruz regarded Hollins as "a fairy godmother." Her Seabright neighbors did not share that opinion when she fenced in her property—the entire point of land at the community's easternmost edge—to create an exclusive outdoor area for club members. Neighbors, having been denied access to the beach, were up in arms. Lawsuits and countersuits ensued until 1935, when financial troubles forced the club's closure. (Above, courtesy of the Geisreiter collection; left, courtesy of Loon Hill Galleries.)

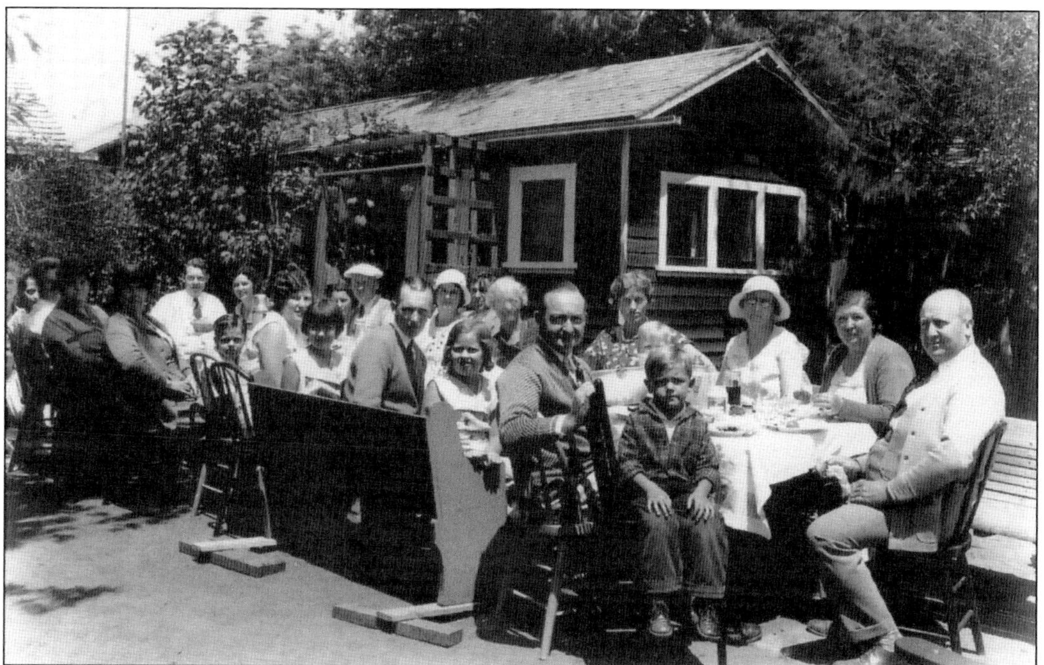

San José couple William and Effy Carper James, front right, bought the quaint 1880s beach bungalow at 218 Seabright Avenue. Throughout the 1930s and from that time on, multiple generations of the James and Carper families gathered for family picnics in this expansive courtyard, typical of the neighborhood's outdoor entertaining. William and Effy's grandson Ron James, the four-year-old at the head of the table, would become the first elected mayor of San José, taking office in January 1967. He continues to retain ownership of the family home. (Courtesy of the James family.)

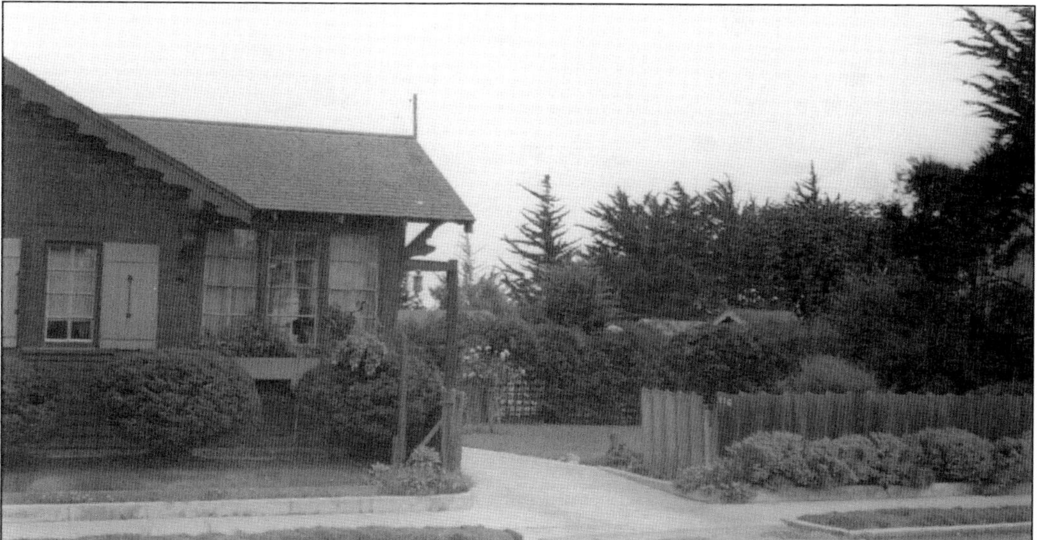

Robert Skelley and his wife, Constance, of Riverside, sold their spacious summer residence at 116 Fourth Avenue (pictured) to registered nurse Ellen Larkin, who promptly converted the home into a guesthouse. Cosy Neuk opened for business in the summer of 1932. Larkin also provided a venue for cultural events, including a showing of world-traveler Ida Geisreiter's color motion pictures of foreign lands. (Courtesy of Beverly Wolfe.)

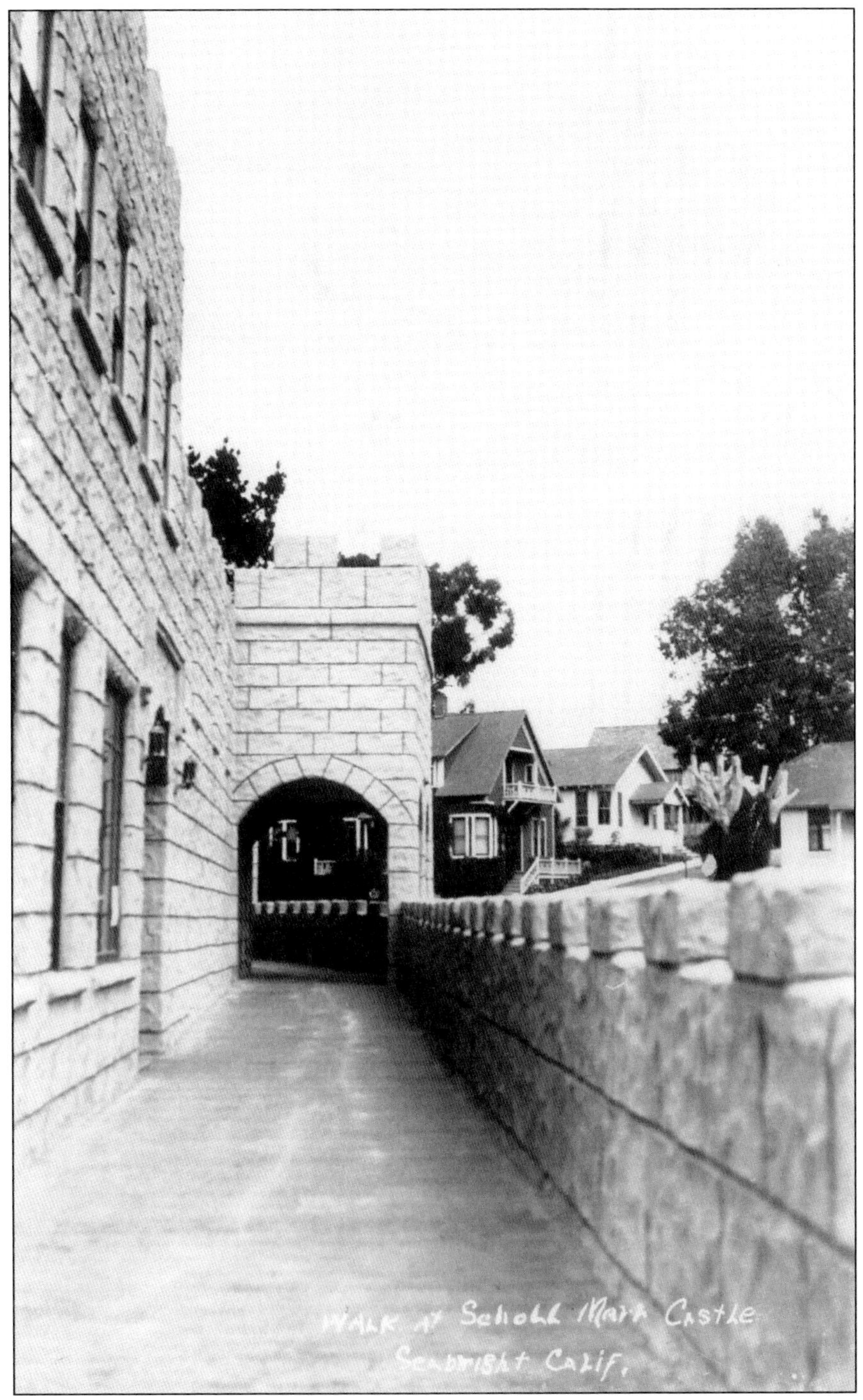

Diners seeking the lovely bay views of the Scholl Marr Castle's restaurant used this corridor from East Cliff Drive, conveniently avoiding sand in their shoes. Patrons enjoyed affordable full-course meals of abalone or fried chicken. Louis Scholl advertised "real" turkey dinners at Thanksgiving "with all the fun but none of the work." The price was $1. (Courtesy of the Ronnie Trubek collection.)

Throughout the Depression, the Seabright cannery of the Santa Cruz Fruit Packing Company provided jobs for hundreds of workers, mostly women. They prepared and packed locally grown pears, peaches, plums, apricots, cherries, artichokes, and spinach. The fancy Santa Cruz and Seabright brands, below, were sold nationwide. When cannery officials announced plans to expand to an adjacent residential block in 1936, the neighbors organized a protest. Their complaints to the city included the loss of sleep due to trucks arriving at night, the stench created by rotting pear peels, and the foul language of workers. When the company agreed to limit trucking and to clean up its refuse piles, locals dropped their objections. (Right, courtesy of SCMNH; below, courtesy of MAH.)

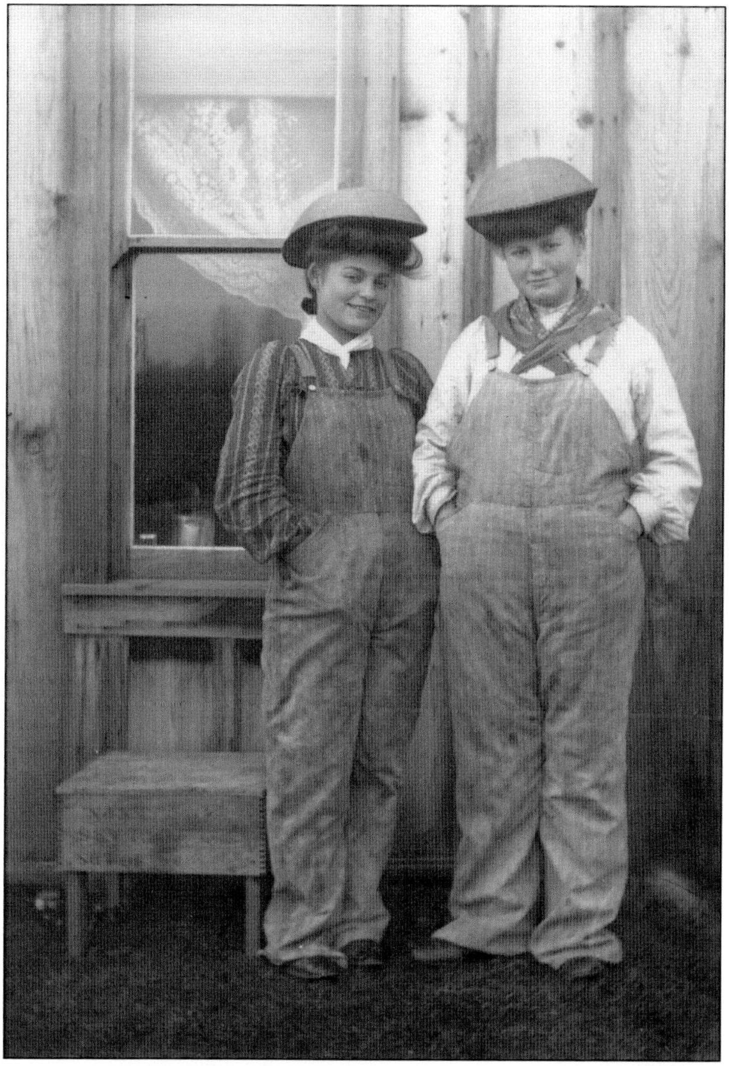

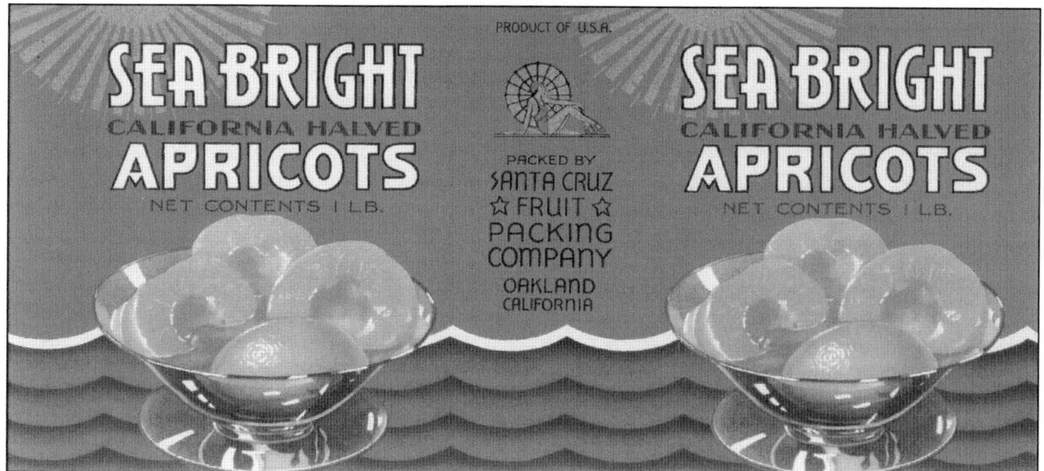

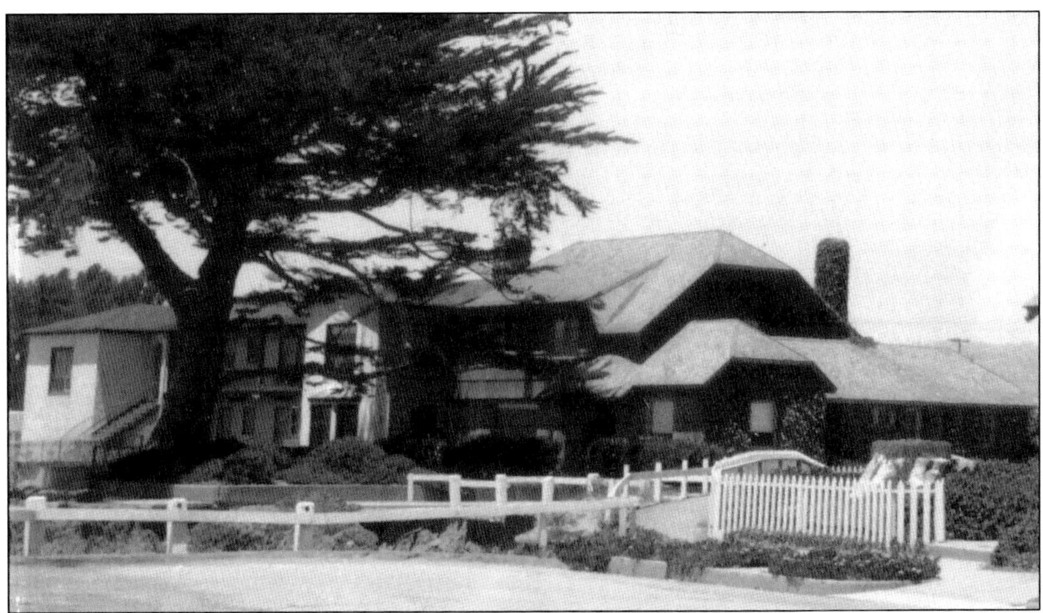

Minnie Chace Hihn had deep local roots as the daughter of a Santa Cruz mayor and widow of Frederick O. Hihn, son of entrepreneur and public servant F.A. Hihn. In 1921, she relocated from downtown Santa Cruz to Seabright. Local architects Walter Byrne and Allen Collins designed her new home at 1711 East Cliff Drive to resemble an English-style thatched-roof house. When the venerable cypress pictured showed signs of decay, she brought in an expert tree surgeon to preserve it, and the tree has been carefully attended by subsequent generations. (Courtesy of SNA.)

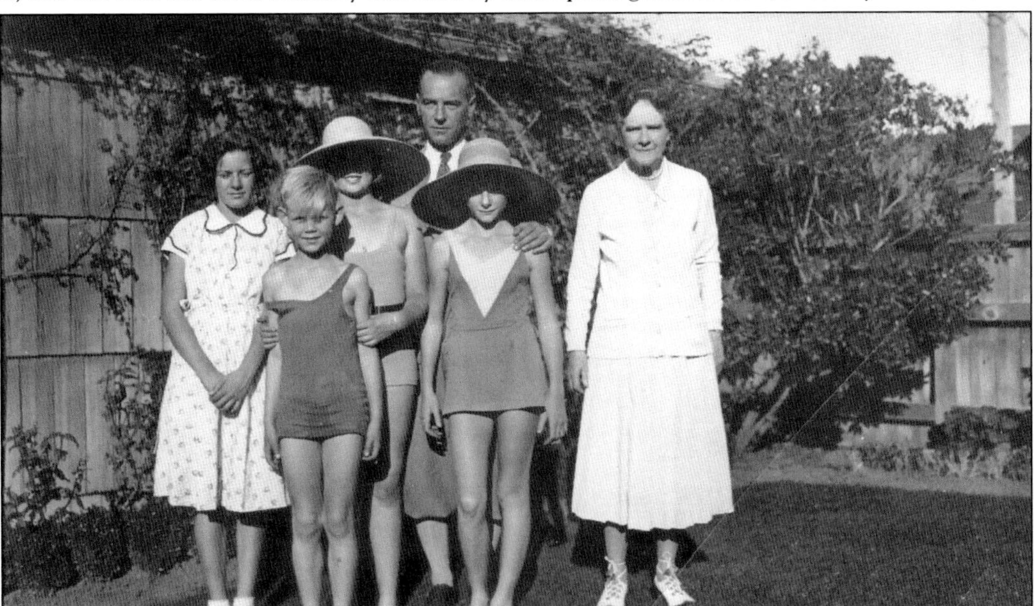

Minnie (at right) poses in her rose-filled garden with her son Frederick D. (in back), his daughter Gloria (second from right), Gloria's neighborhood pals Jim Boone (with blond locks), and his sister Mariellen (directly behind him), and an unidentified visitor (far left). A native San Franciscan, Gloria spent summers visiting her grandmother and eventually lived in the home year-round. (Courtesy of Mariellen Boone.)

These playful beachgoers are probably oblivious to the eroding cliff directly behind them. Wave action had undermined the softer deposits of sandstone, leaving an overhanging ledge at the top of the cliff. In December 1931, a powerful storm attacked another weakened bluff at nearby Fourth Avenue, causing a section of East Cliff Drive to collapse. After surveying the damage, city engineers permanently closed that section of the scenic roadway. (Courtesy of the Lionel T. Lenox collection.)

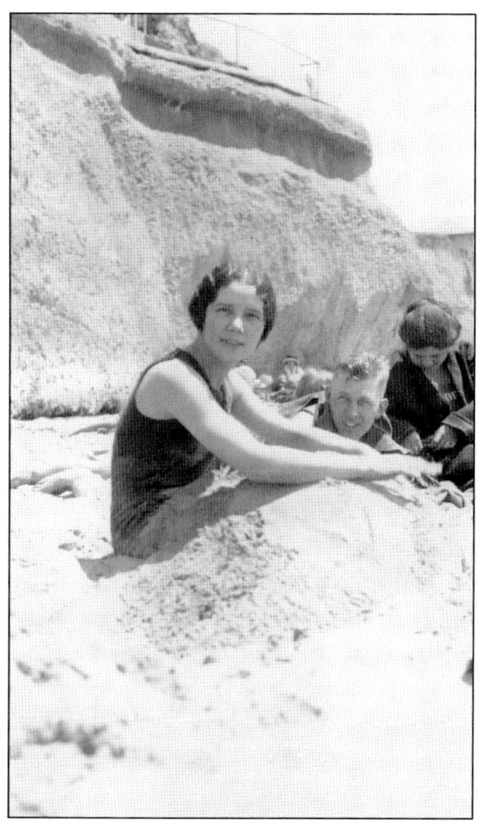

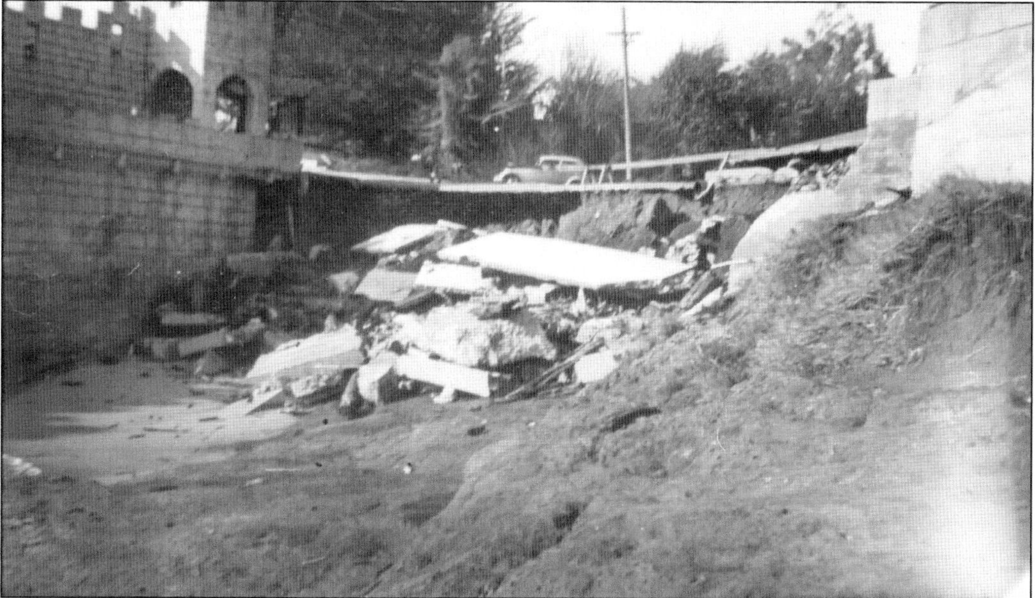

Cliff erosion increasingly threatened Seabright streets and sidewalks. A downpour in January 1938 caused the collapse of East Cliff Drive at the Cove (pictured). The city repaired the damage, but in 1939, another piece of the drive fell onto the beach a few blocks away at Second Avenue. (Courtesy of SNA.)

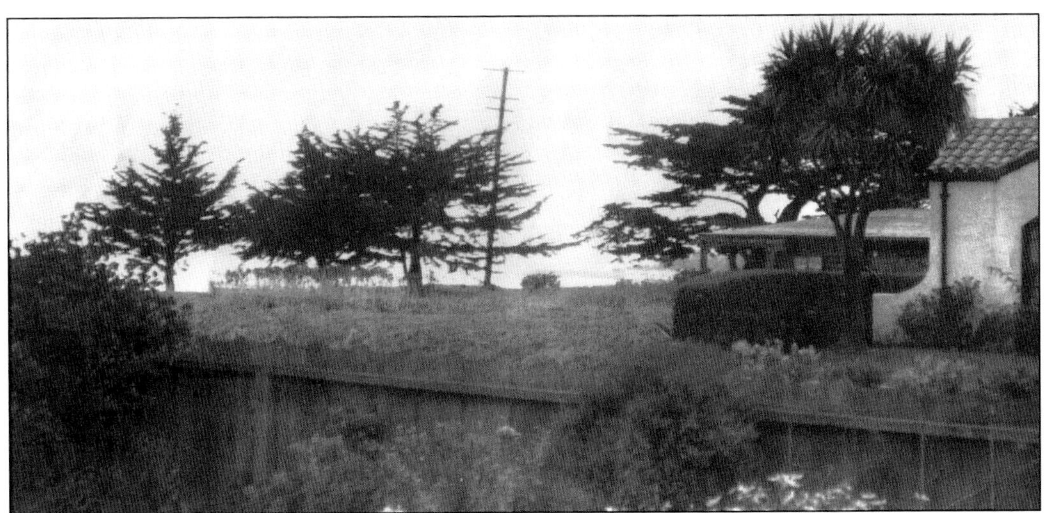

George and Isabella Gow joined Seabright's "Fresno Colony" when their summer home was completed in 1933, complete with servant quarters and a two-car garage. From the living room of the Spanish-style residence at 113 Fourth Avenue, they enjoyed an unobstructed view of the bay—no one expected the front lot, subject to cliff erosion, would ever be built upon. The Gows' close friend from Fresno, Nan Barton (see page 44), owned the cottage next door at 1907 East Cliff Drive. (Courtesy of Beverly Wolfe.)

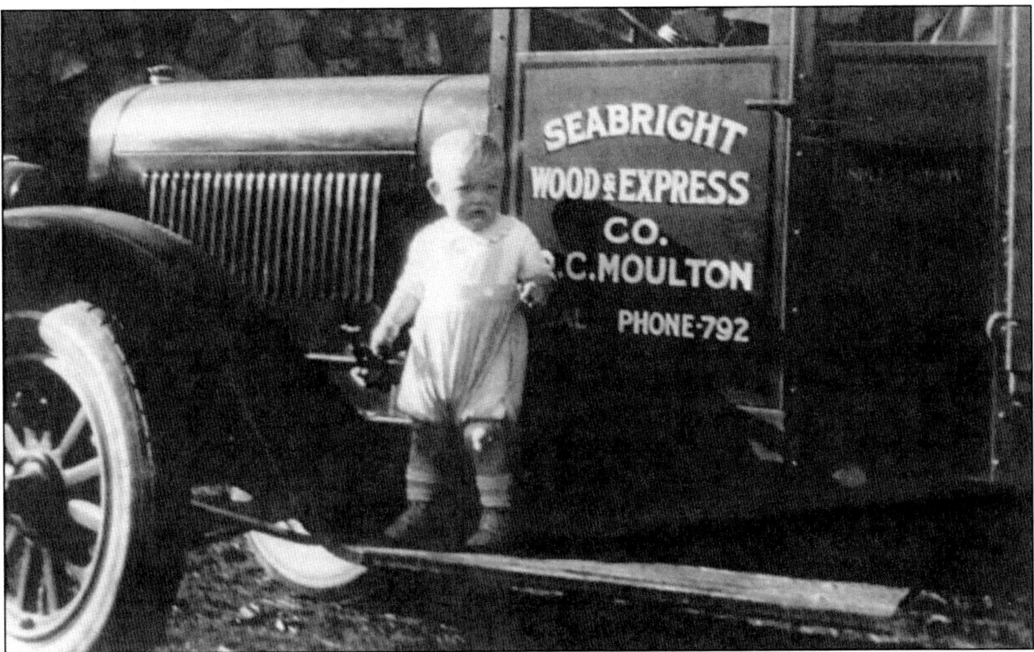

Seabright native Kenneth "Mo" Moulton, born in 1926, poses in his father's woodyard on Seabright Avenue. The pickup truck, which replaced Oliver C. Moulton's horse-drawn wagon, enabled him to expand into express hauling, which included the heavy trunks of summer visitors. As a teenager, Mo had a full-time summer job at the cannery and excelled in Santa Cruz High School sports. After commencement in 1944, he enlisted in the Navy and volunteered for submarine duty, earning the right to wear the "double-dolphin" insignia of the Submarine Service. (Courtesy of SNA.)

Originally from Merced, J. Douglas Wagner, right, and wife, the former Marjorie Saunders, inherited her mother's summer house at 303 Atlantic Avenue in 1934, where they would raise their orphaned niece and nephew—Mariellen and Jim Boone. Across the street from their new home, the family observed the constant turnover in a barracks-like block of low-rent apartments. When land in front of the complex became available, Wagner bought it and hired prominent local architect Lee Dill Esty to design a building worthy of the site. Each of the five living rooms in the Spanish Eclectic, Monterey Revival–style La Solana Apartments offered an unobstructed bay view. La Solana was to be "A Real Home for Santa Cruzans." Permanent residents were welcome—transient vacation-seekers need not apply. (Both, courtesy of Mariellen Boone.)

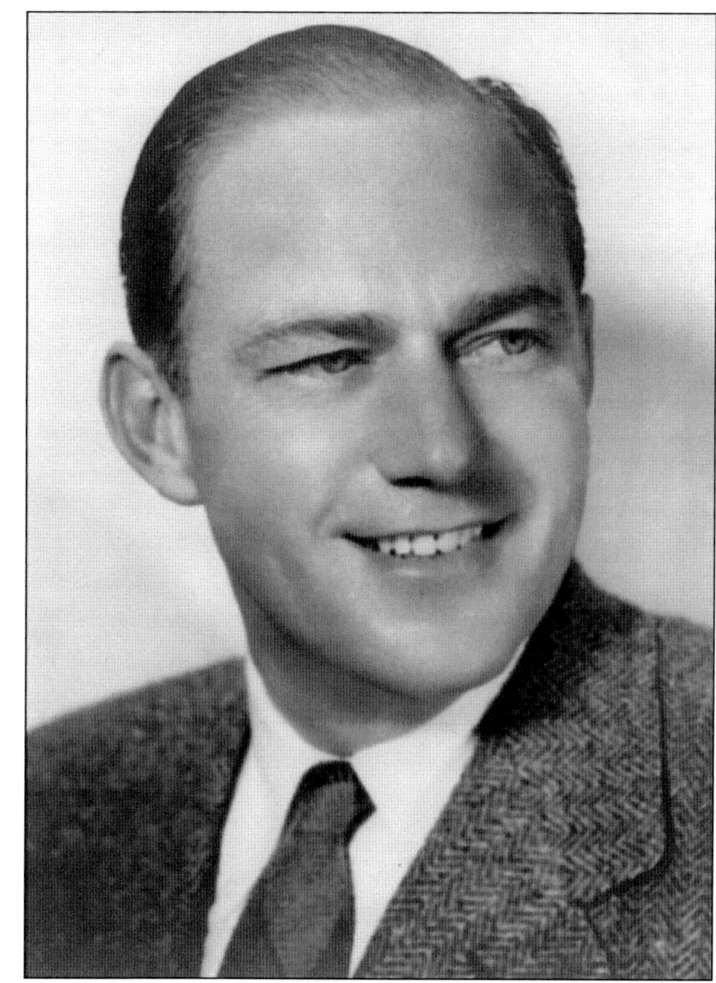

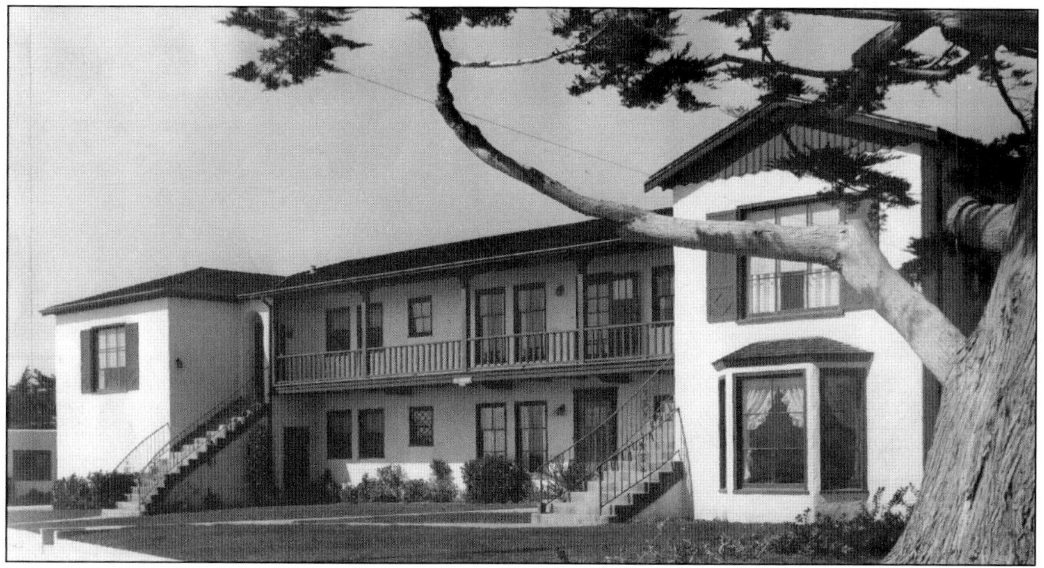

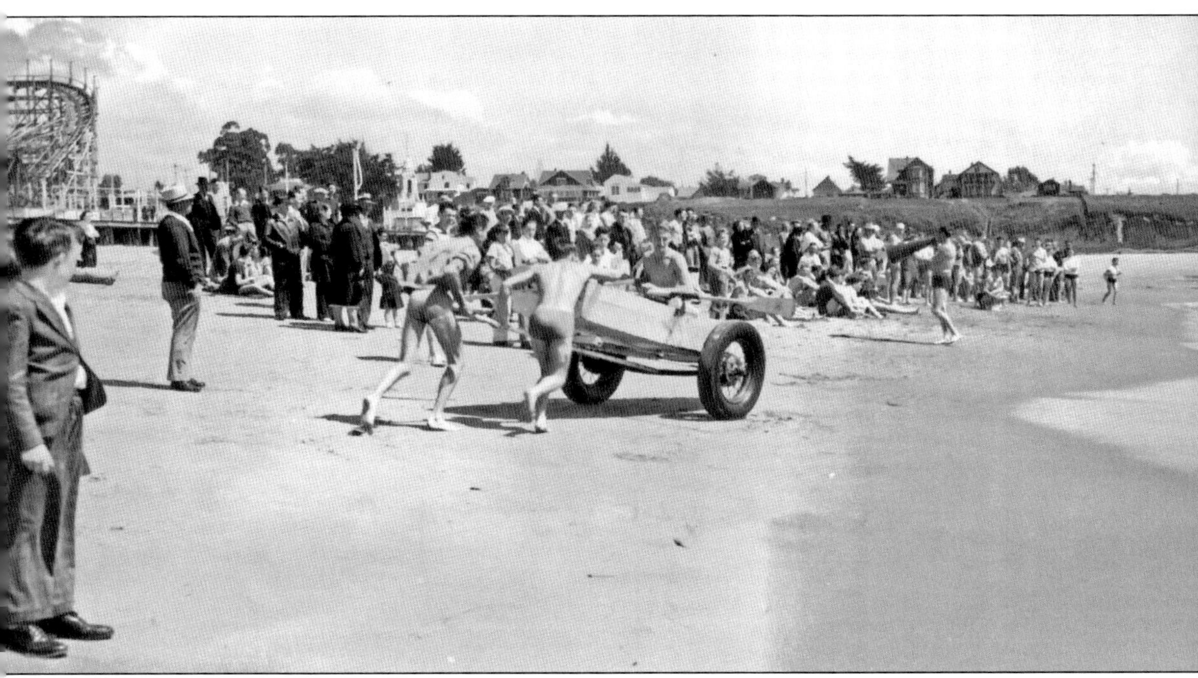

The heroic death of Harold Stewart (see page 71) led to an expansion of the local lifeguard corps and in 1935, Marion Blake became Seabright's first official guard. The Seaside Company provided boats to help carry endangered swimmers to shore, as did Louis Scholl, who mounted his on a rubber-tired dolly, shown here. In April 1939, the Red Cross staged this event at Santa Cruz Main Beach to promote a new lifesaving tool—the hollow surfboard. Thanks to world-renowned surfer and inventor Tom Blake, hollow boards, much lighter than traditional ones, could be quickly and easily brought into service. In the background, East Cliff Drive homes overlook the San Lorenzo River with the Ocean View House in the middle at right. A few homes have been added since the early 1900s, but the Seabright building boom has substantially slowed. (Courtesy of SNA.)

The growing popularity of surfing in Santa Cruz owed much to young enthusiasts, seen here spending time at the Cove. High school track star Rich Thompson, far left, helped organize the Santa Cruz Surfing Club in August 1939. Many members, including club president Harry Mayo, crafted their own boards in shop class. Before long, female surfers, led by Pat Collings, second from right, formed a club of their own. Also pictured are Eugene "Jeep" Allen, between Thompson and Collings, and P.B. "Smitty" Smith, far right. The Jory house (see page 31) sits at the intersection of East Cliff Drive and Seabright Avenue, at the far left. (Courtesy of Santa Cruz Surfing Club Preservation Society.)

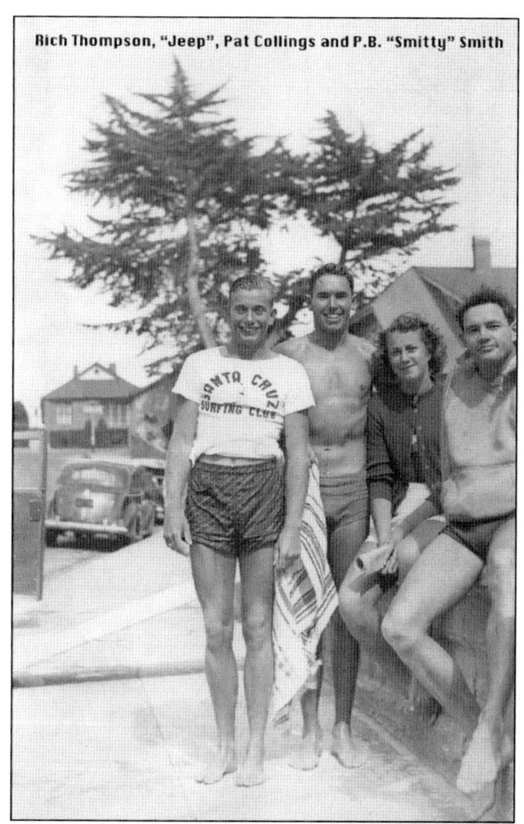

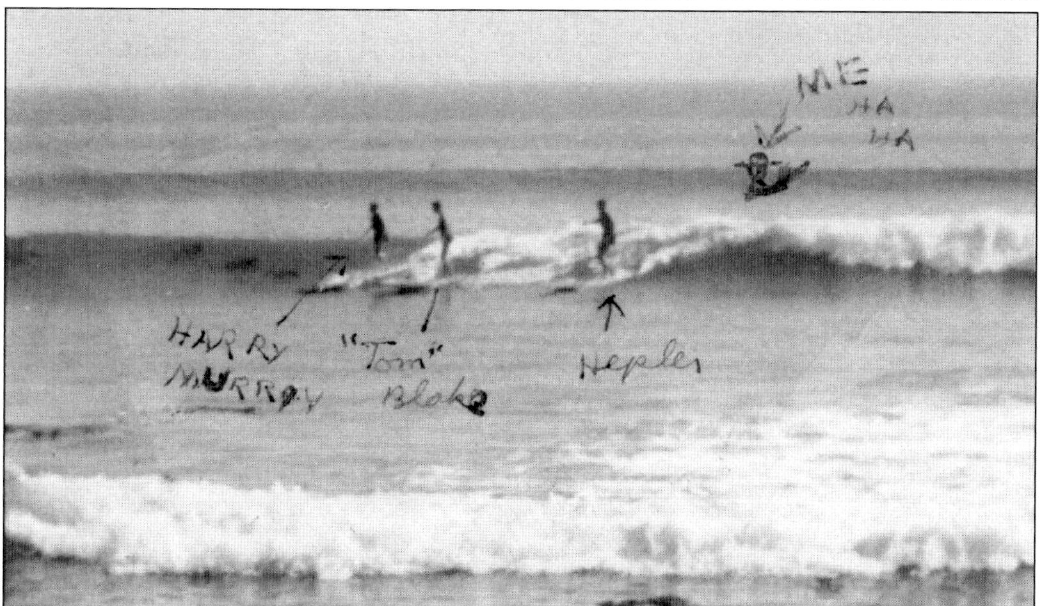

Members of the Santa Cruz Surfing Club often carried cameras to the beach with their boards. This view, taken off Seabright Beach, presents a bit of a puzzle. Is the "Tom" Blake noted on the image the legendary surfer and Malibu lifeguard, or has the photographer assigned a nickname to local lifeguard Marion Blake? (Courtesy of Santa Cruz Surfing Club Preservation Society.)

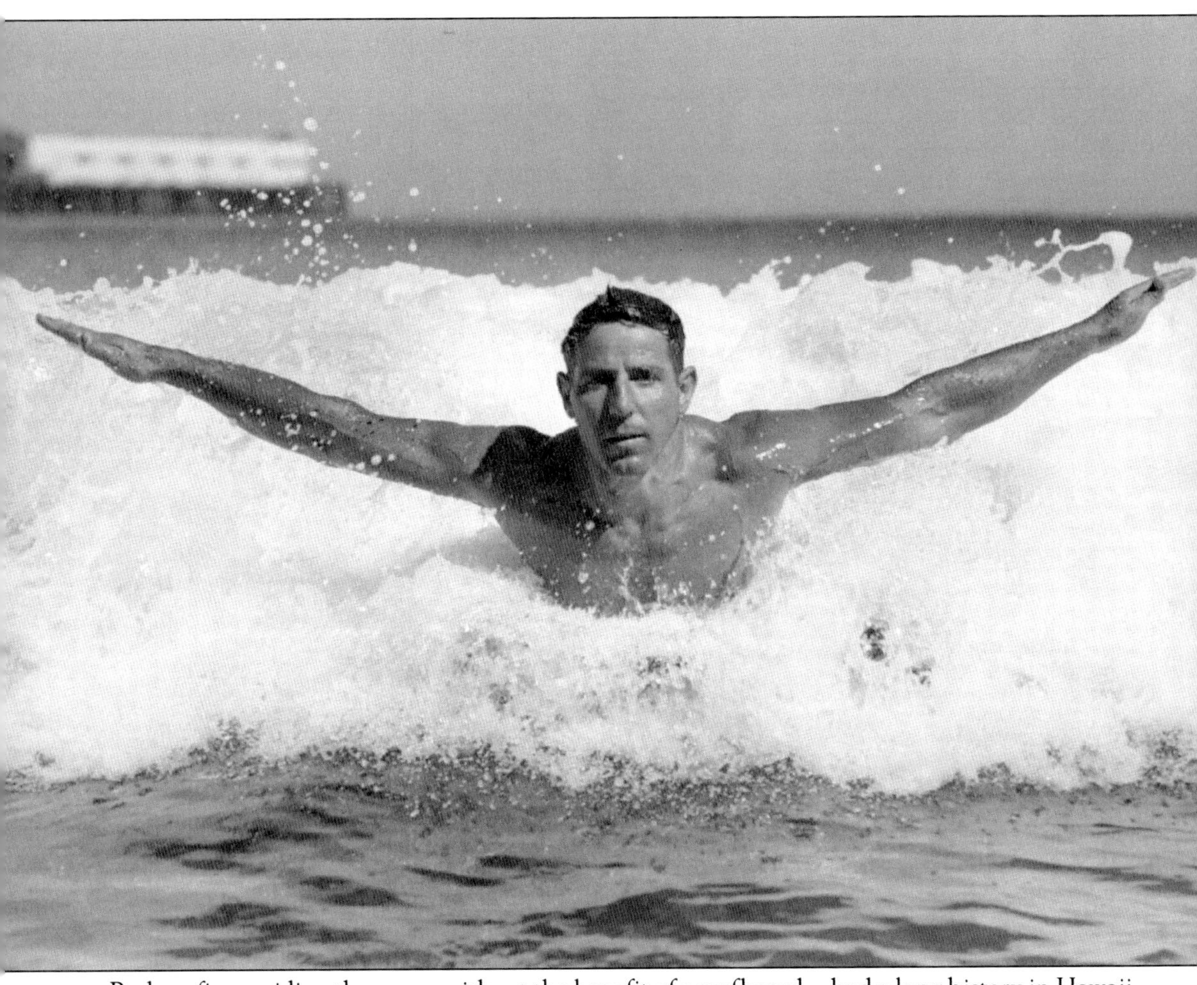

Bodysurfing—riding the waves without the benefit of a surfboard—had a long history in Hawaii. During the early 1930s, the sport caught on in California, and Seabright offered an ideal spot: the narrow stretch between Pinnacle Rock and San Lorenzo Point. Warren "Skip" Littlefield, of the Seaside Company, believed that Santa Cruz's future as a surfing destination was "second only to Honolulu." To publicize the idea, he enlisted photographer Ed Webber, a Seabright native, to document the thrill of bodysurfing. Don "Bosco" Patterson, star of aquatic exhibitions at Santa Cruz Main Beach and Boardwalk Plunge, agreed to pose for a shoot. Webber perched on Littlefield's shoulders on and off for two days to capture this image of Patterson completing a ride. Littlefield labeled it "The Action Photo of the Generation," and it appears in the July 1941 issue of the American Automobile Association's magazine *Motorland*. Patterson's demonstration confirmed bodysurfing's status as a Santa Cruz sport. (Photograph by Ed Webber, courtesy of Santa Cruz Beach Boardwalk Archives.)

Six

Service at Home and Abroad

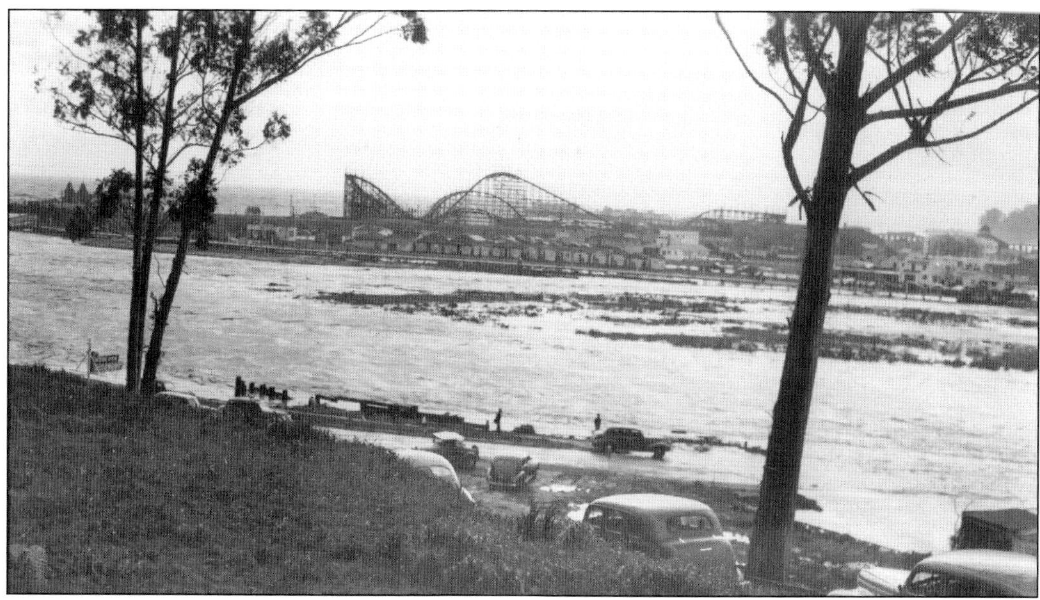

The dawning of the 1940s brought hopes of a return to the boom of the 1920s after a decade spent in the Great Depression. But in Santa Cruz the era began with two consecutive winters of devastating storms. This Ed Webber photograph from February 1941 shows the San Lorenzo River with overflowing banks at lower East Cliff Drive, across from the Boardwalk. Wood piled up at Seabright Cove faster than it could be gathered, while sections of the drive lost more ground. Meanwhile, news of the escalating world war convinced Americans to prepare for the worst. In the summer of 1941, several young men who would have been seen at the Castle Beach began heading elsewhere for military training. (Courtesy of Covello & Covello.)

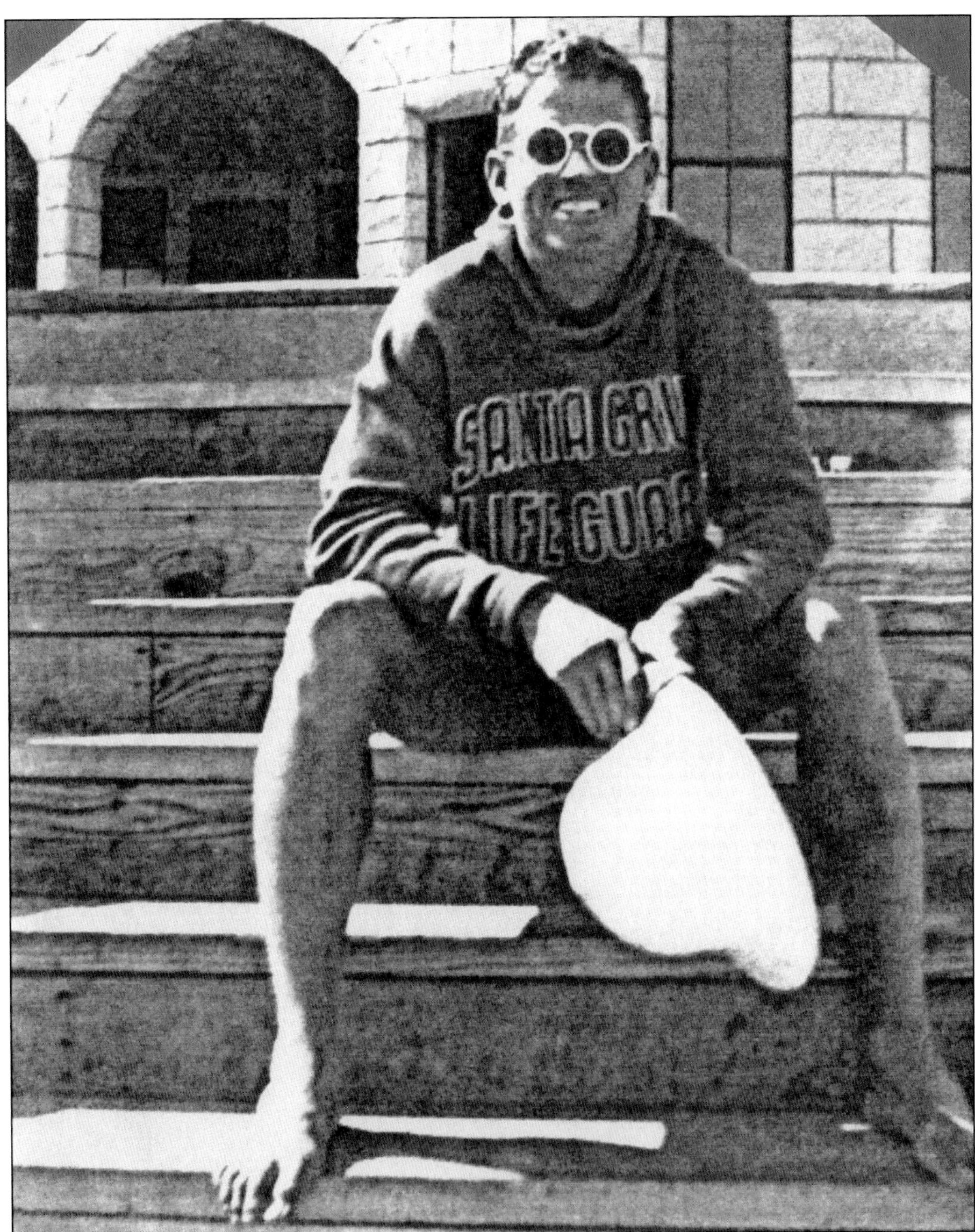

The Mee brothers of San Francisco, Hubert and Fred, spent all their childhood summers in Seabright with family friend Beatrice Milward on Pilkington Avenue. Older brother Hubert (pictured on the Castle steps), a University of California, Berkeley student in the late 1930s, earned a summer job as a Castle Beach lifeguard. Hubert joined the Navy and became an officer in June 1941, assigned to the USS *Quincy*. His ship supported the Marine Corps assault on Guadalcanal the following summer, but a Japanese counterattack sank the ship within an hour. Hubert, one of the few officers to survive, spent four hours in shark-infested waters and helped save the lives of fellow crewmen before being picked up by a destroyer. (Courtesy of the Mee family collection.)

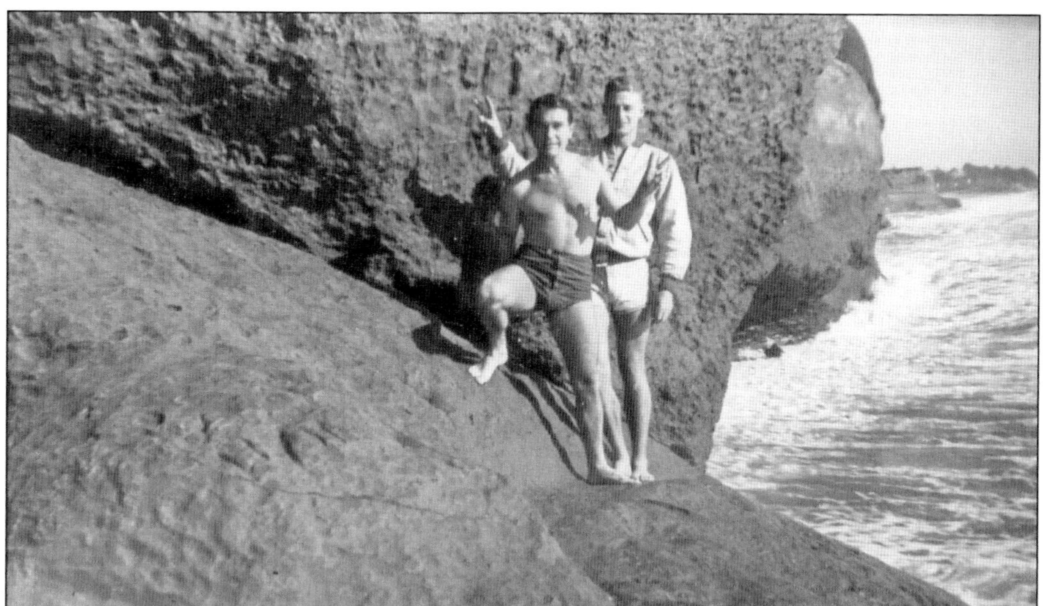

In January, 1942, a month after the attack on Pearl Harbor, Stewart Cureton (left) and Fred Mee flash the V sign for "victory." Mee notes on the back of this snapshot taken of the cliff on Castle Beach: "Yes, we did go in for a swim." Cureton had braved the chilly water from early boyhood, while staying at the family's summer home at what is today 1591 East Cliff Drive. (Courtesy of the Mee family collection.)

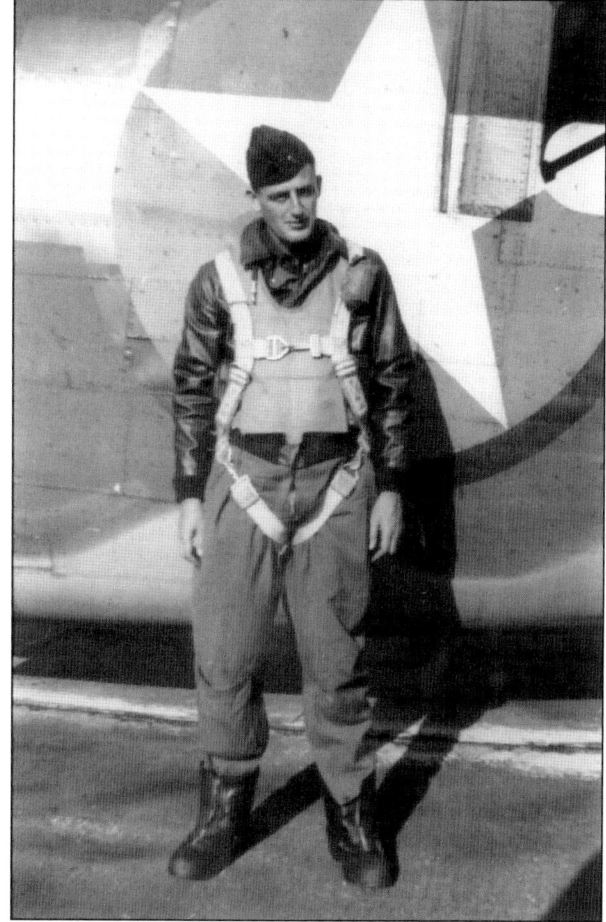

In the summer of 1942, Fred Mee showed his lifesaving prowess by diving into the Seabright surf to help distressed local surfer Malcom Sinclair reach shore. A year later, as an Army Air Forces lieutenant, Mee served as a bomber's navigation officer. Hit by flak, the plane disintegrated, but Fred recovered consciousness in time to open his parachute. He spent several months as a POW in Romania before returning to Seabright, where he made his permanent home. (Courtesy of the Mee family collection.)

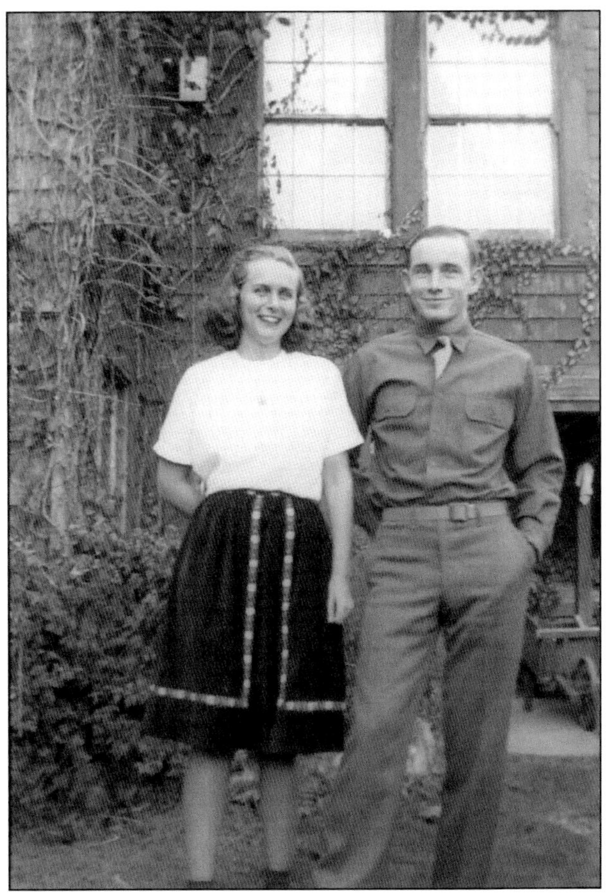

Dick Dunham (see page 71) left Seabright in November 1941 to become a private in the Army Air Corps. Assigned to a bomber crew, he served as both radar operator and waist gunner. Two years later, Sergeant Dunham returned home on furlough, having recently been awarded an air medal. Stopping in San Francisco, he married his college sweetheart, Dorothy McLean, who was then working as a secretary for the War Production Board. In his third year, Dunham (below, first row, second from left) spent time in Newfoundland hunting for Nazi submarines and received a second air medal. The couple honeymooned at 110 Mott Avenue (at left), where they later raised two sons—Roger and Larry. Dorothy and Larry still live there, preserving one of Seabright's most historic homes. (Both, courtesy of the Dunham family.)

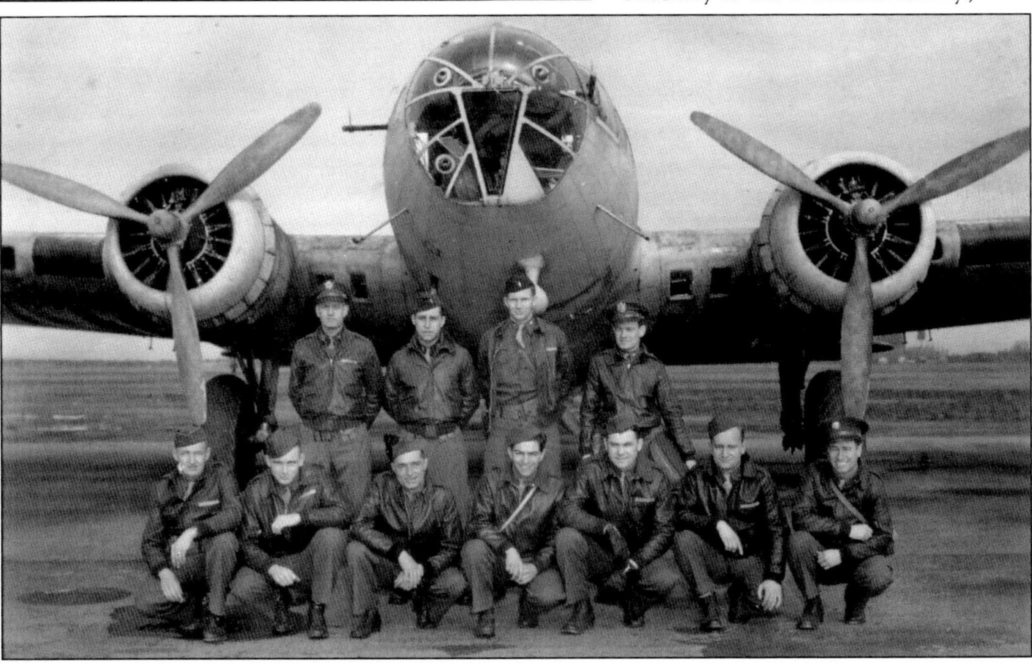

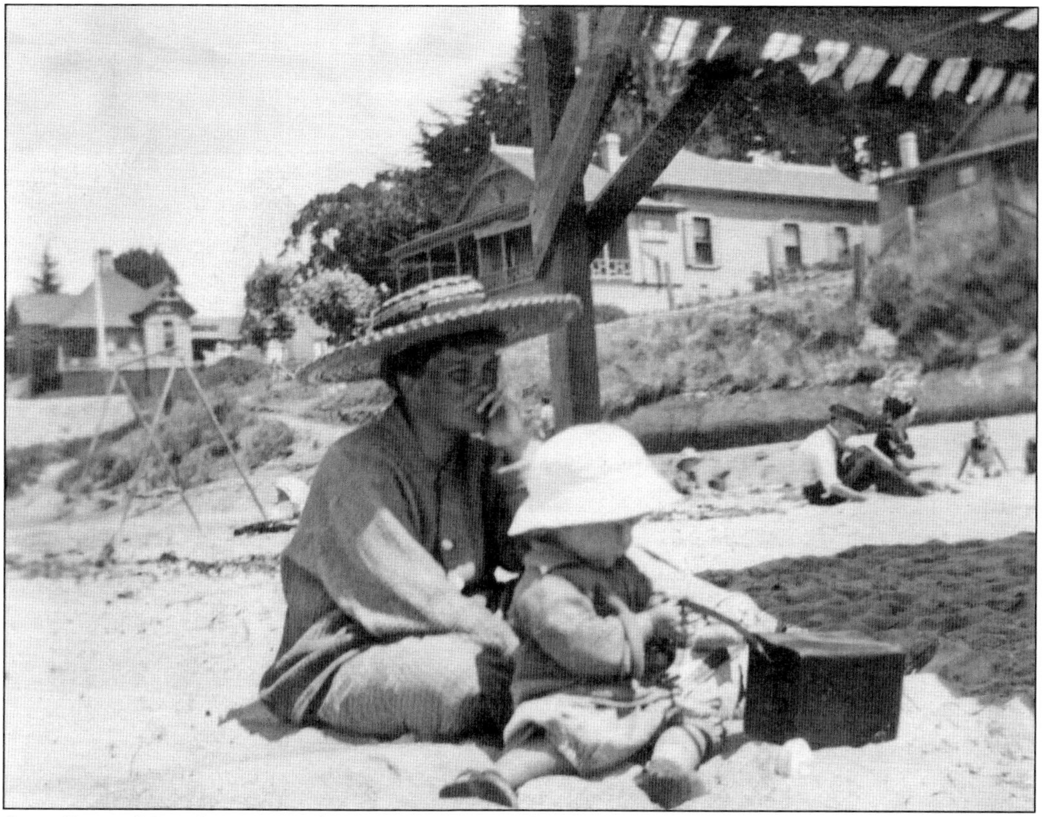

Starr Pait, of San José, seen above at age two with her mother, Bertha, in 1913, spent summers and vacations at the family beach house on Mott Avenue. Twenty years later, she pursued postgraduate work in Munich. Within two years, she married Werner Guerke, a German-born businessman living primarily in Costa Rica. In 1941, Werner was blacklisted and, subsequently, labeled as one of the "thirty-five most dangerous enemy aliens." He, Starr, and their young daughters, Heidi and Ingrid, were forced to leave Costa Rica and interned in Crystal City, Texas. By 1946, Werner no longer had the "enemy alien" label, but deportation to Germany loomed. A group of Starr's Seabright friends intervened, petitioning the Department of Justice on Werner's behalf: "His deportation and separation from his family would deprive us of an intelligent, cultured, responsible resident." From then on, the family lived on Mott Avenue where Werner taught Heidi (right) and Ingrid biking fundamentals. Years later, Starr's abilities as a linguist led her to translate early California documents for Special Collections at the University of California at Santa Cruz. Today, Heidi and her husband, Bruce Donald, make their home on Brook Avenue. (Both, courtesy of Heidi Donald.)

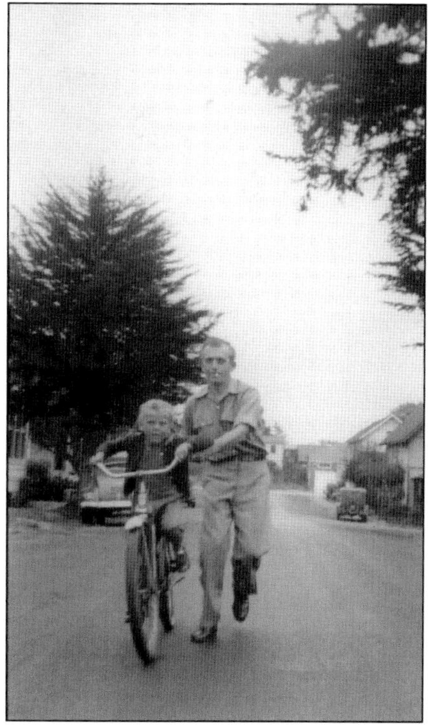

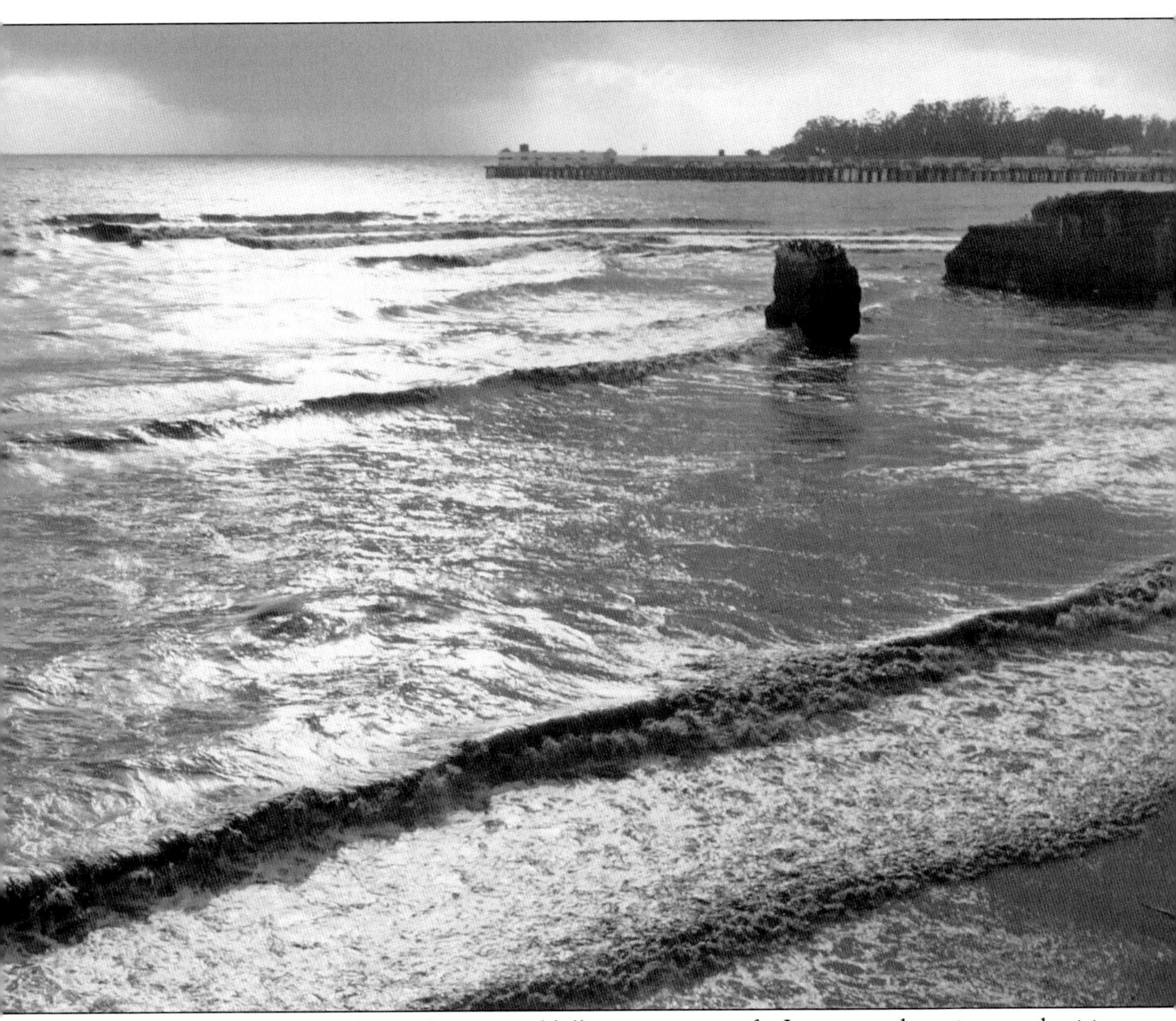

Fearing that the lights of coastal cities would illuminate targets for Japanese submarines, authorities imposed blackout regulations in the first months of the war. Tony Day, a longtime local businessman, served as the neighborhood's Civil Defense leader. "When the Air Raid Warden comes to your home," citizens were advised, "do what he tells you. He is for your protection." Observing the view from East Cliff Drive in the spring of 1943, a *Sentinel* reporter waxed nostalgic: "In bygone years, before Pearl Harbor, when there was no blackout in this town and vicinity, it was indeed pleasant to go to San Lorenzo Point and watch the giant beacon at intervals all through the night and the lights at the casino and the giant dipper glittering in the darkness." Months later, the War Department relaxed its vigilance and the outlines of Santa Cruz reappeared. (Photograph by Ed Webber, courtesy of Santa Cruz Beach Boardwalk Archives.)

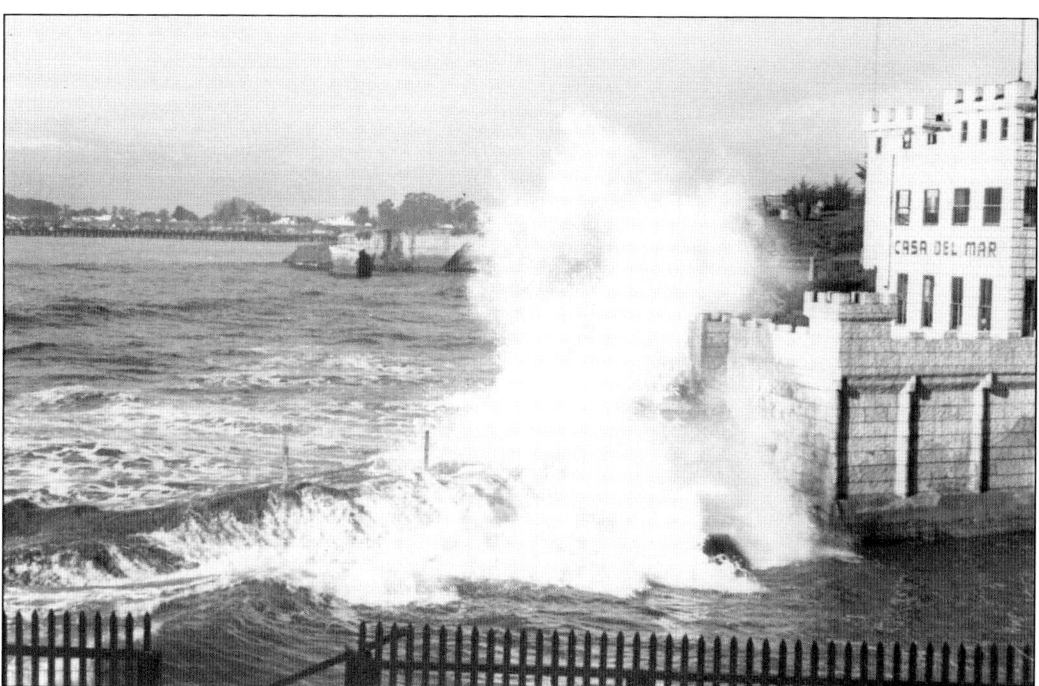

Louis Scholl, at 54, contributed to the war effort by serving as chief engineer at Camp Stoneham in Contra Costa County, where one million soldiers passed through on their way to war. When Scholl returned to Seabright in 1944, he married Adeline Hagen, a USO organizer, and surprised his friends by putting the Castle, his own creation, up for sale. Purchaser W.E. Dodge gave the resort a new name—Casa del Mar—but his ownership quickly ended when neighbors fought a plan to sell liquor. (Courtesy of the Geisreiter collection.)

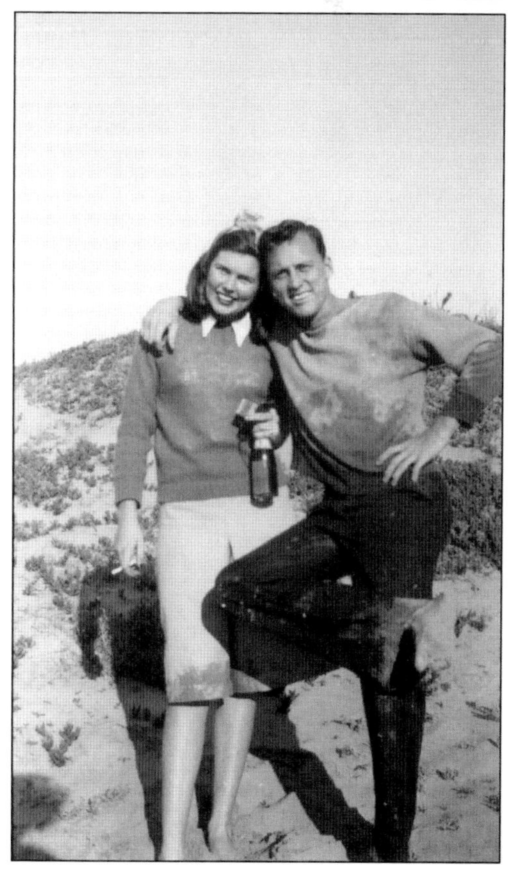

Mariellen Boone grew up in Seabright, where Jack Pagen returned each summer with his family to their home at 416 Atlantic Avenue. Best friends since childhood, here Mariellen and Jack celebrate summer fun before Jack enlisted in the Marines as a pilot and flew missions in the Pacific until September 1945. Jack's Marine buddy Brooks Pierce married Mariellen in 1947, and Jack married Janet Hanscom. (Courtesy of Mariellen Boone.)

The sands of time run endlessly and the grain has now sifted through which marks the going of 1945—the coming of 1946! The old year brought with it some good things, the greatest of all being the war's end. Now may 1946 bring us more good things than the world has ever enjoyed.

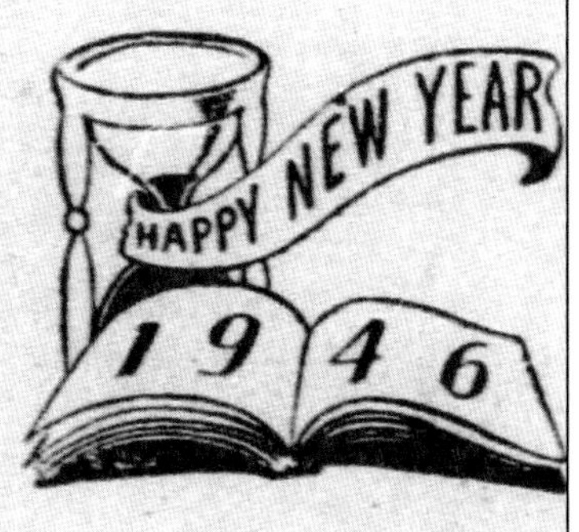

TONY DAY'S MARKET

CHOICE MEATS OF ALL KINDS & CHEESE

THE MEAT DEPARTMENT

(EASTON HILL, Owner)

436 Seabright Ave. Phone 1430

Since the mid-1920s, Tony Day had provided Seabright with meat and groceries. The mutual loyalty between him and his customers withstood the challenges of the Great Depression as well as the wartime rationing rules. To celebrate the war's end, Tony placed this advertisement in the *Santa Cruz Sentinel* New Year's edition for 1946. Soon after, meat manager Easton Hill bought the market while Tony retained ownership of the liquor store next door. His son Norman Day, an Army veteran, became a partner and eventually opened his own Day's Market at 522 Seabright Avenue—still operating under that name at the same location. (Courtesy of the Brown collection.)

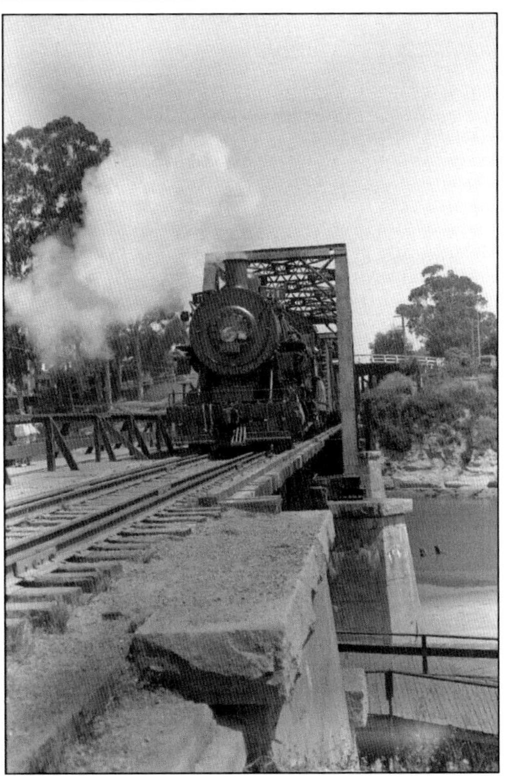

Southern Pacific Locomotive No. 2585, pulling one of three daily freight trains, crosses the San Lorenzo River from Seabright in August 1946. Although passenger service had ended almost a decade earlier, freight trains with carloads of produce stopped at the cannery, made possible by a spur track. (Photograph by Ed Webber, courtesy of Santa Cruz Beach Boardwalk Archives.)

Hyperrealist Claude Buck painted this portrait of Margaret Rogers (right) in 1944. Known for her Monterey Bay seascapes, Rogers presided over the Santa Cruz Art League's gallery in the Tyrrell House basement for more than 30 years. One of the art league's cofounders and stalwarts, Rogers's close friend Cor de Gavere owned a bungalow overlooking Woods Lagoon. She considered the Santa Cruz environment ideal for an artist. One of her most expressive paintings in this self-portrait (below). (Both, courtesy of MAH.)

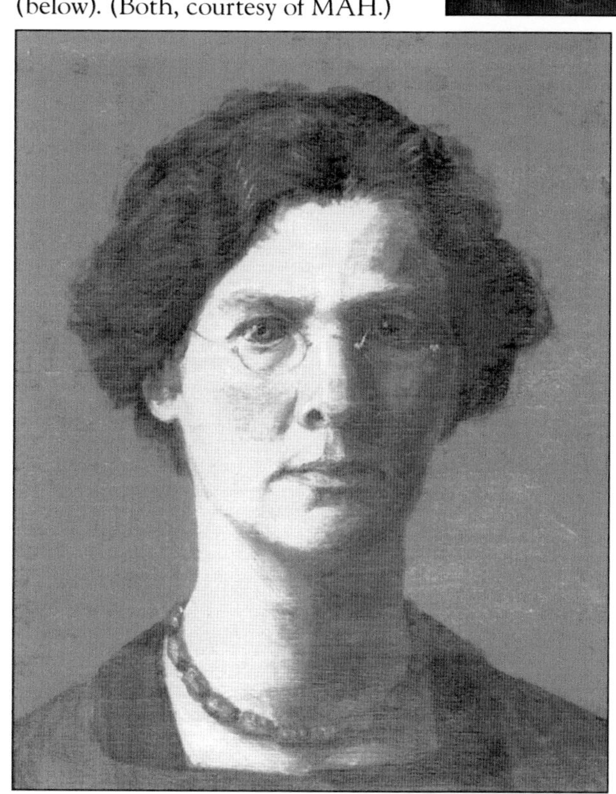

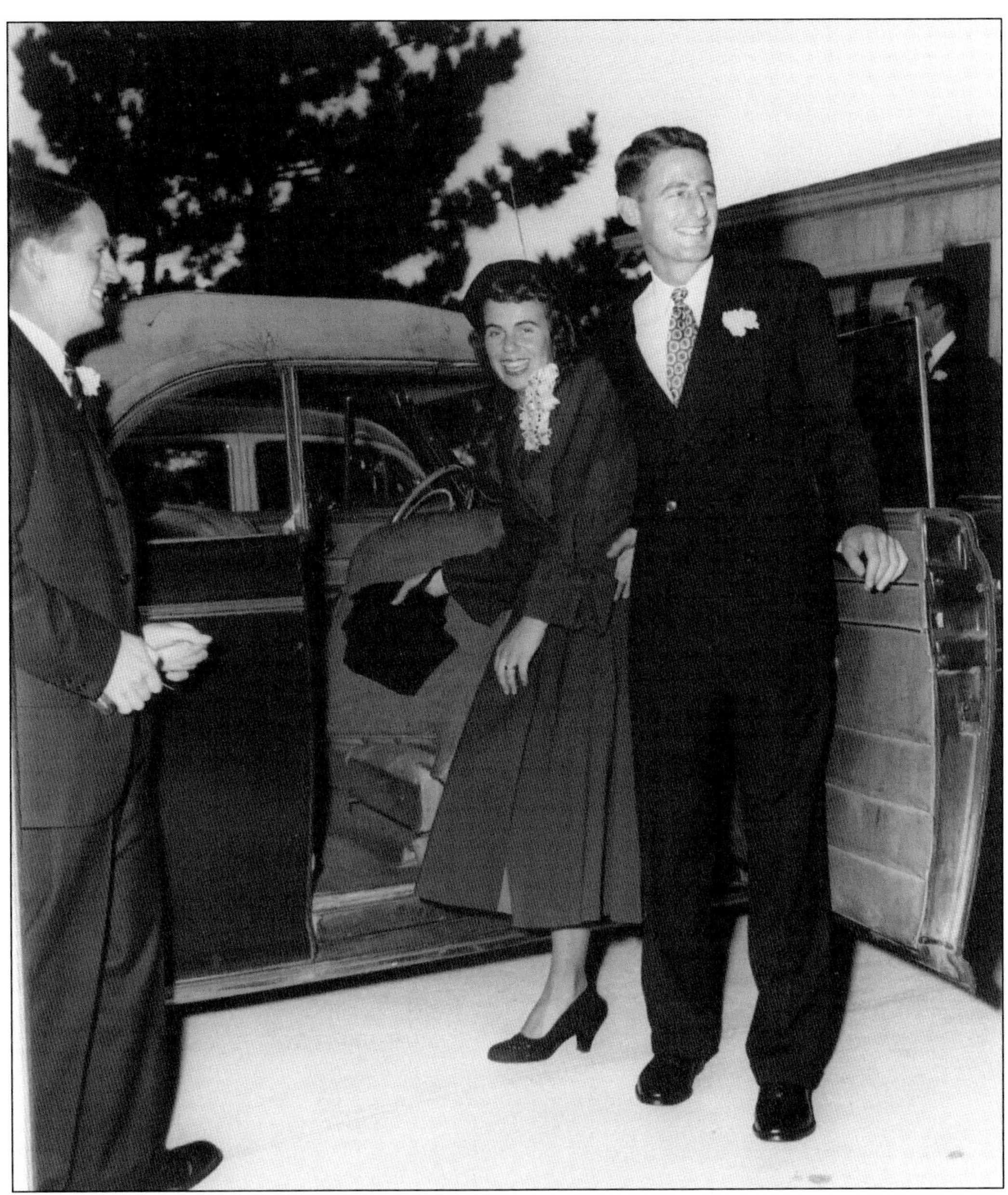

When nurse Marian McKinney, of Live Oak, met San Franciscan Fred Mee at Scholl Marr Castle, romance bloomed, a not uncommon occurrence at that beach. Hubert Mee, left above, and his wife, Sally, lived at 114 Alhambra Avenue at the time of his brother Fred's 1948 nuptials. A subset of guests consisted of the following native Santa Cruzans and Fred's summer beach buddies from the Bay Area and beyond: Peter and Pat Pagen Abell, Le Baron and Nancy Bliss, Stewart and Lillian Cureton, Louis and Frances Gripenstraw, Lloyd and Scott Hebron, Jack and Janet Pagen, Louis and Adeline Scholl, Warren and Sibille Wessendorf Thal, and Joseph and Gloria Hihn Welsh. This group, a circle of friendships that coalesced around Seabright, endured for another 50 years. Today, members of the next generation of some of these families have homes in the area, continuing the deep-rooted friendships of their parents. Marian McKinney Mee lived at 110 Fourth Avenue, the home she and Fred built, for 40 years. (Courtesy of the Mee family collection.)

Teamwork by this local lifeguard corps—clockwise, from top left, Ted Johnson, Neil Frank, Doug Thorne, Rich Thompson, Bill Lidderdale (sergeant), and Danny O'Brien, saved a life in 1950. Pulled unconscious from the heavy surf at Twin Lakes Beach, teenager Charlotte Kessler received artificial respiration from Thorne, stationed at Seabright and assisted by Johnson and O'Brien. On their days off, these guards watched over the Boardwalk's saltwater plunge. (Courtesy of Doug Thorne.)

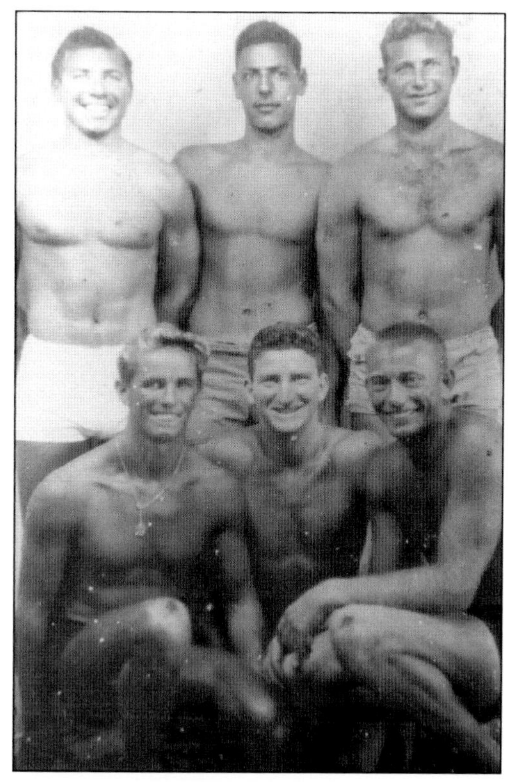

Sam Reid, Hawaii paddleboard champion of 1931, leads the Santa Cruz beach lifeguards—from left to right, Shannon Bunjes, Bill Lidderdale, Danny O'Brien, Reid, Henry Ingerman, Lou Padini, and Doug Thorne in this early-1950s photograph. Reid was one of the first owners of a Tom Blake surfboard when, according to Blake's biographer, Sam and Tom shared "the honor of being the first surfers to ride Malibu Point in September of 1926." Sam's favorite board, of solid California redwood, is displayed at the Santa Cruz Surfing Museum. (Photograph by Ed Webber, courtesy of Santa Cruz Beach Boardwalk Archives.)

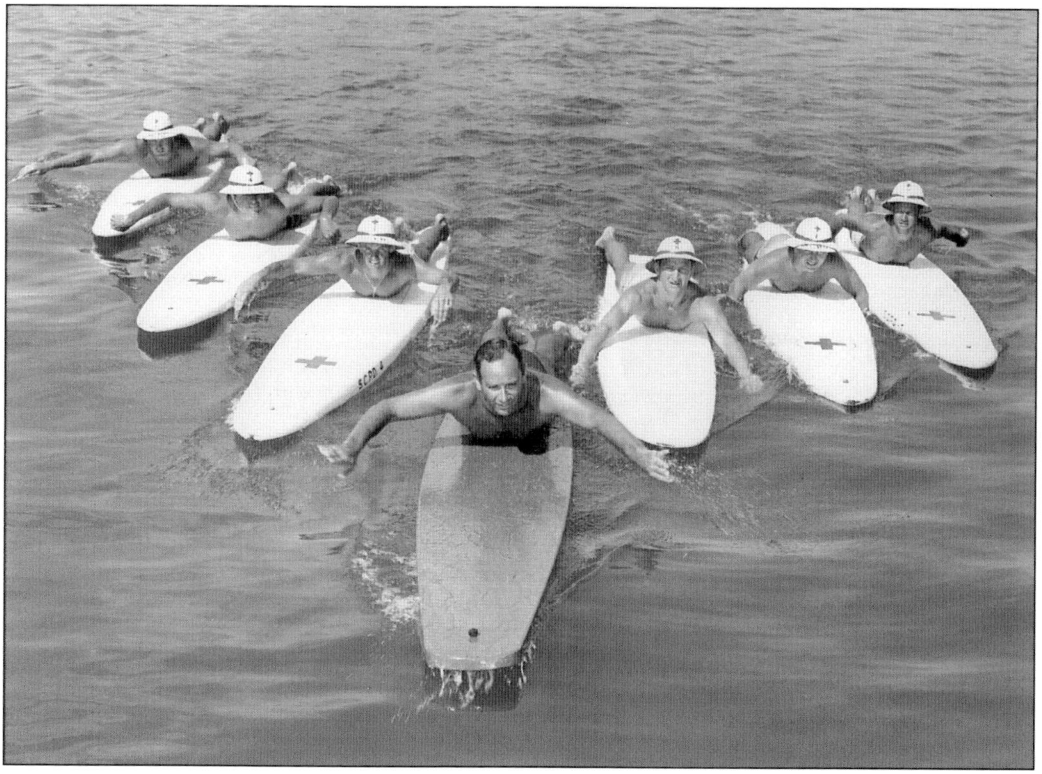

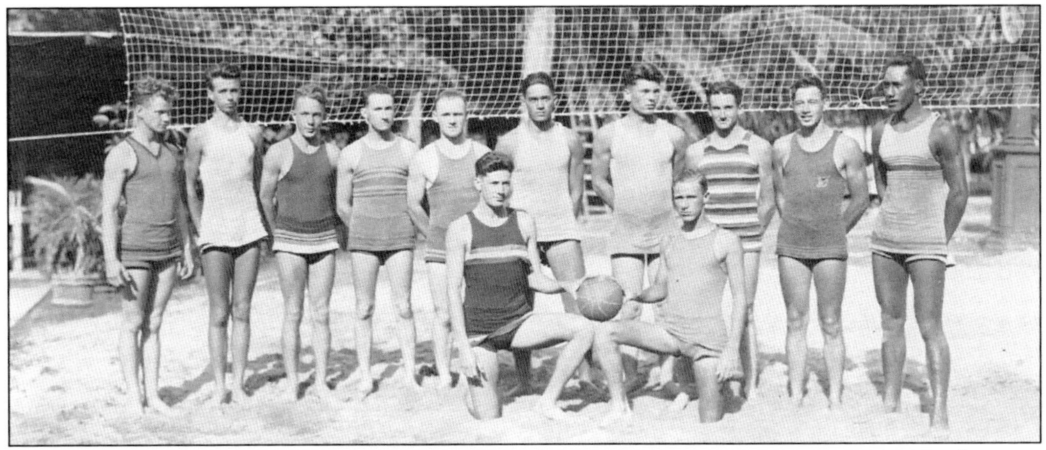

When the Hall family, of Stockton, bought a beach house on Cypress Avenue in 1940, eight-year-old Don began hanging out at Castle Beach watching teenagers, including Kenny "Mo" Moulton and Bill Lidderdale, play beach volleyball. Eventually, Don joined in, and by age 18 (below), he was considered by most to be the best player in Santa Cruz. In 1952, his Stockton YMCA team made it to the finals of the nationals, and Don was selected as an all-American. Then, thanks to his summers on Castle Beach, an unlikely door opened. As a Navy sailor stationed in Honolulu, he reconnected with his Seabright friend Mo, who worked for Honolulu Gas. Once Mo introduced the talented volleyball player to influential members of the exclusive Outrigger Canoe Club (OCC), Don became a member, an ideal venue for his game. Beach volleyball had originated at the OCC in 1915, and that year, the club's regular players (shown above) included the renowned Duke Kahanamoku, (far right). OCC affiliation more than paid off for Don: His USA team won the gold medal at the 1955 Pan American Games, and he competed in the world championships the following year. (Above, courtesy of Outrigger Canoe Club; below, courtesy of Don Hall.)

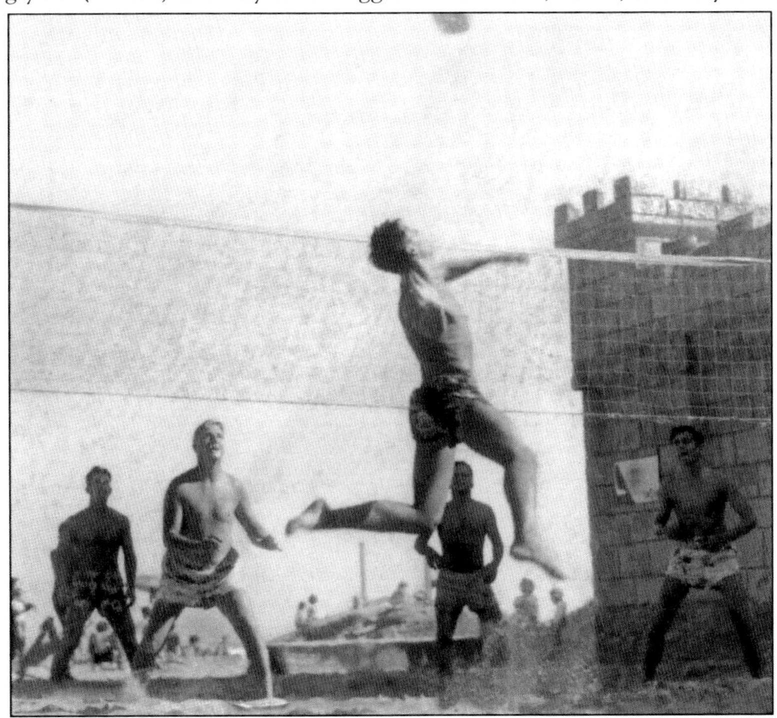

Seven

OUT WITH THE OLD, IN WITH THE NEW

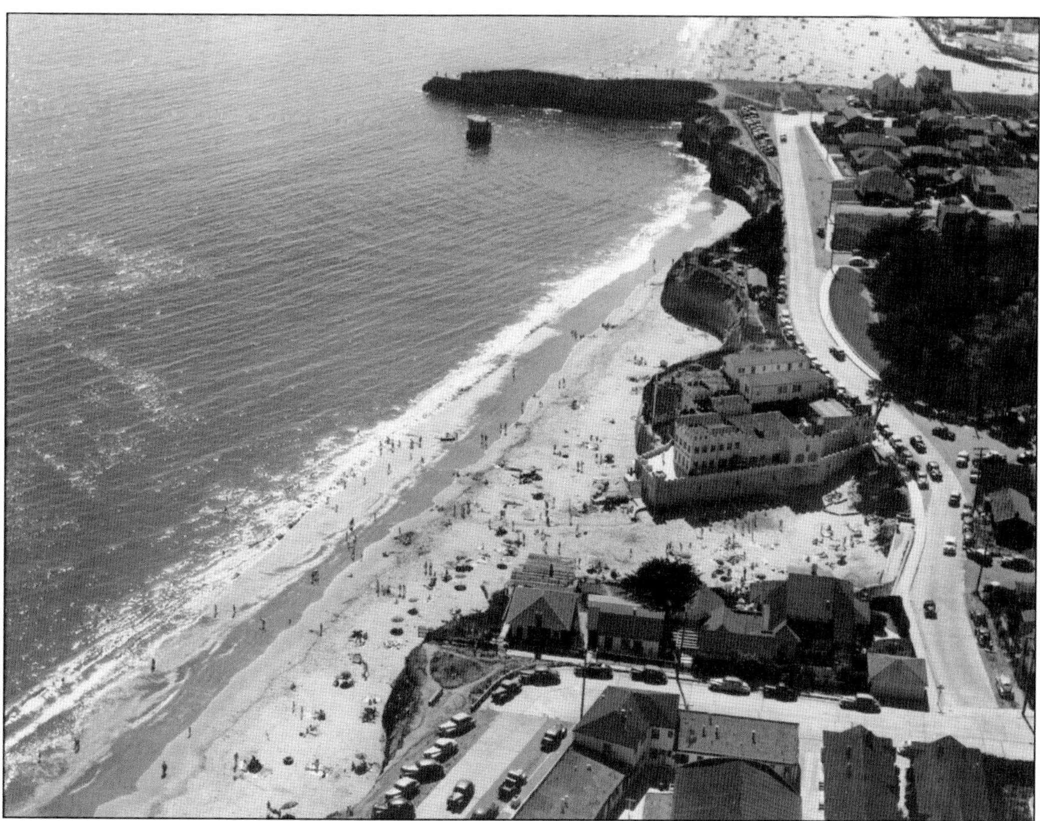

Familiar landmarks appear in this July 1948 aerial view with the Castle and its namesake beach at the hub of Seabright life, at center. Immediately across East Cliff Drive, a grove of old cypress trees hides the library and museum buildings. At uppermost right, the Ocean View house overlooks the San Lorenzo River's mouth, while a lone bodysurfer can be seen between Pinnacle Rock and San Lorenzo Point. (Photograph by Ed Webber, courtesy of Santa Cruz Beach Boardwalk Archives.)

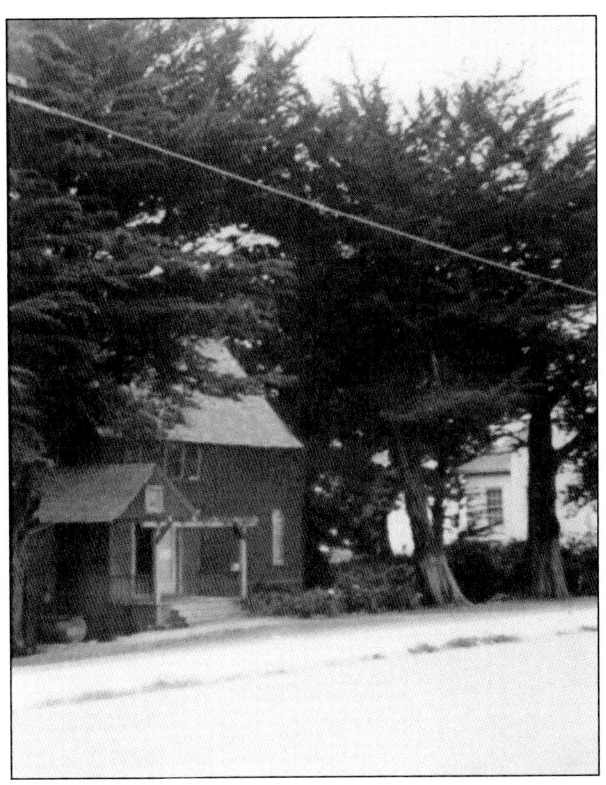

For more than two decades, the city museum's collections had been housed in the increasingly dilapidated Tyrrell House, far left. Officials agreed to let Santa Cruzans vote on a special sales tax to fund a new building, but the proposition lost three to one. A unique opportunity presented itself when the library board voted to close the Seabright Branch, at right. Friends of the museum jumped at the chance to secure the location and promised unhappy Seabright booklovers "minimum library service." In August 1954, the museum reopened in the former library building with five rooms of displays compressed into half as much space. Below, curator and librarian Laura Flickinger, at left, shows off one of the many Native American artifacts displayed in the new exhibit rooms. (Left, courtesy of SCMNH; below, photograph by Ed Webber, courtesy of Covello & Covello.)

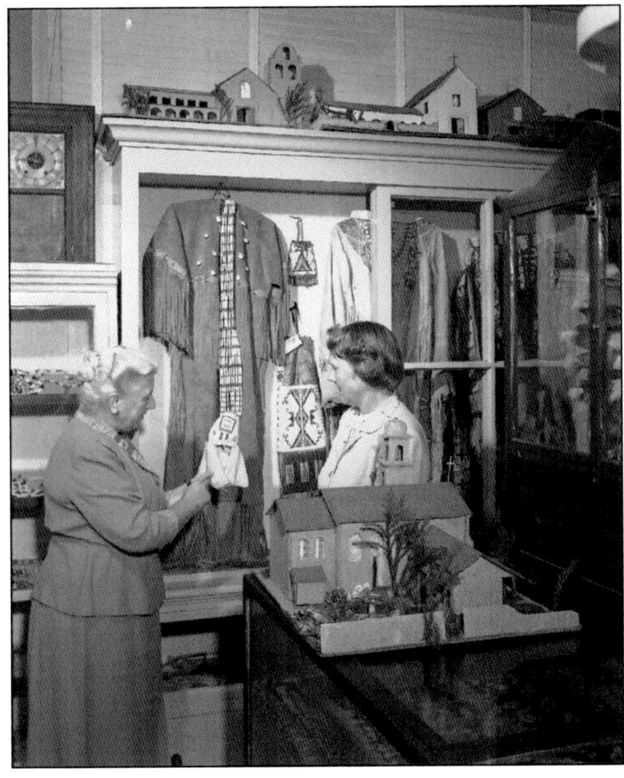

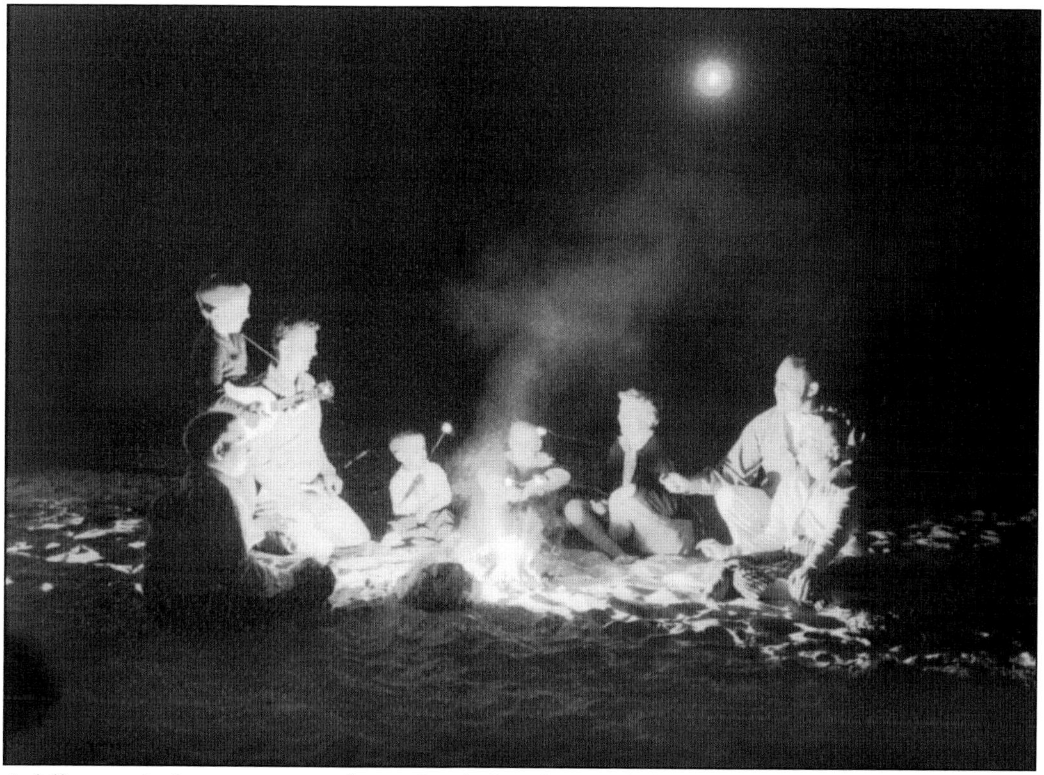

A full-moon Indian summer night on Castle Beach provided an ideal setting for a marshmallow roast. Bud and Carolyn Prindle and four-year-old son Pete, with marshmallow at left, enjoy an evening with friends in 1955. The Prindle home at 1306 East Cliff Drive, adjacent to the Castle, had a perfect view of Pinnacle Rock bodysurfers. The sketch below, a Pete Prindle original, illustrates one of the popular variations on basic bodysurfing technique, which is angling across the wave. (Above, photograph by Ed Webber, courtesy of Covello & Covello; below, courtesy of Pete Prindle.)

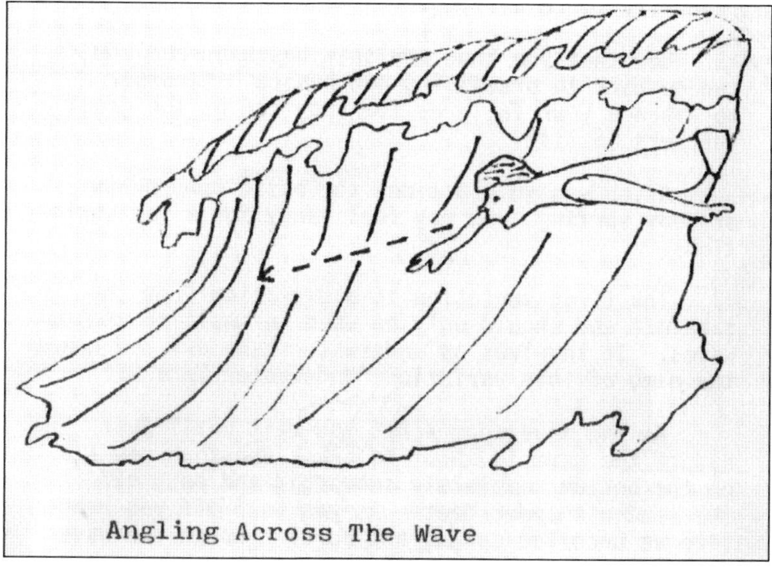

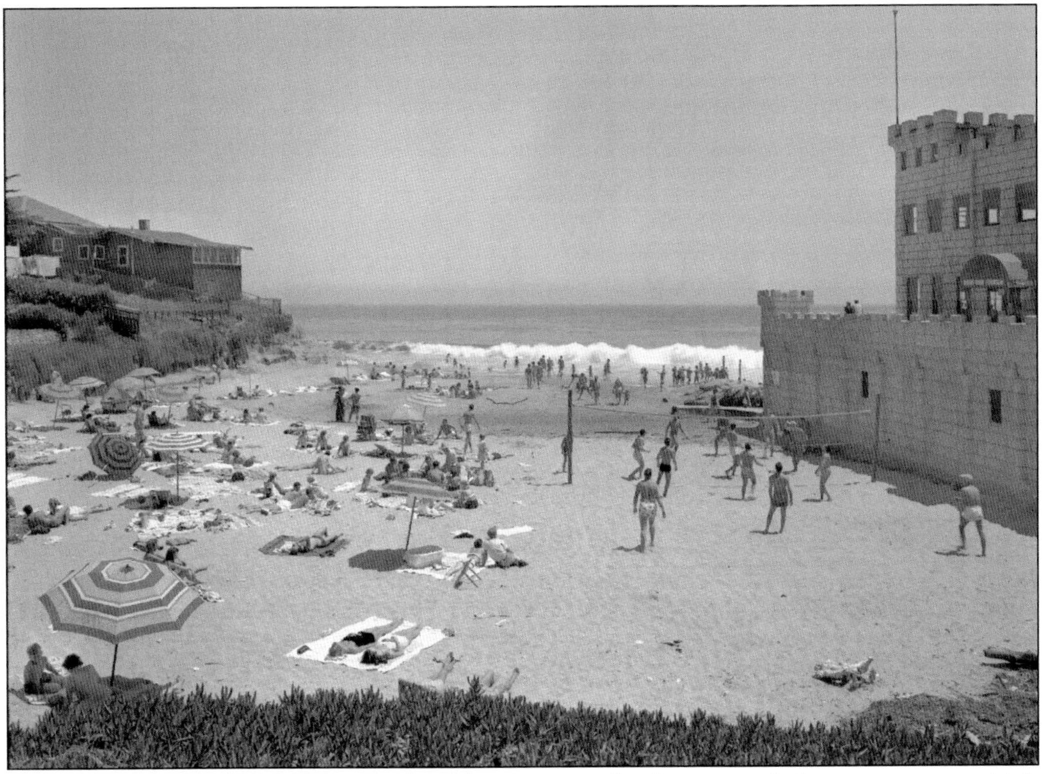

Castle Beach volleyball enthusiasts, local businessmen by day, created their own team, which included Dick Alderson, Chuck Berryessa, Barry Bliss, Joel Brown, Stewart Cureton, Bob Hultzen, Jim Huxtable, Fred Mee, Charlie Miller, Junior Morgan, Ken and Lee Moulton, Warren and Ed Penniman, Bob Pio, Bud Prindle, Bob Rittenhouse, Horace Street, and Doug Thorne. Their commitment to after-work camaraderie lasted for several decades and coalesced into a formal name—Sons of the Beaches (SOBs). Official membership cards, below, were enjoyed by all. (Above, photograph by Ed Webber, courtesy of Covello & Covello; below, courtesy of Robert Rittenhouse.)

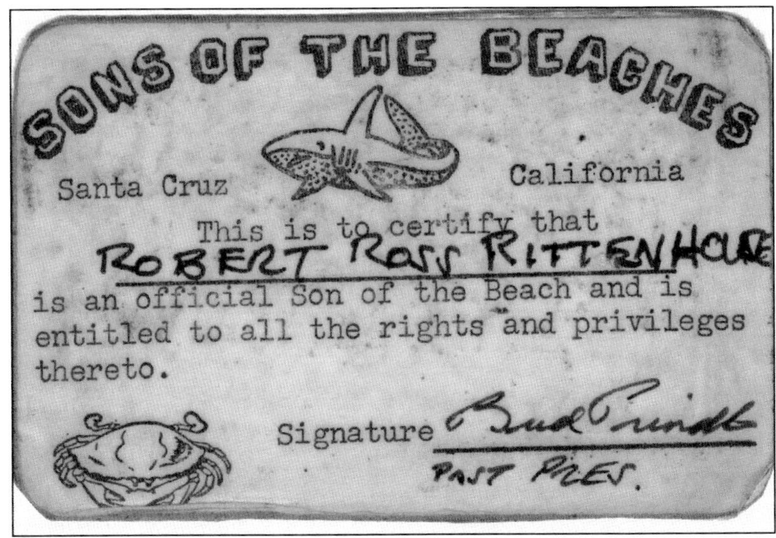

SONS OF THE BEACHES

Santa Cruz California

This is to certify that

ROBERT ROSS RITTENHOUSE

is an official Son of the Beach and is entitled to all the rights and privileges thereto.

Signature Bud Prindle

PAST PRES.

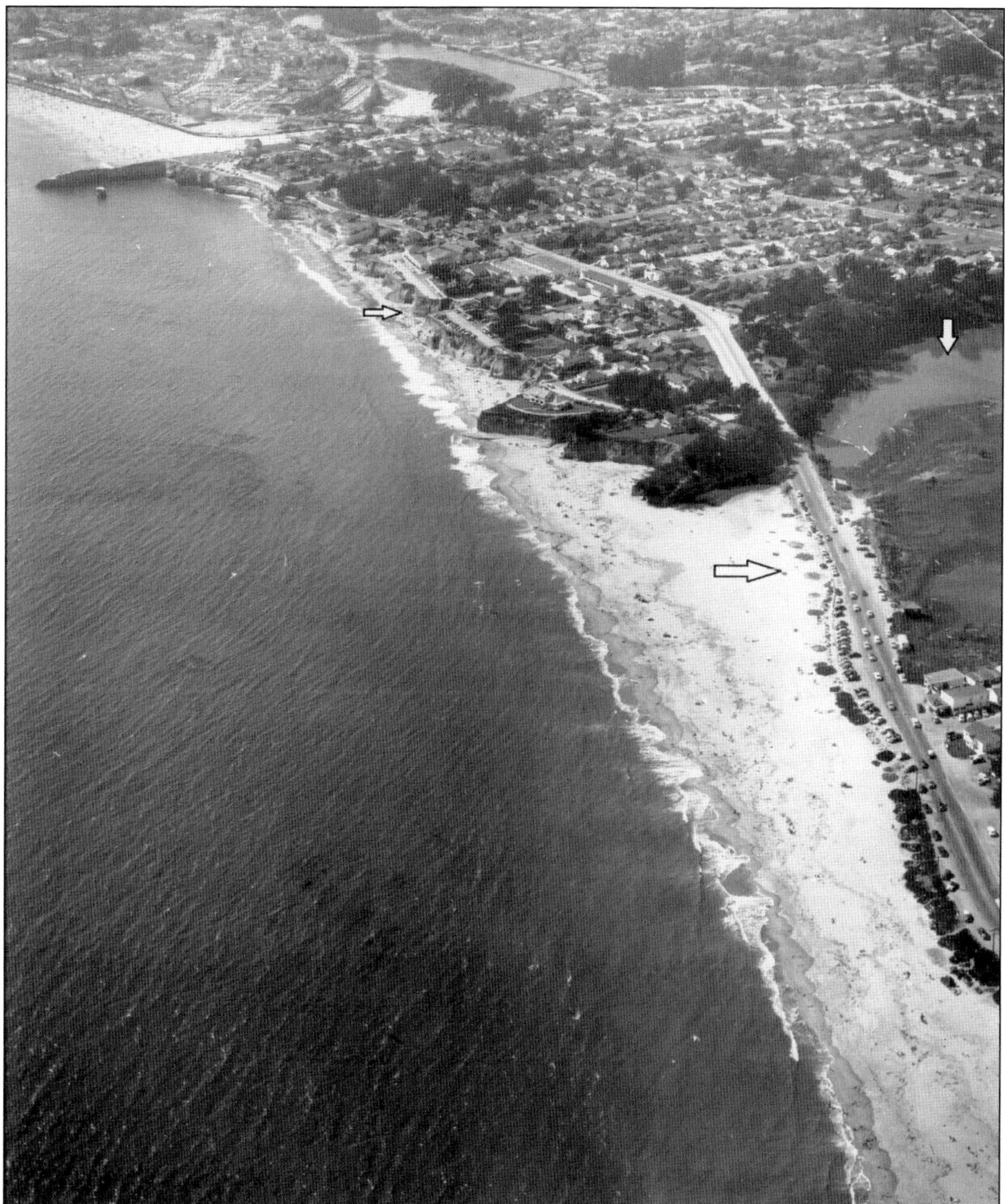

In 1955, the Army Corps of Engineers' long-awaited erosion study concluded that the sandstone cliffs of Seabright (top arrow) were vanishing into the bay at the rate of one foot a year. What would be the future of Seabright Beach and the adjacent Twin Lakes area? Local officials considered two separate plans, which were ultimately compatible. The engineers' plan, supported by commercial fishermen and the Santa Cruz Yacht Club, called for a small craft harbor at Woods Lagoon. There, two stone jetties would protect the entrance while gradually adding sand to the beaches, preventing further cliff erosion. Meanwhile, county and state planners purchased the Twin Lakes beachfront (bottom arrow) to create permanent public access, a top priority. Supporters of the harbor plan were satisfied when officials agreed to include Woods Lagoon (middle arrow) in the deal and hold it in reserve for the future harbor. (Courtesy of SNA.)

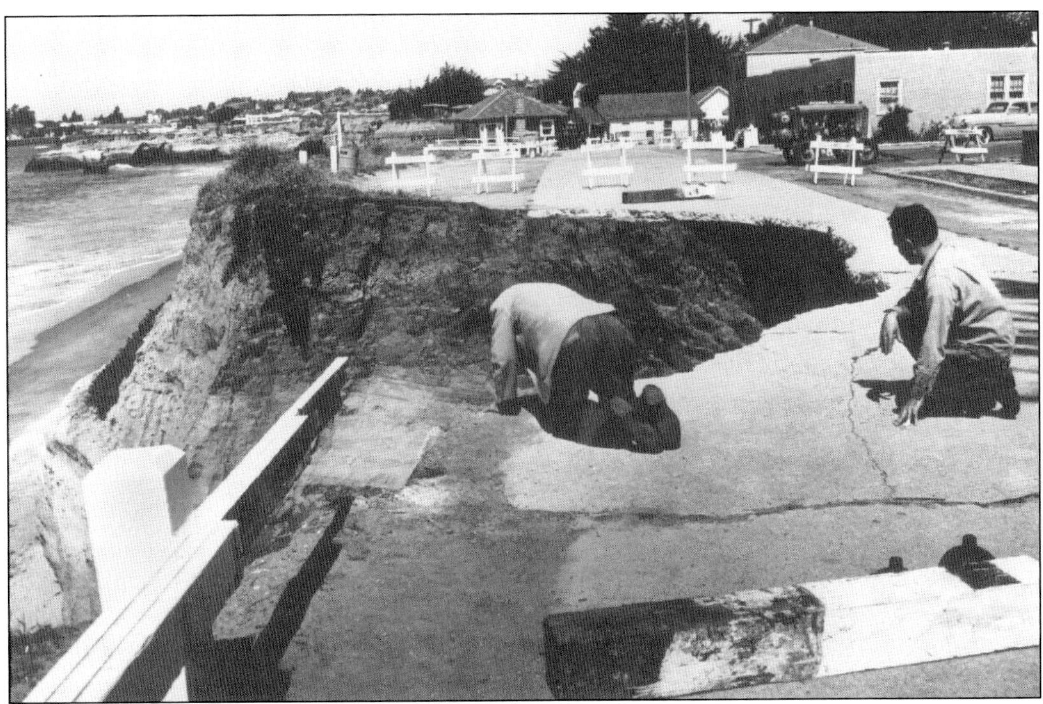

The never-to-be-forgotten Christmas flood of 1955 inundated downtown Santa Cruz and left Castle Beach a wood-strewn lagoon requiring bulldozers for drainage. Months later, the deluge had dire consequences for East Cliff Drive, sections of which were already closed to through traffic due to previous erosion. On the evening of June 3, 1956, the corner of East Cliff and First Avenue gave way, crashing to the beach below. Fortunately, none of the residents of the nearby La Solana Apartments had parked a car along the cliff. (Courtesy of SCMNH.)

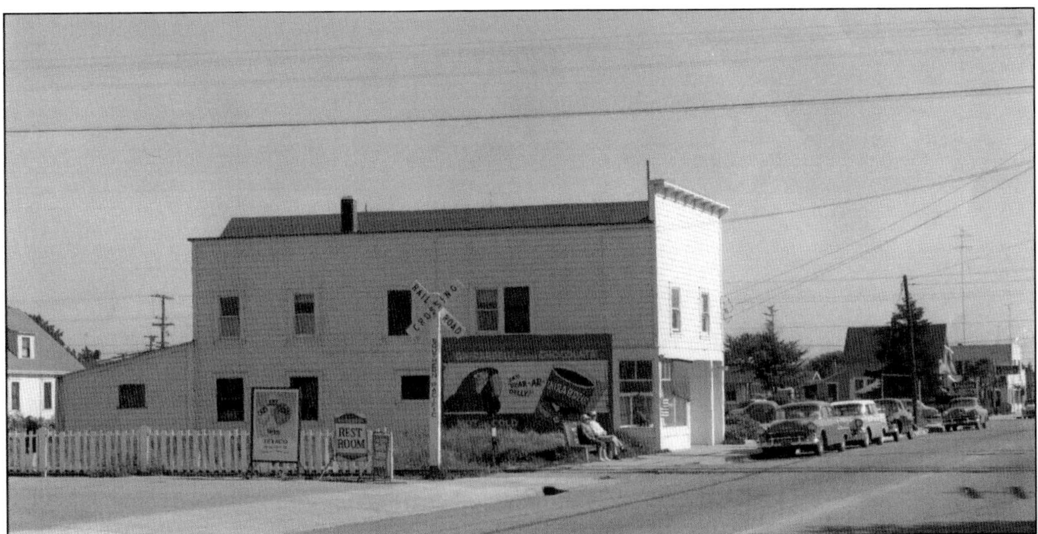

The once thriving business district on Seabright Avenue gradually disappeared. The driveway of a Texaco station, at left, marks the site of the old Southern Pacific depot. Once surrounded by similar structures, including the Seabright Hotel, the now lone two-story building served as the local post office. Before long, the wrecking crew would come for it as well. (Courtesy of SNA.)

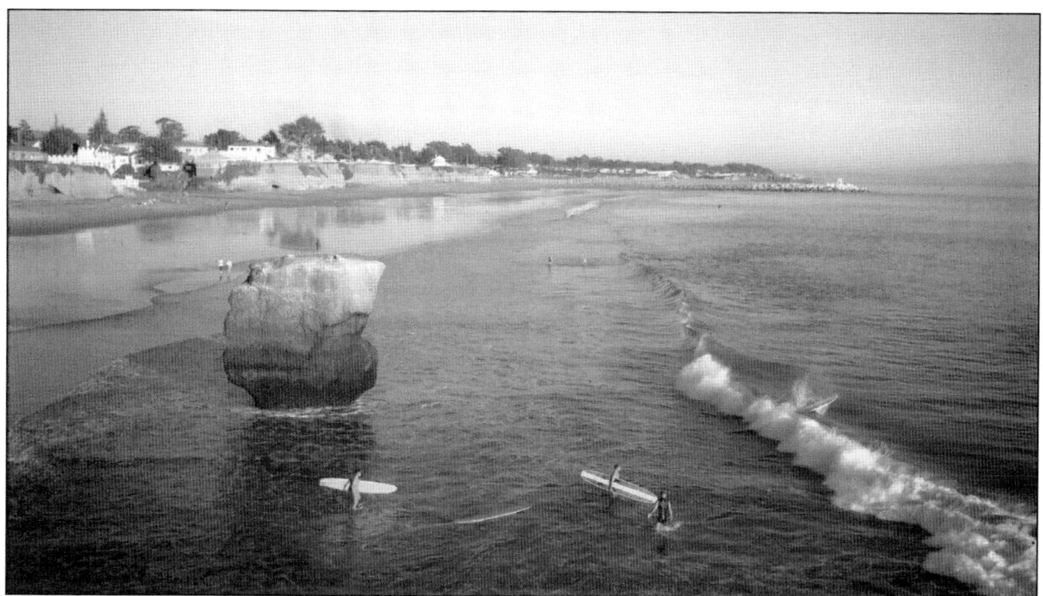

The opening of Twin Lakes State Beach in 1957 increased the number of surfers and swimmers at Seabright, above, testing the skills of the elite lifeguard corps. Once again, the 25-foot-long tunnel, "the Blow Hole," beneath San Lorenzo Point proved especially dangerous. On two consecutive summer afternoons, veteran lifeguard Al Wiemers and associate George Kovalenko, below at center, swam through the opening to rescue several victims. Skip Littlefield, supervisor of beach safety, below at right, wanted to eliminate the danger by blowing up the cliff face. The owner of the property refused to grant permission but agreed to sell it to the state to protect the cliff. (Above, courtesy of Bill Davis; below, courtesy of SNA.)

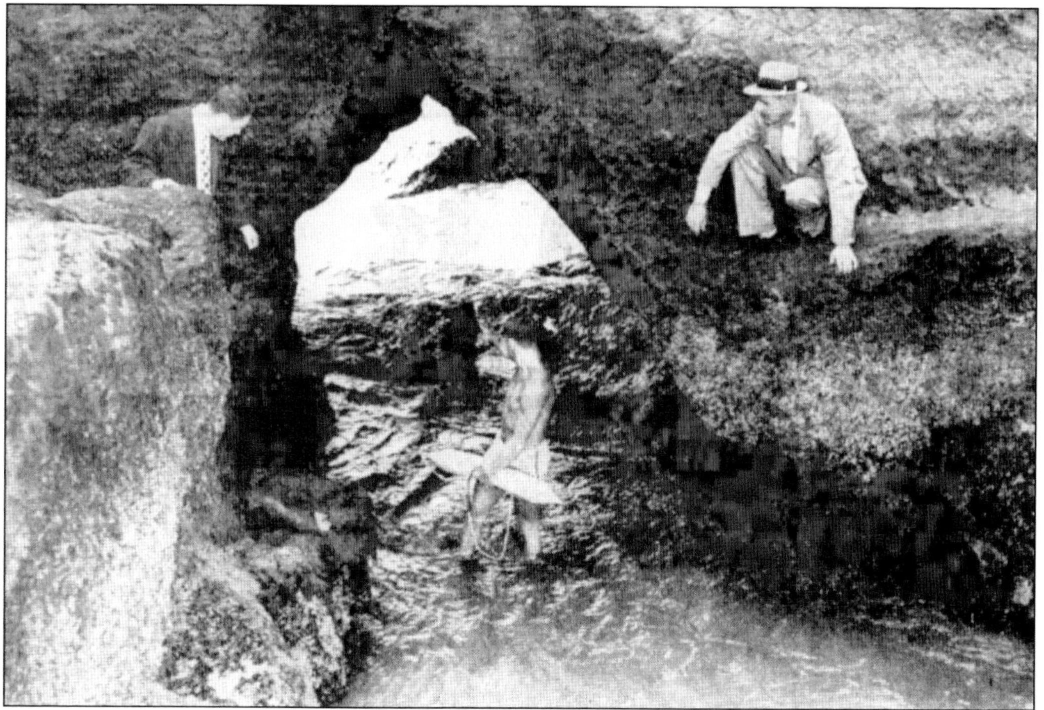

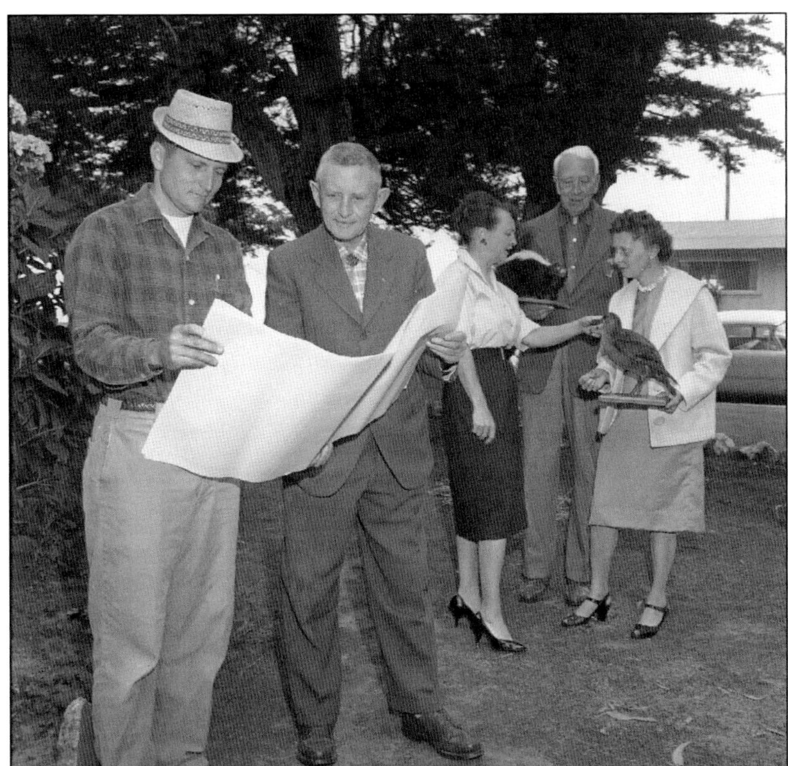

The museum enjoyed a renaissance when Dr. Glenn Bradt became board chairman in 1961. An expert on beavers, the retired zoologist went to work to provide adequate display space. Bradt, second from left, reviews plans for a new wing to house the Hecox natural history collection. Dorothy B. Hunt, far right, displays one of its artifacts—a stuffed Sooty Shearwater. (Courtesy of Covello & Covello.)

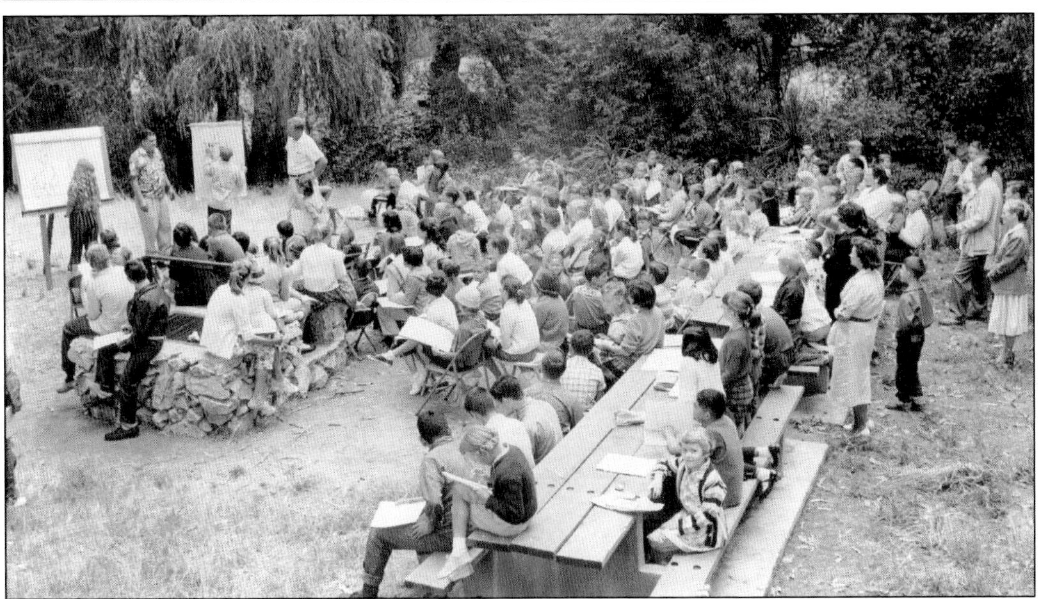

By the end of the decade, the city had installed barbecue pits and picnic tables, making Tyrrell Park (pictured) an inviting venue for large events. When artist Ralph Gray, who offered kids free summer art classes at his studio on Seabright Avenue (now the La Posta restaurant) could no longer accommodate the crowds, Santa Cruz Parks and Recreation stepped in. The expansive location enabled Gray to give basic arts education to thousands of children and their parents. (Courtesy of SCMNH.)

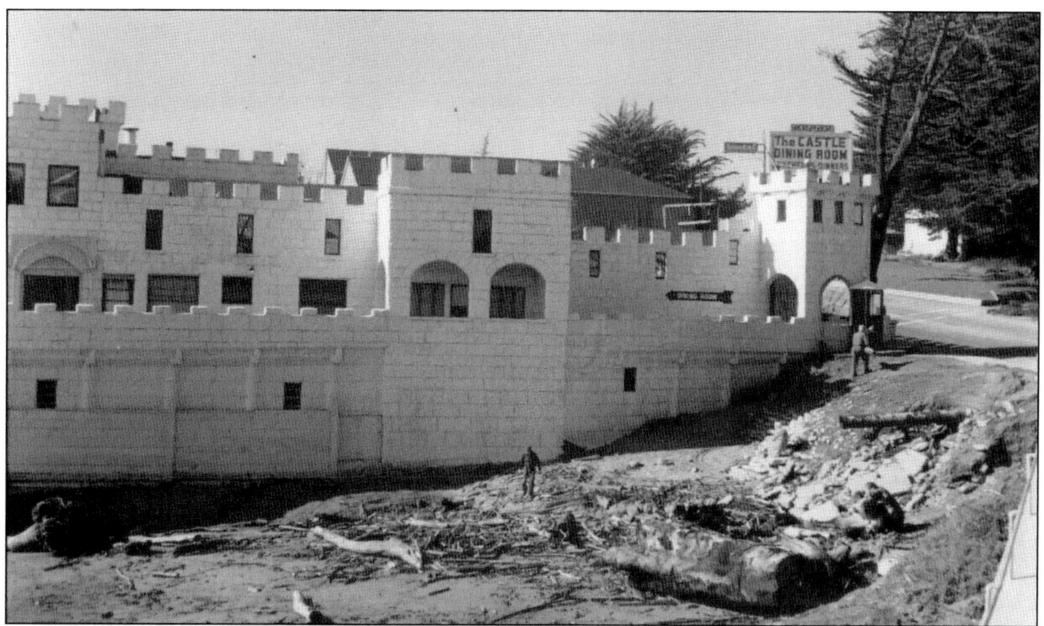

Fred Russell, formerly a Boardwalk concessionaire, acquired what was then simply named the Castle in 1955 and managed the restaurant, with his wife, Pearl, and daughter-in-law Mary as the chefs. The family specialized in smorgasbord, offering 60 different foods and four hot dishes in the famous bay-view dining room while continuing to run the downstairs snack bar, which was well known for its burgers and snow cones. (Courtesy of Don Hall.)

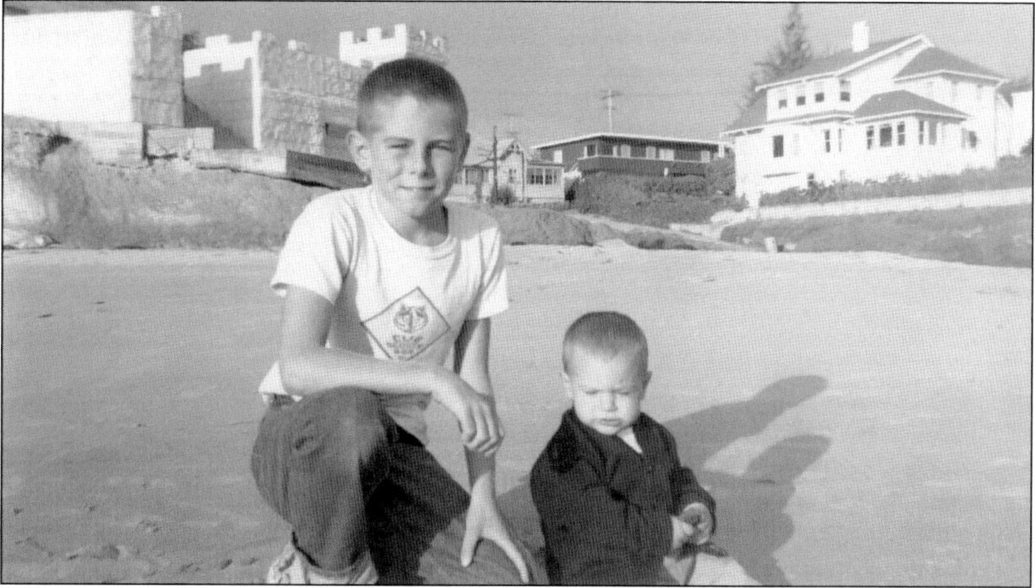

In 1960, only a handful of youngsters lived in Seabright year-round. Larry Dunham, age 10, at left, mastered the challenging Seabright waves early on with coaching from lifeguard Al Wiemers and became a well-known swimmer and surfer. At age 13, he landed his first job at the Castle Snack Bar. His neighbor, Bobby Hall, age one, whose family still lives on Forbes Street, checks out the beach—where he would one day play volleyball like his parents did and bodysurf. (Photograph by Don Hall, courtesy of the Dunham family.)

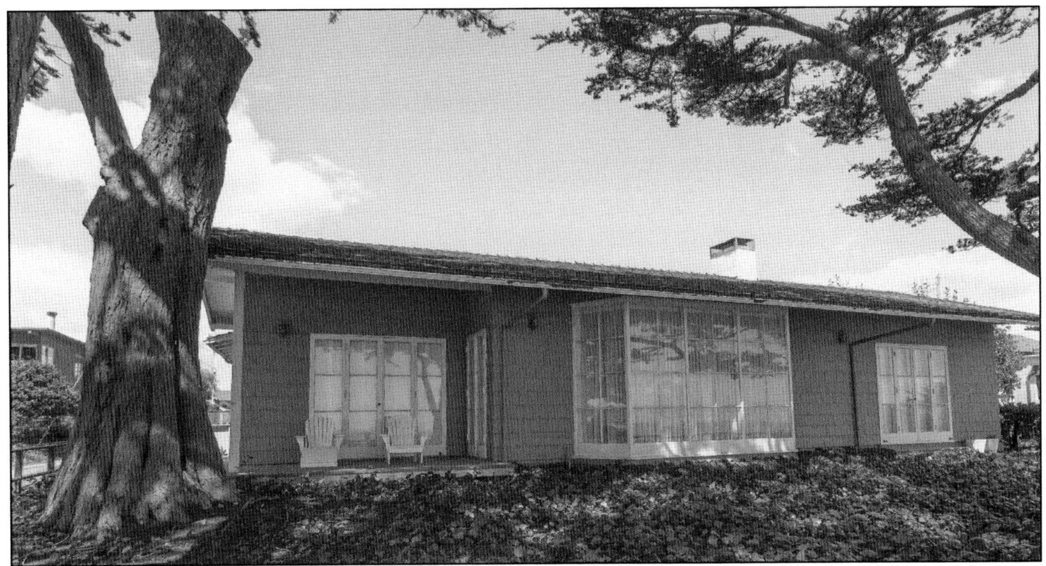

Russell Giffen, Fresno rancher and longtime Seabright summer vacationer, prospered as the nation's "Cotton King." In 1950, he bought Laguna Vista at 206 Fourth Avenue (see page 44). The three buildings on the property created an ideal compound where the Giffens' four children and many grandchildren spent their summers. Then, in 1957, Russell and his wife, Ruth Price Giffen, enlisted Wurster, Bernardi, and Emmons to design their own beachfront home a block away at 109 Fourth Avenue (above). The interior courtyard, designed by Thomas Church, provided the perfect spot for entertaining—and still does today. Decades earlier, Fresno families were among the first homeowners in Seabright, and yet their overwhelming influx in the 1950s and 1960s felt like "a stampede" to some native Seabrightans. (Photograph by Joe Michalak.)

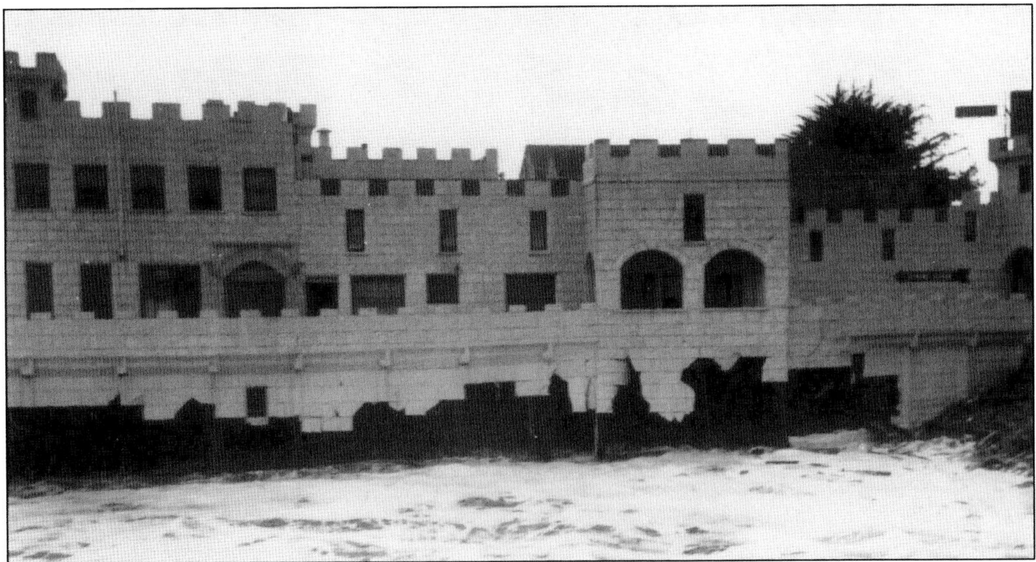

Stucco, cleverly applied, created the illusion that the lower walls of the Castle consisted of stone, but winter storms regularly revealed plain wooden boards, easily dislodged by incessant bashing from incoming logs. Once the Russell family had repaired the severe damage of 1960, shown here, they sold the Castle to the Jack Ritchey family, who would be its final owners. (Courtesy of Don Hall.)

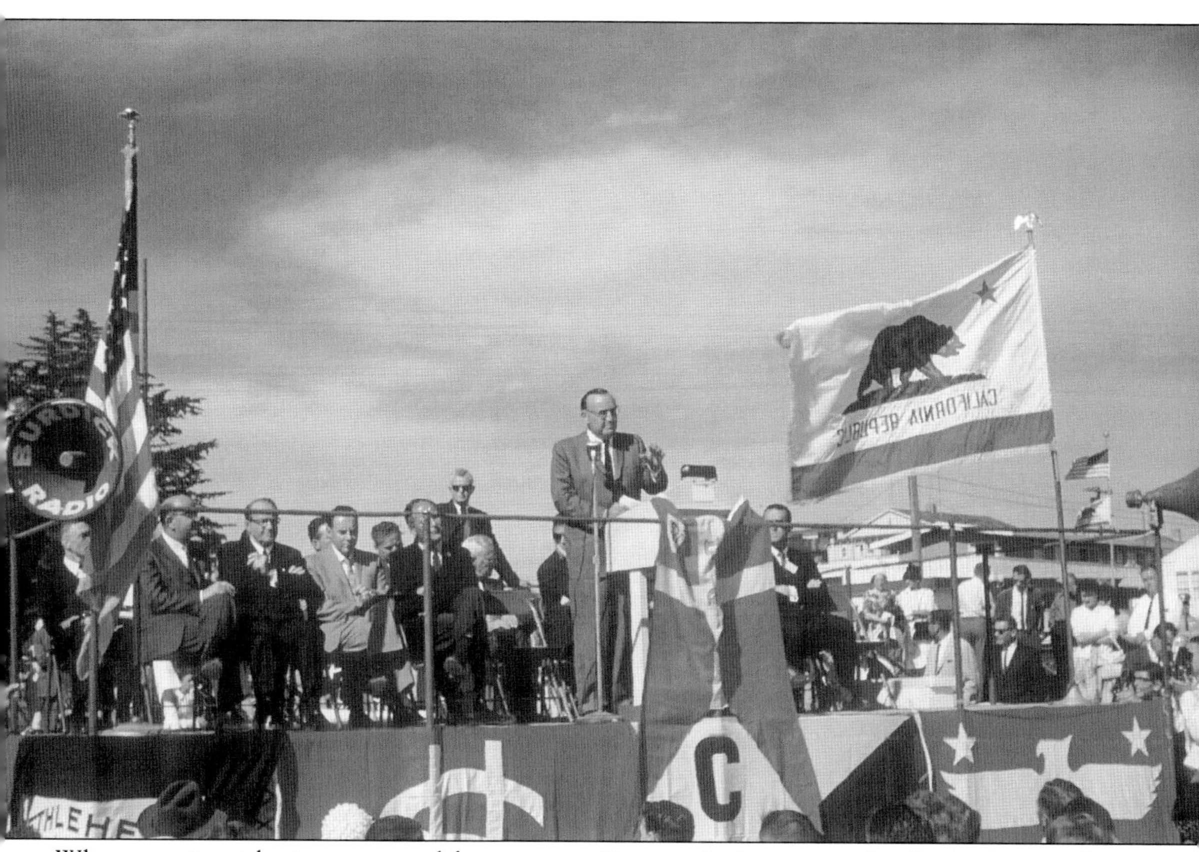

When prominent businessman and future mayor Norman Lezin, among the dignitaries seated above, welcomed a crowd to the 1962 ground breaking of the Santa Cruz Small Craft Harbor, he ushered in a new era long in the making. More than a dozen years had passed since the Army Corps of Engineers endorsed the project. Santa Cruzans had successfully organized one of California's three coastal port districts—a rare form of public agency empowered to negotiate with state and federal authorities. The state agreed to a long-term lease and provided nearly $2 million in loans, but progress stalled when President Eisenhower vetoed a bill funding the project. The election of John F. Kennedy brought new hope. First-term Democratic governor Edmund G. "Pat" Brown hurried to Washington and lobbied for legislation, which the president signed in September 1961. At the ground breaking, Brown, above at center, shared his vision for state parks and beaches. It was a heartfelt, personal, as well as a political, message, given the governor's strong family ties to the region. His sister-in-law lived in Pasatiempo, and his daughter Kathleen was attending boarding school in Monterey. (Photograph by Les Long, courtesy of Santa Cruz Port District.)

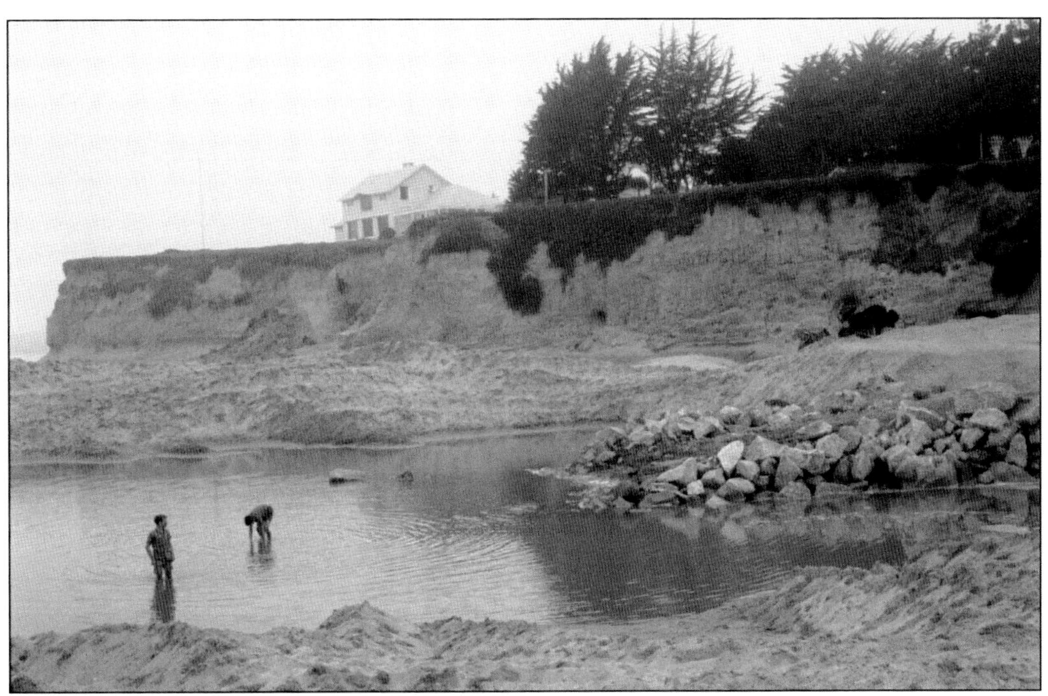

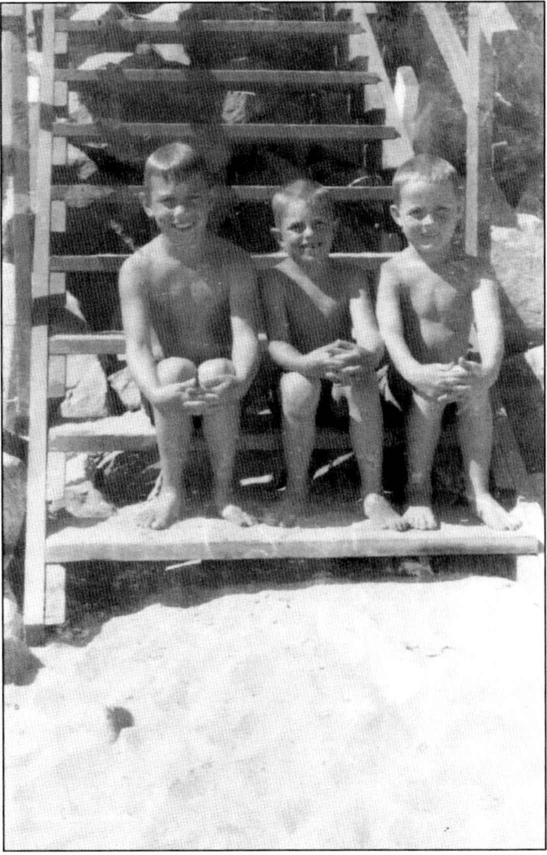

In the summer of 1962, two boys play in the former mouth of Woods Lagoon. Bulldozers had cut a channel, sending its water rushing into Monterey Bay. The pile of rocks are the first of 11,000 truckloads—176,000 tons of stone in all—used to build two jetties, creating an entrance for the Small Craft Harbor. Atop the bluff, the 1914 Pioda house (see page 56) overlooks the changing scene. (Photograph by Les Long, courtesy of Santa Cruz Port District.)

A wooden staircase near Third Avenue dated from 1910, but it often washed away during storms. Three Fresno buddies—from left to right, Chris Martin, John Woolf, and Stewart Randall—found the stairs convenient in the late 1950s. The Jack Woolf family already owned a Seabright home when, in the mid-1960s, they acquired the 1909 Brown House, a two-story Craftsman bungalow, close to the stairs on East Cliff Drive. Fresnans called the area "Fresno Beach," while native Santa Cruzans insisted on "Fourth Avenue." Lifeguards used the names interchangeably. (Courtesy of Mary Randall Peterson.)

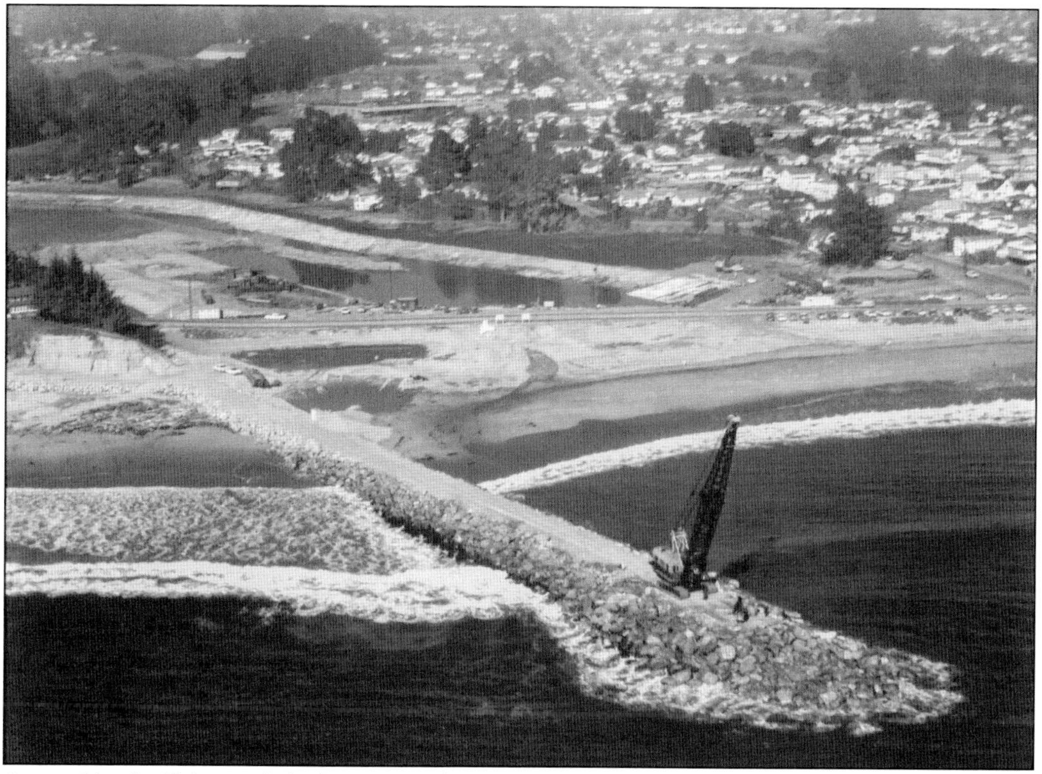

Assisted by the "Monster," the largest crawling crane in California, construction crews kept the jetty project moving forward, as shown in this January 1963 snapshot. Army engineers guaranteed that the massive stone breakwaters would not only protect the channel into the harbor but also would solve Seabright's cliff erosion problem by ensuring sand buildup on the west-side beaches. (Above, courtesy of Jay Johnson; below, photograph by Les Long, courtesy of Santa Cruz Port District.)

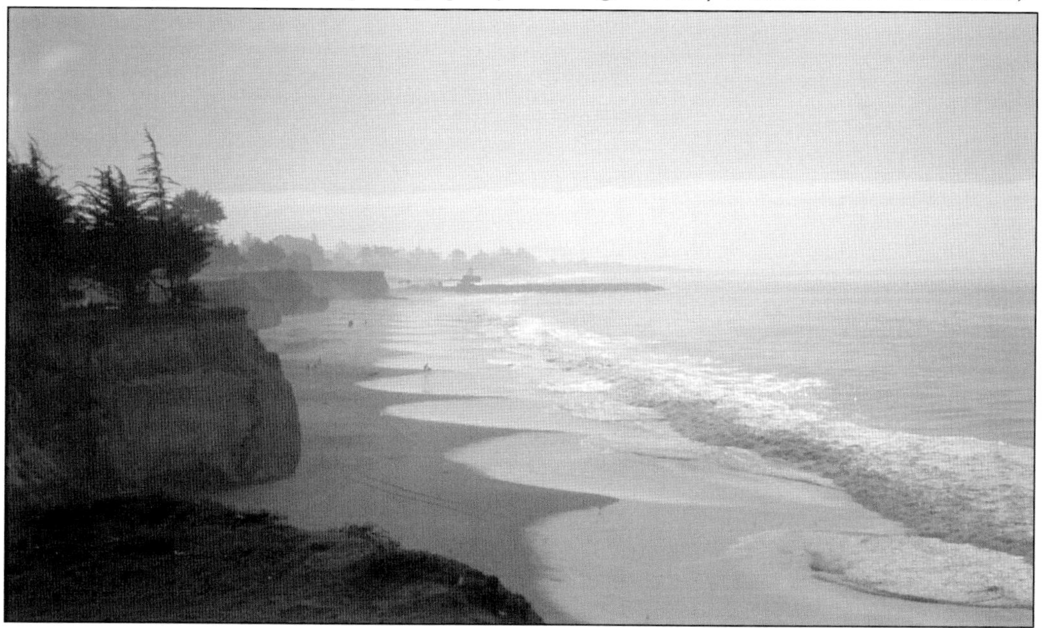

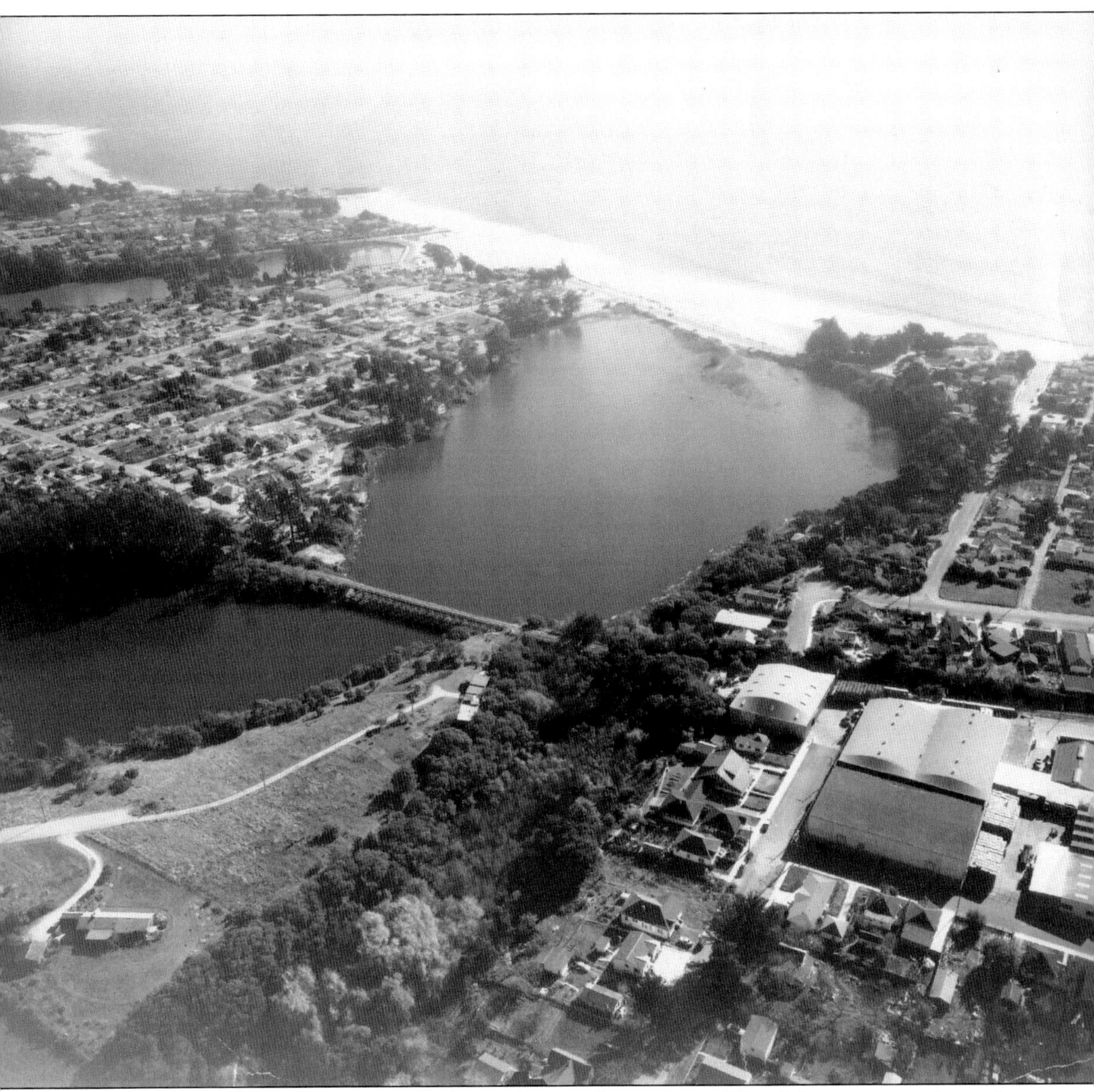

Taken before the harbor's opening, this 1950s aerial view shows Woods Lagoon stretching along the eastern edge of Seabright and the western edge of Live Oak. At center, the Southern Pacific trestle crosses the water at its original 19th-century location. The many spacious buildings of the cannery complex are seen at center, right. On the far side of the tracks, Fourth Avenue runs toward the bay. The wooden bridge that extended East Cliff Drive from Seabright to Twin Lakes by way of Atlantic Avenue has been replaced by a roadway. (Courtesy of SNA.)

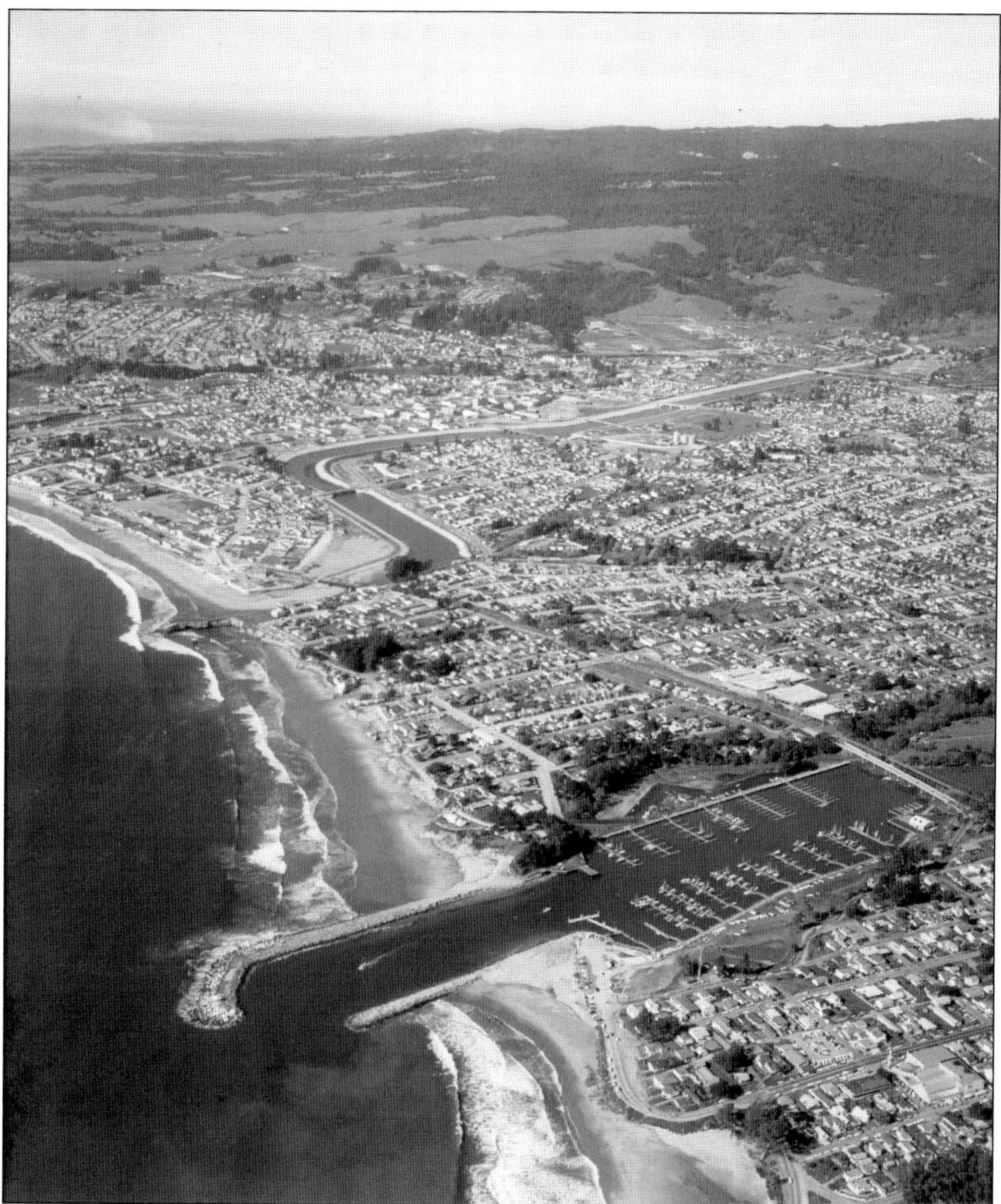

Taken after the harbor's completion, this aerial view was captured by Vester Dick in early 1964. At right, the Glenn Coolidge Bridge, commonly referred to as the Murray Street Bridge, parallels the Southern Pacific trestle, bringing traffic by way of an expanded Murray Street past the cannery. The old road from Seabright to Twin Lakes has been removed. At top, another project of the Army Corps of Engineers—concrete flood control levees—contain the winding San Lorenzo River, a direct result of the 1955 flood. (Photograph by Vester Dick, courtesy of Covello & Covello.)

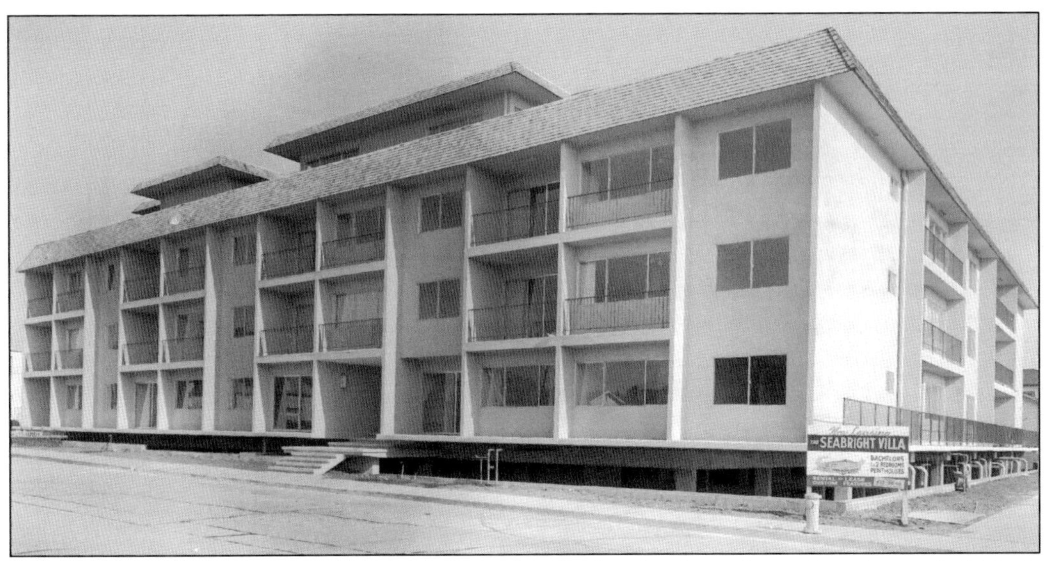

When the planning department used the term "Seabright slums," it referred to a full block of single-story motel/apartments on Atlantic Avenue, catering to transient summer tourists. No one objected when a developer announced plans to replace some of the buildings with an upscale apartment building. Seabright Villa opened in June 1964, the first and only high-rise in the neighborhood. Advertisements for "Santa Cruz' Most Luxurious Apartments" feature its year-round heated pool (seen below). After a handful of divorced men became residents, the complex acquired the nickname "Heartbreak Hotel." In 1973, the 44 units were transformed into condos, and Annalisa Streich became the sole apartment dweller who moved back in. Still living at 220 Atlantic Avenue today, she is known by some as the "Mayor of Seabright Villa." (Both, courtesy of Covello & Covello.)

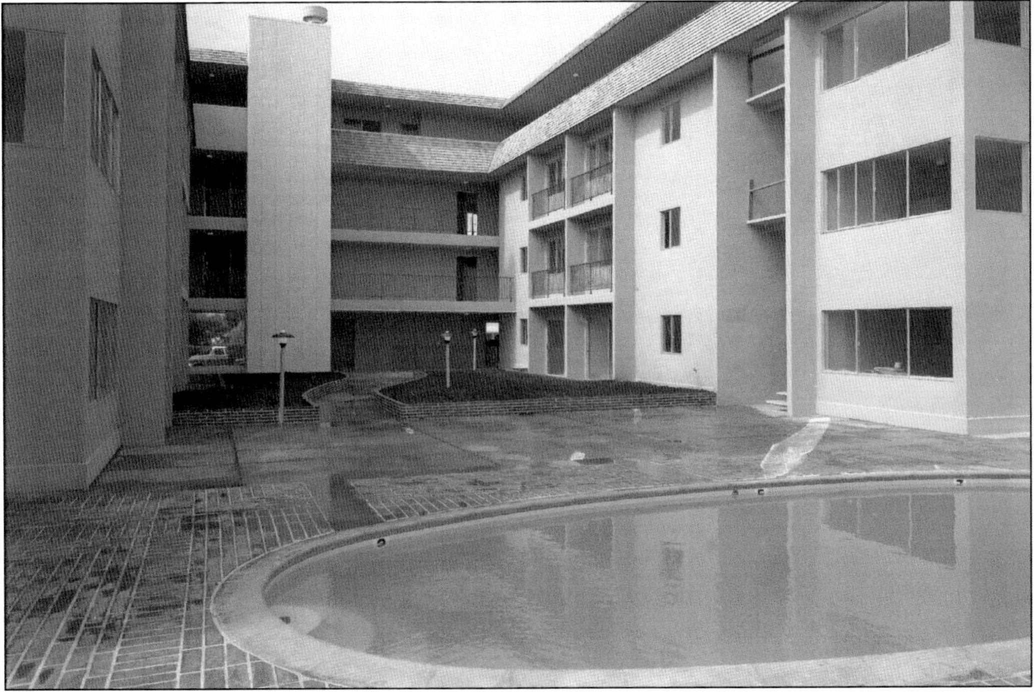

A day of ceremonies marked the opening of the Santa Cruz Small Craft Harbor on April 18, 1964. Bands played "Ruffles and Flourishes" as dignitaries spoke warmly of the achievement by local backers like Worth Brown, Malio Stagnaro, and Louis and Al Haber. A regatta of yachts, fishing boats, and cruisers braved choppy water, parading from one end of the bay to the other. Here, Seabright native Marty Mee surveys the 350-slip harbor. (Courtesy of the Mee family collection.)

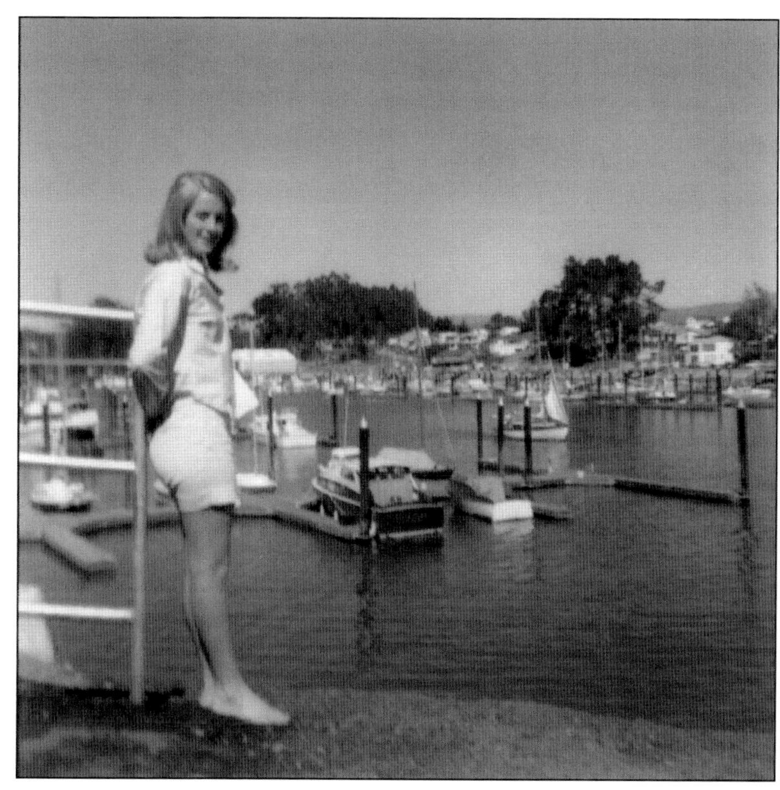

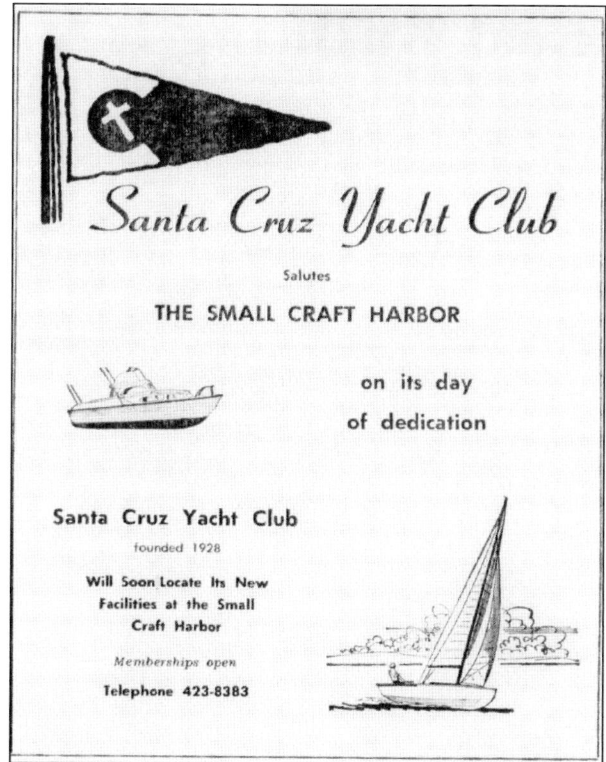

The Santa Cruz Yacht Club (SCYC) enjoyed its home on the municipal wharf for more than 30 years, until the Santa Cruz Port District began construction. Club members, longtime supporters of the port district idea, purchased a bungalow at 244 Fourth Avenue. Although some in the vicinity protested that the neighborhood was purely residential, the project won approval because yacht clubs had to be built adjacent to water. Within six months of the harbor's grand opening, SCYC members celebrated at their new location overlooking the docks, where the club has continued to thrive in the decades since. (Courtesy of the Brown collection.)

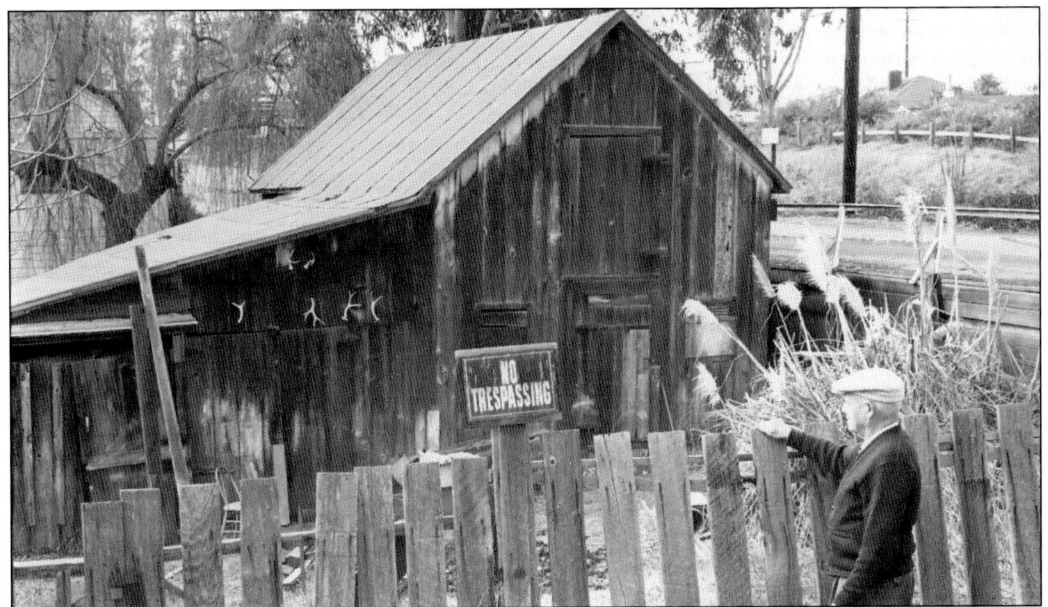

Longtime resident Leo Kincannon, above right in the early 1960s, bids farewell to one of the neighborhood's last barns. When Foster Mott developed the neighborhood in the 1880s, he refused to allow barns on residential streets. His solution was to set aside a separate block of stable lots. Each buyer of a cottage lot also received a place to house horses and carriages on Brook Avenue. To clean the stalls, stable hands simply shoveled the refuse into Pilkington Creek, which ran behind the buildings. (Courtesy of MAH.)

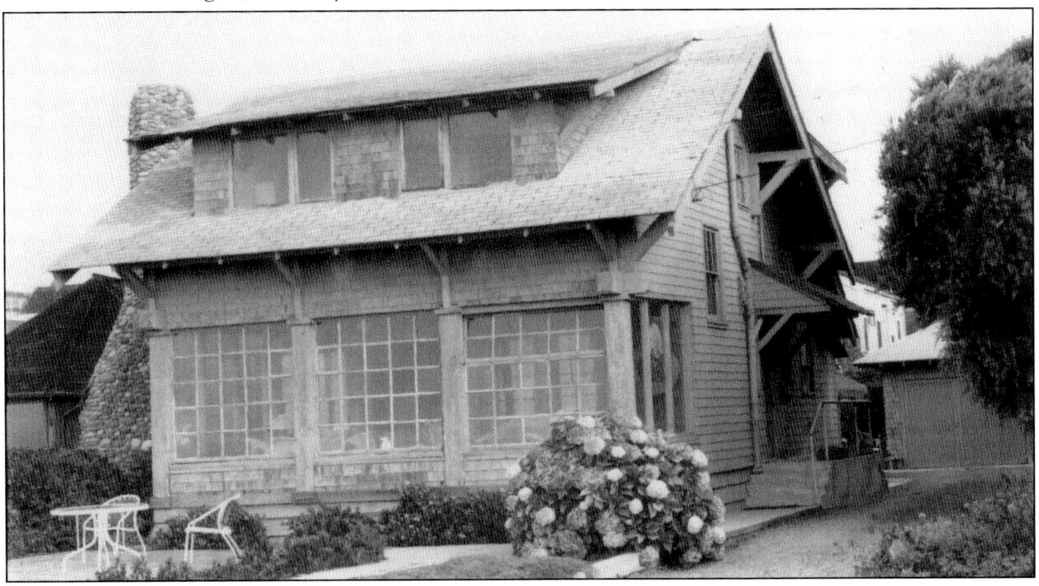

Malio Stagnaro initially received approval to build a six-story high-rise at East Cliff Drive and Second Avenue, a block away from Seabright Villa. The apartment complex would be on his extensive property, which included this single-family, bay-view home. Locals objected, arguing it would change the character of the neighborhood, contrary to the city's master plan. In June 1966, the planning commission turned down the required zoning change and the neighborhood rejoiced. (Courtesy of SNA.)

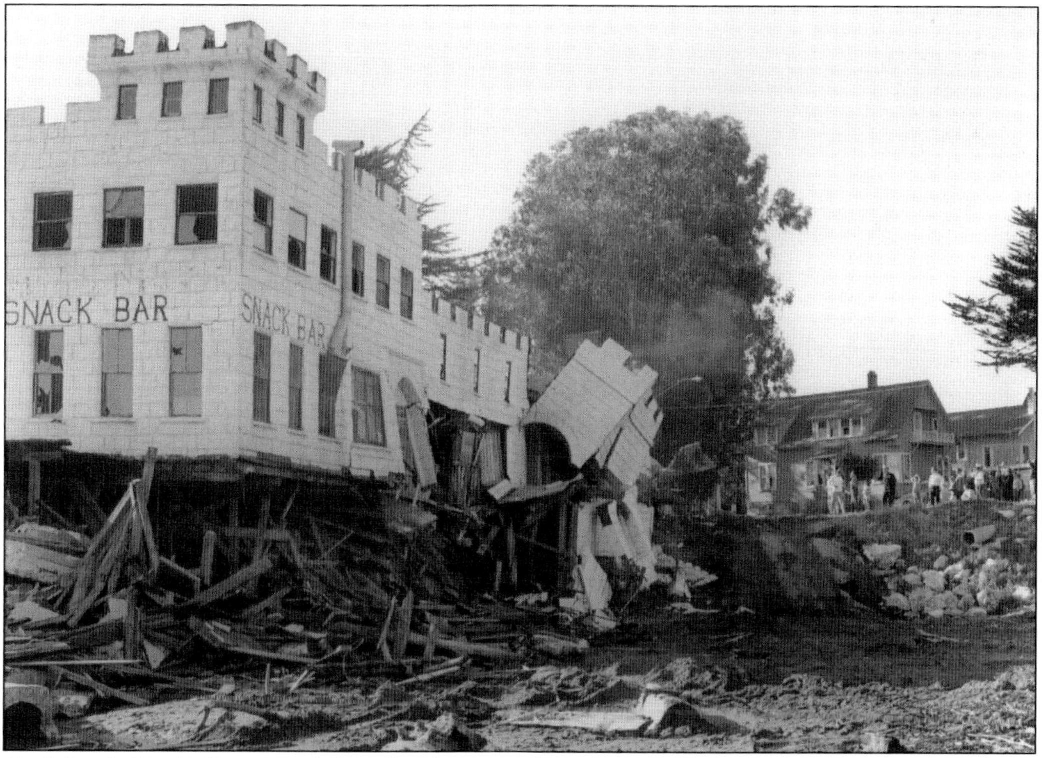

On March 24, 1967, mournful Seabrightans gathered to say farewell to their beloved Castle, damaged by a fire two years earlier. Demolition proved difficult. Louis Scholl had built well, and extra bulldozers were required to finish the job. Piled high, the fragments of the iconic structure fed a huge beach bonfire that lasted well into the night. (Courtesy of SNA.)

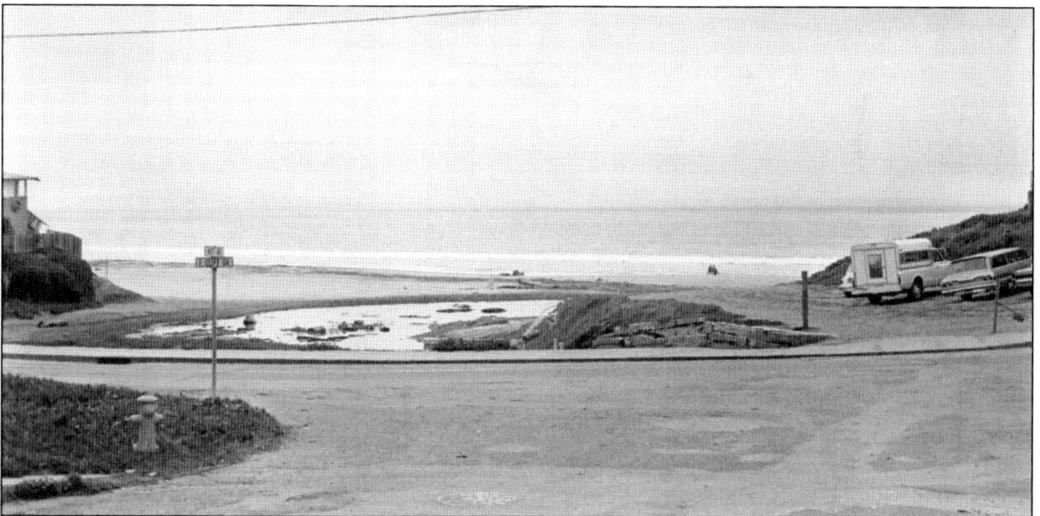

Castle owner Joe Ritchey hoped to fill the now empty site, above right, with a plush six-story apartment building, a goal supported by the planning commission. Outraged neighbors rallied to stop the project, successfully arguing that it would destroy Seabright's "special character" and encroach upon the public beach. In August 1970, Joe and his parents reluctantly agreed to sell their property to expand the state beach. (Courtesy of MAH.)

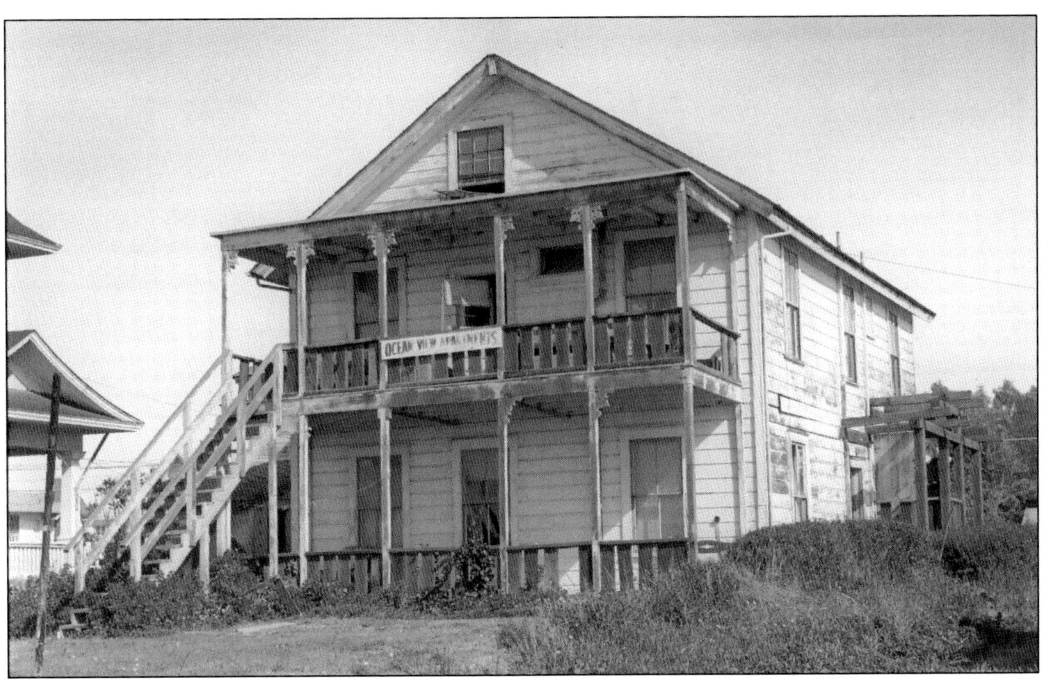

Another Seabright landmark passed into history in the fall of 1967. When the wrecking crew arrived, it demolished the neighborhood's first boardinghouse, the Ocean View, overlooking the San Lorenzo River. Farther down East Cliff Drive, the altered view was jaw-dropping. The harbor's west jetty had trapped tons of sand that would have drifted down the coast. The process transformed the once narrow beach into a sweeping expanse from San Lorenzo Point to the harbor. The long row of freshly deposited seaweed (center) shows the new high tide mark, which, five years earlier, had been the approximate limit of low tide. At long last, the cliffs had a buffer against the attack of winter waves, but far sooner than the Army Corps of Engineers had predicted. As the beach continued to grow, down-coast residents of Capitola complained bitterly about "sand-stealing." (Above, courtesy of Capitola Museum; below, courtesy of Al Mitchell.)

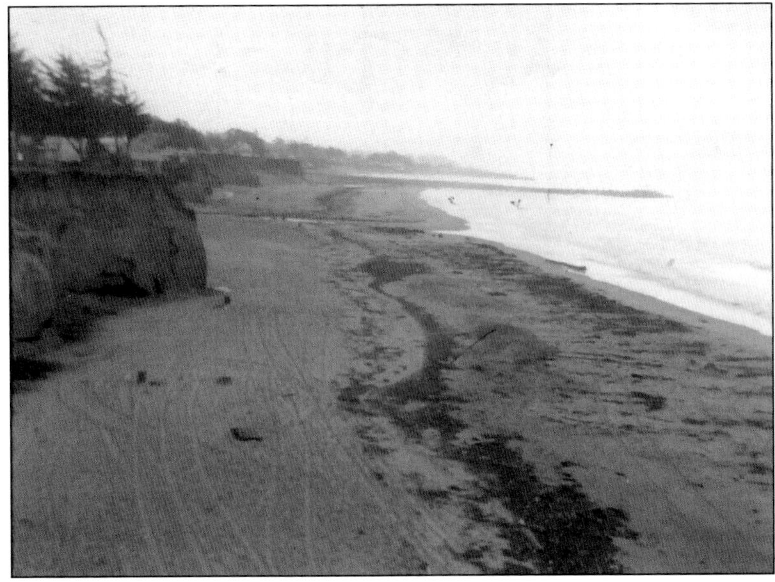

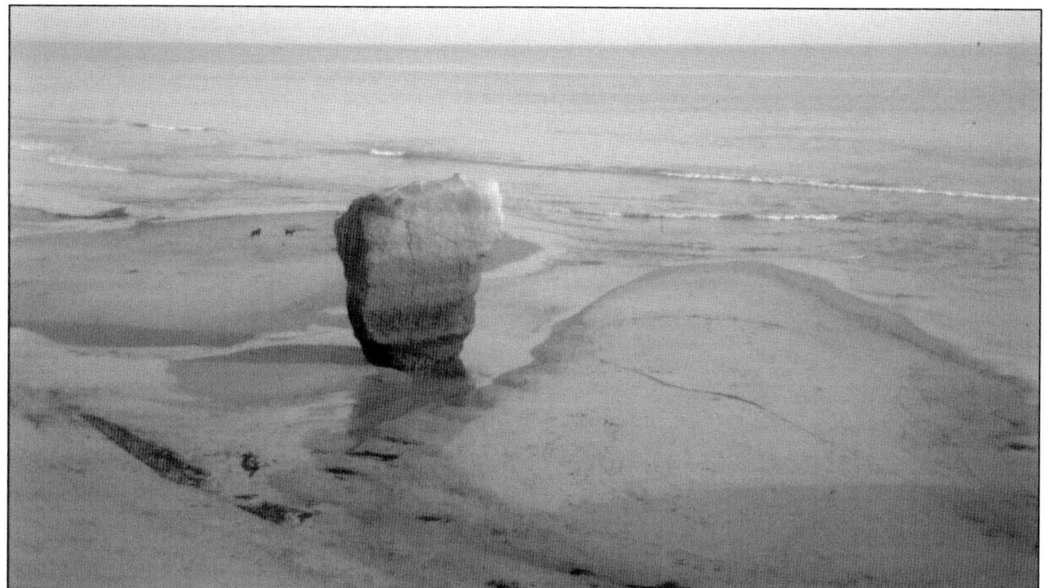

Sand accumulation changed the wave breaks, and landmark Pinnacle Rock became part of the beach. Unhappy bodysurfers went elsewhere. Mounds of sand also filled the Blow Hole, removing the perpetual threat to swimmers. While this challenge for lifeguards abated, a new one arose. Daredevils or newcomers would dive off the point into the water below. "People didn't realize how much the beach expansion had changed the ocean depth, lessening it by as much as six feet," recalls former lifeguard supervisor Al Mitchell. (Courtesy of Bill Davis.)

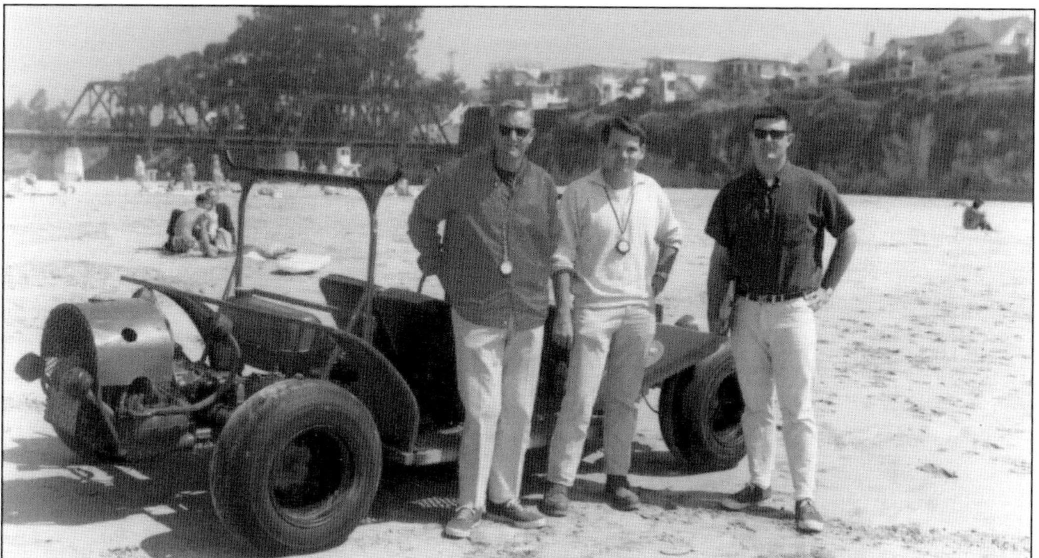

Near the mouth of the river, Al Mitchell, Stormy Strong, and Dean Hovey (far right) pose by *The Ready*, a red beach jeep designed by Hovey to enhance lifeguards' response time. During one month in the summer of 1969, Mitchell and his crew pulled three out-of-town divers from the Seabright surf, suffering from broken necks. "I don't know how we're going to keep them off [the point]," he complained to reporters. "A fence wouldn't do it." Even today, signs and fences are ignored. By the early 1970s, Mitchell had led rescues for a dozen men who dived off the point—11 survived. (Courtesy of the Sam Reid collection.)

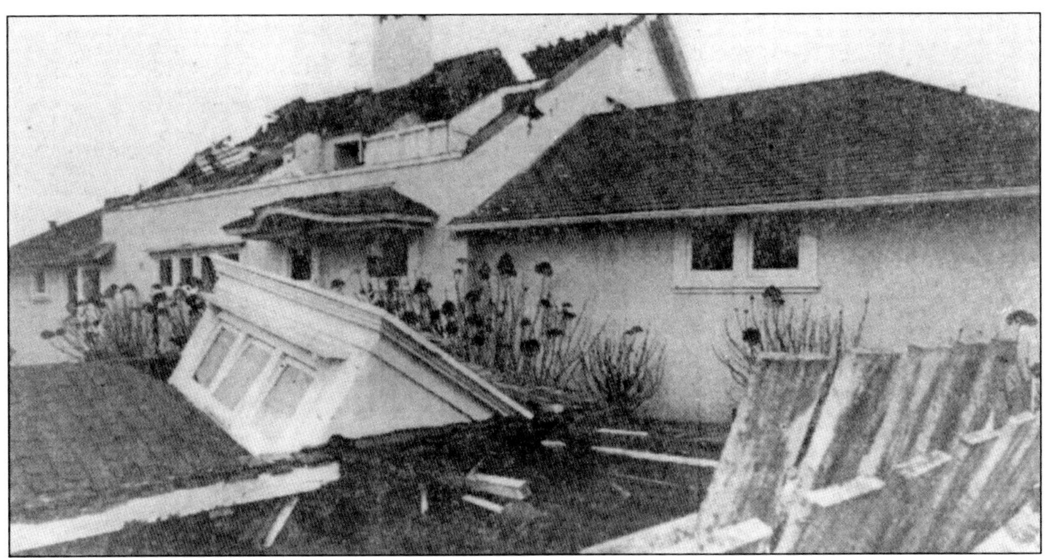

While their children played with cousins on Fresno Beach, Sumner and Carolyn Giffen Peck, owners of the 1914 Pioda house, kept a wary eye on the eroding cliff beneath their summer home. After a dozen years and many thousands of dollars for a reinforced seawall, the Pecks sold the property and moved on. The new owner decided to replace the existing structure, and to avoid demolition, he sold it at a charity auction. A landmark in its own right, the building collapsed when a crane attempted to lift it. (Courtesy of SNA.)

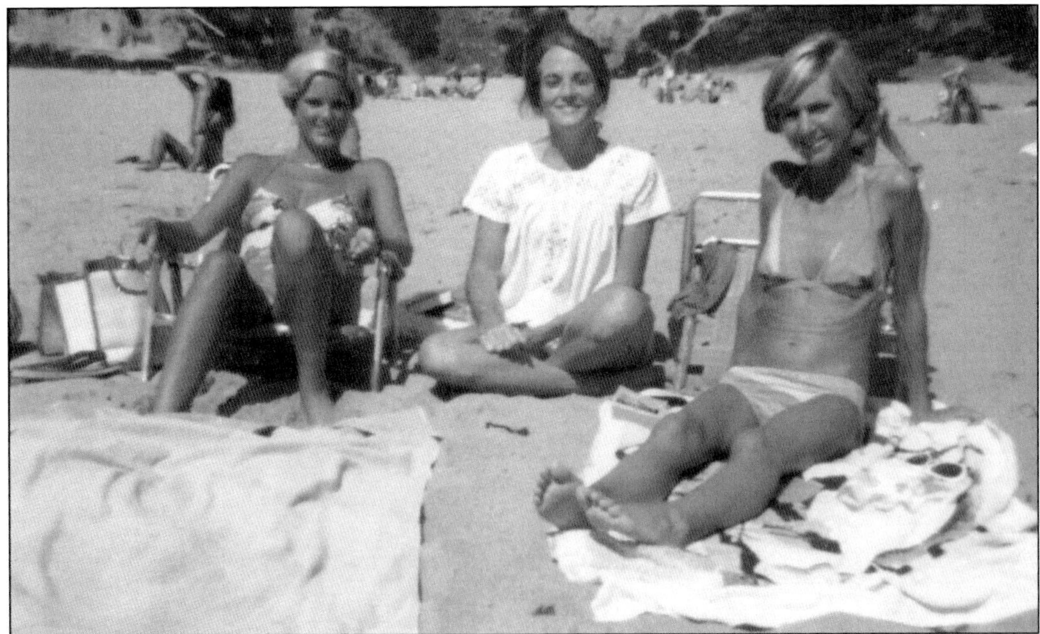

Pictured from left to right, Mary Randall, Patty Docker, and Judy Maupin—Fresno friends—spent many childhood summers together on Fourth Avenue/Fresno Beach. In early-1970s bathing attire, they show how much had changed or "vanished" since the Edwardian-era bathing costumes (see page 42). Today, all three women live in Seabright, regularly walking the west jetty. For Mary and Judy, the love of Seabright began when their grandparents, Giffens and Gows, took them to the beach as toddlers in the 1940s. (Courtesy of Mary Randall Peterson.)

Eight

Seabright Today

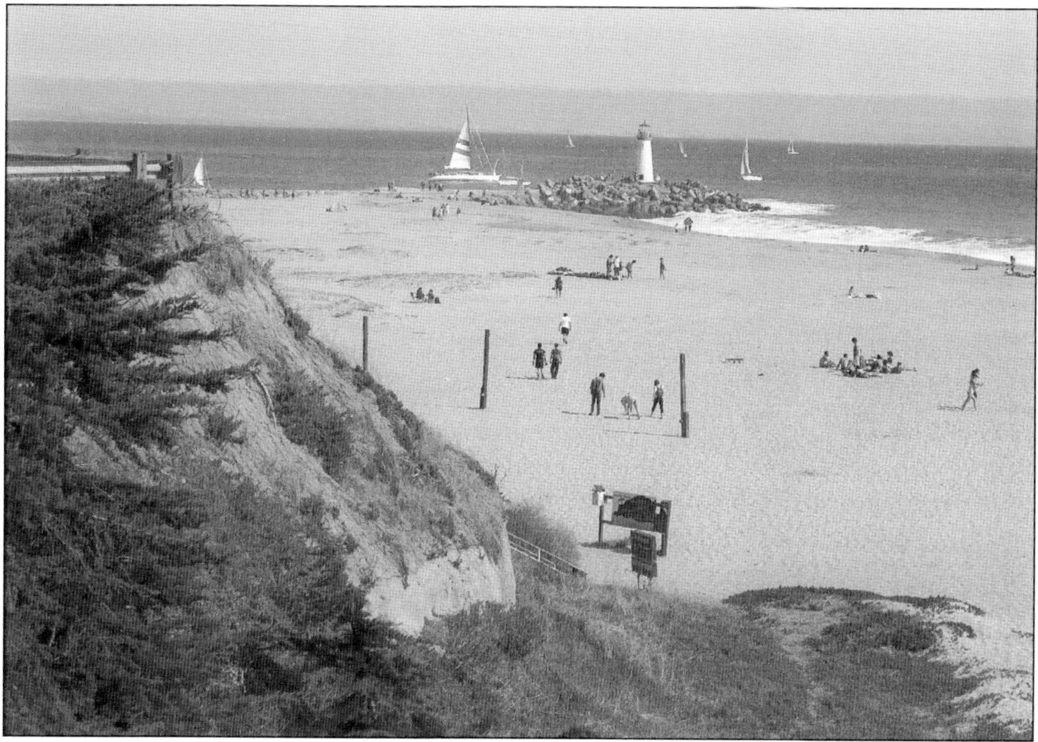

The successful campaign mounted by Live Oak residents Bill Simpkins and Jim Thoits raised $380,000 for Walton Lighthouse, which began operating in June 2002. Charles Walton, a major donor, asked that the structure be named for his brother Derek, a World War II merchant mariner lost at sea. The adjacent beach, now three times its width since harbor construction, continues to grow as sand accumulates. Seabright native Pete Prindle and his Santa Cruz High School buddies took advantage of the expansion in the late 1960s; they created volleyball courts near the foot of the Third Avenue stairs, at center, accommodating the next generation of players. (Photograph by Joe Michalak.)

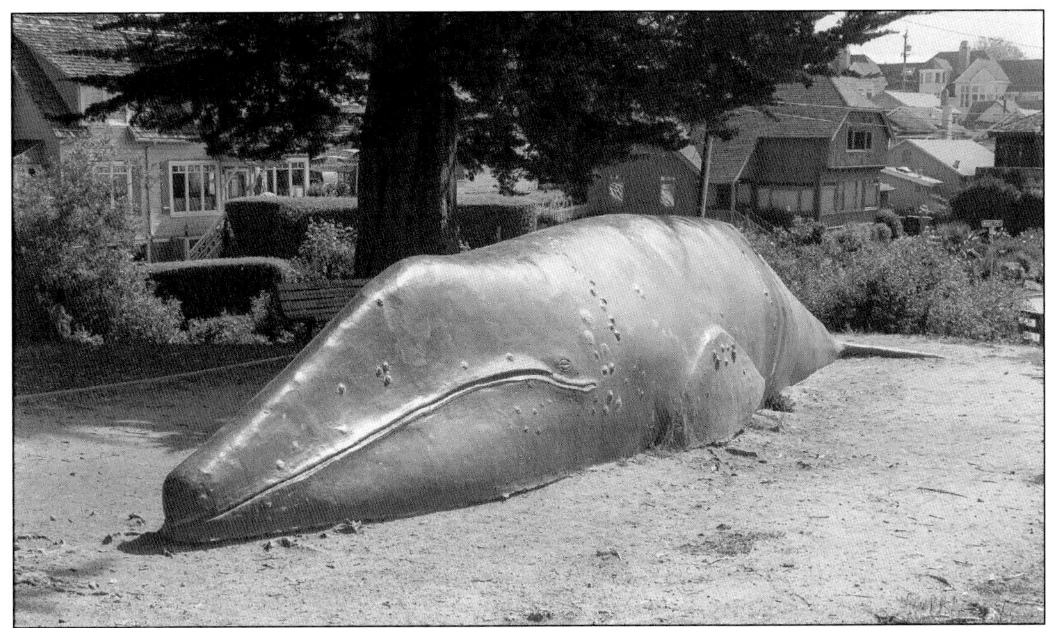

A true-to-life replica of a female gray whale inhabits the front lawn of the Santa Cruz Natural History Museum and can be immediately seen by passersby on East Cliff Drive. Designed by international marine artist Larry Foster, the model provides children with playful education. The beautiful, graffiti-proofed mammal, frequently teeming with youngsters, gives the institution an easy-to-remember identity—"the Whale Museum." (Photograph by Joe Michalak.)

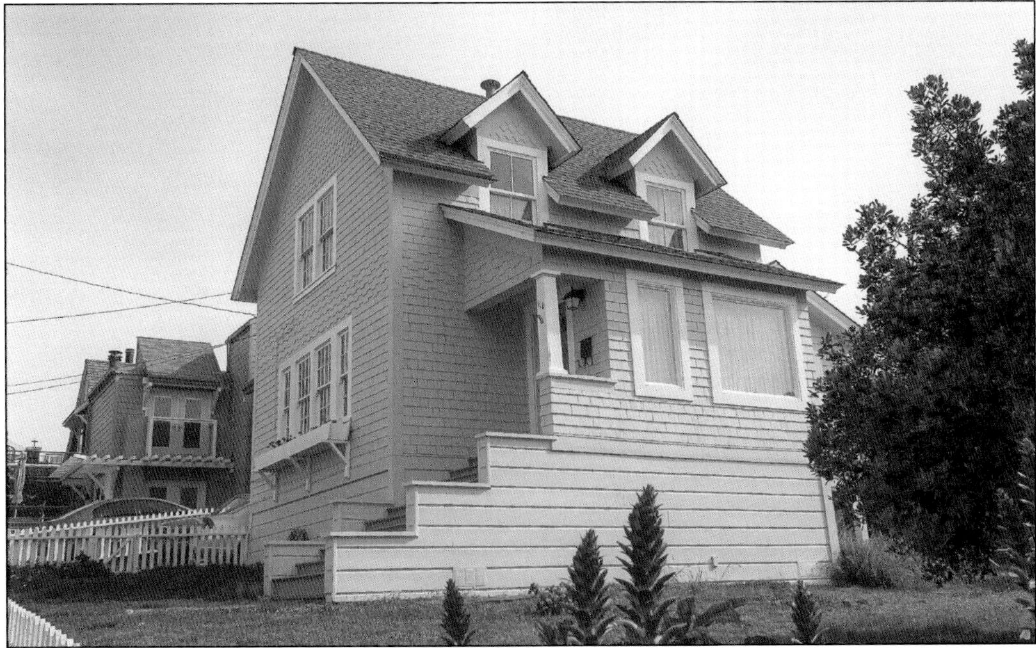

When constructed in 1888, the two-story home of Susan A. Tyrrell looked out at Monterey Bay from its New England-style dormer windows. The basic integrity of the building has benefited from stable ownership. Susan Tyrrell lived there for its first three decades, and in 1930, the Dunham family moved in and still resides there today. (Photograph by Joe Michalak.)

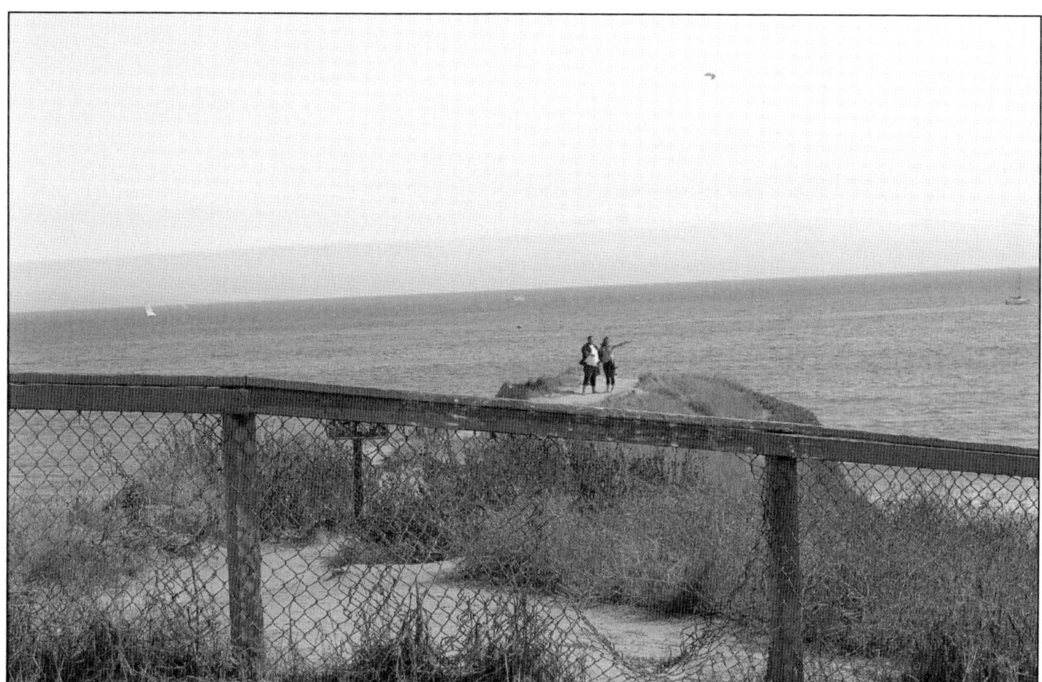

Willful trespassers daily violate restrictions designed to provide safety and to protect the fragile sandstone cliffs at San Lorenzo Point and East Cliff Drive. Wooden warning signs often feed bonfires, and metal ones are marked with graffiti. As seen above, alterations to the fence provide unofficial access for pedestrians. The potential for irreparable damage by humans, like the man descending the cliffs to the beach, below right, continues to worry neighbors and environmentalists. (Photographs by Joe Michalak.)

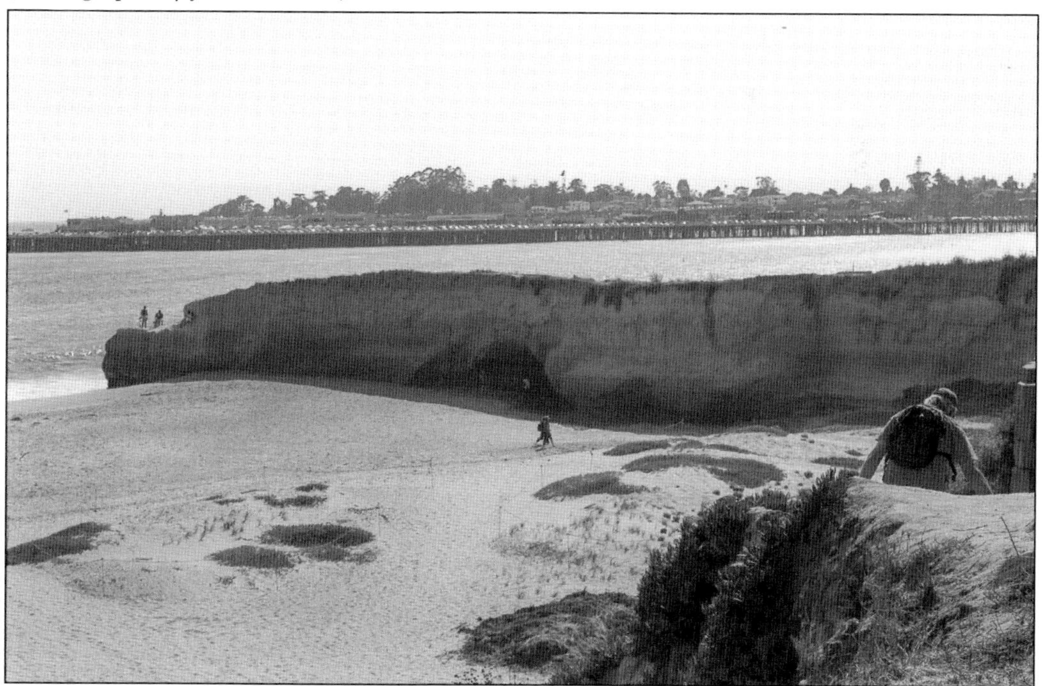

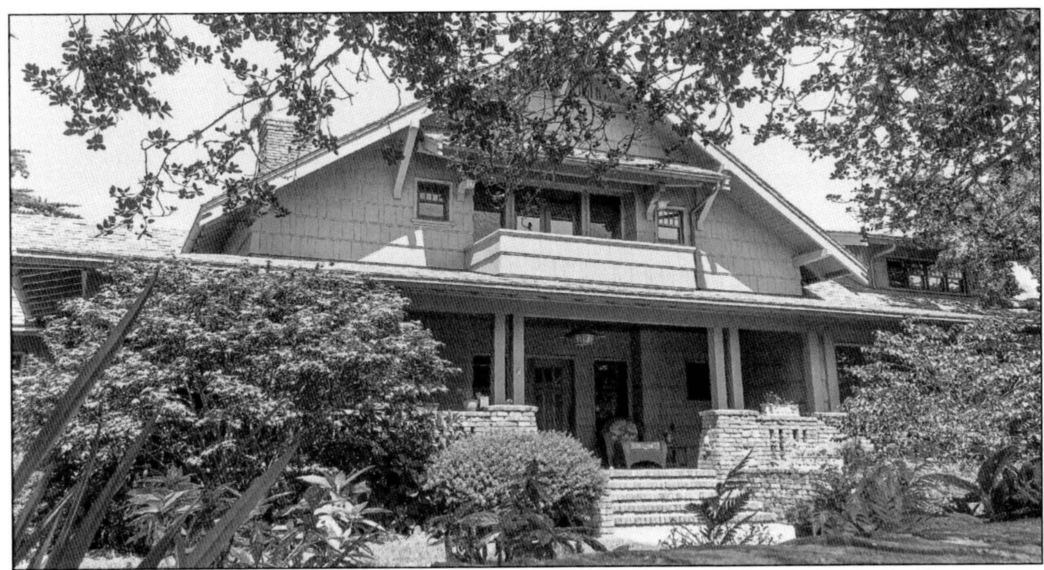

The estate at 210 Fourth Avenue, known as "the Giffen Compound" since 1950, was replaced in the 1990s by Ken and Jill Gimelli, of Hollister. The new home, designed by Clark Shultes, won critical praise in the *Sidewalk Companion to Santa Cruz Architecture*—"exquisite . . . the best period revival building in the city since 1921." (Photograph by Joe Michalak.)

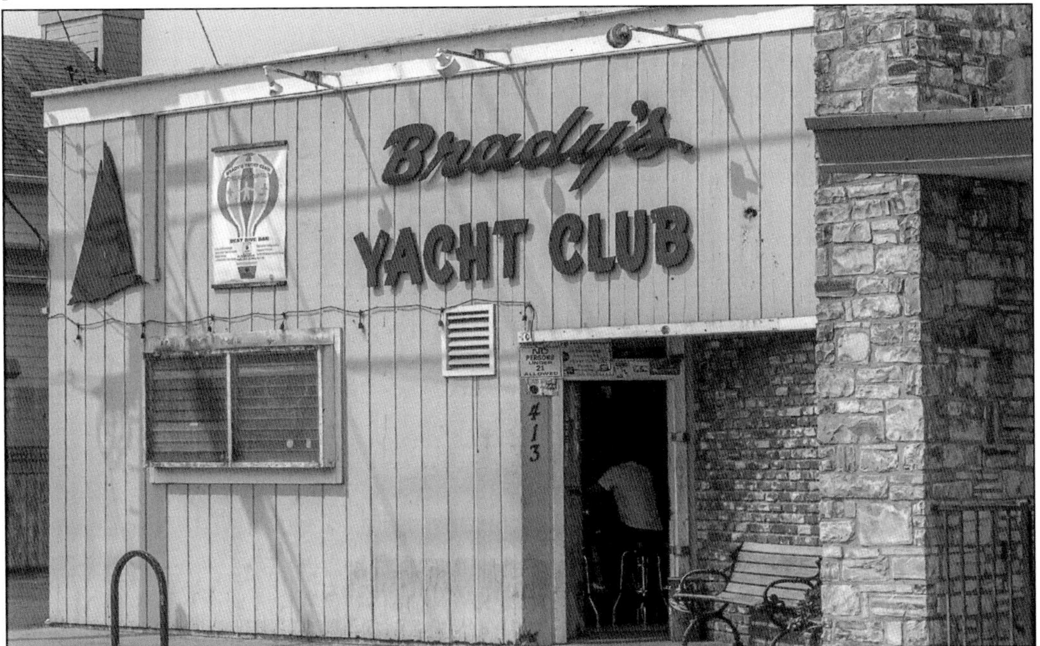

Pioneer Foster Mott, who banned alcohol from his Seabright development, would have been appalled by the neighborhood's best-known bar. The area remained free of saloons until after Prohibition, when Johnny's Place at 444 Seabright quietly began selling drinks. When it became Joe's Place, the new owner advertised it as a "cocktail lounge." Abbott A. Brady, who bought the business in 1944, adopted the more anonymous 444 Club. The completion of the Small Craft Harbor inspired yet another new name—Brady's Yacht Club, which endures more than 50 years later. The current owner advertises the location as a classic dive bar. (Photograph by Joe Michalak.)

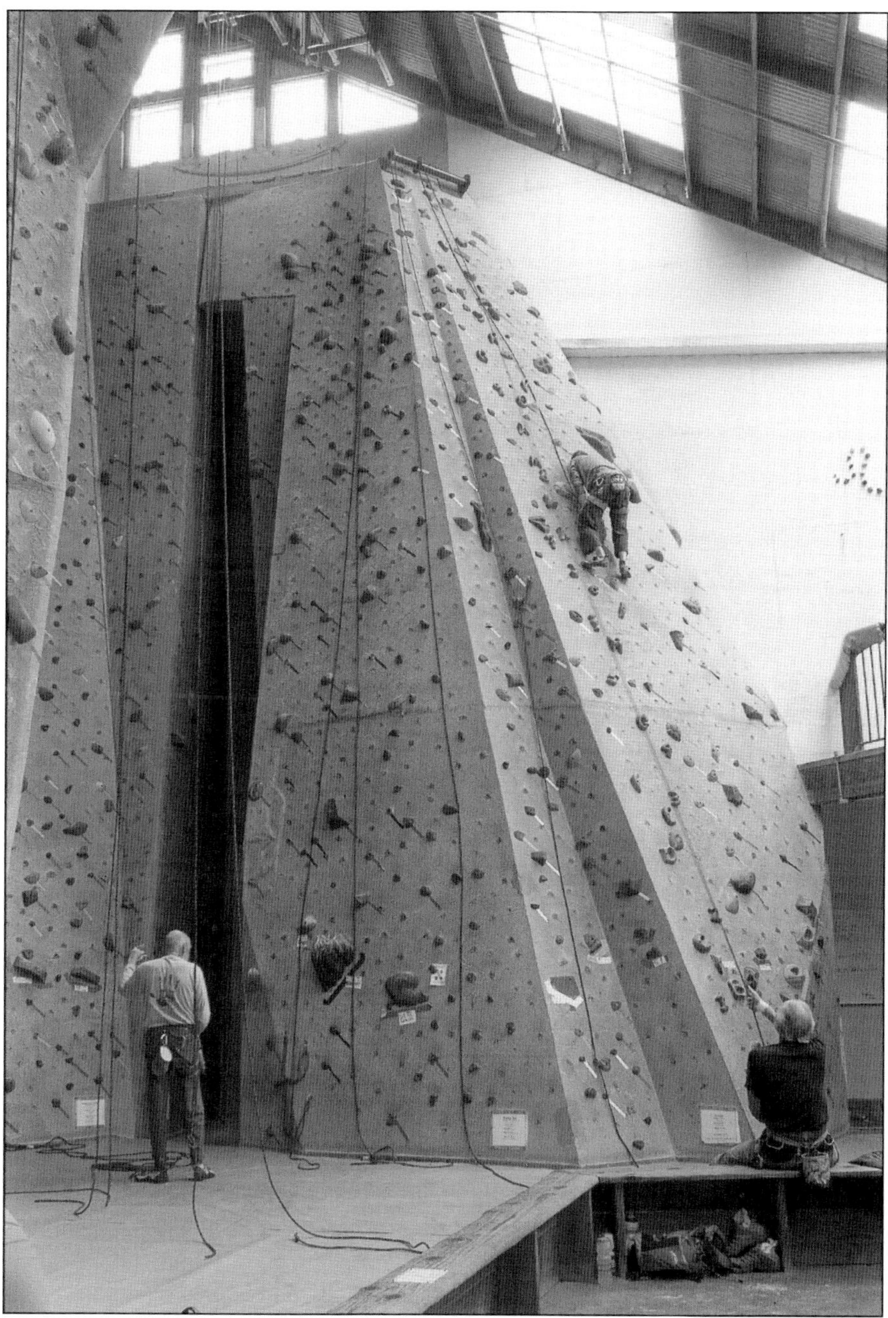

At the Seabright Cannery, established in 1914, the workforce processed pears until the plant shut down in March 1989, causing neighborhood concern over what businesses would fill the vacant structure. Later that year, after the Loma Prieta earthquake, Beckmann's Bakery moved in to stay. Entrepreneurs, including a sailmaker, gradually repurposed the lofty spaces. The Pacific Edge Company came up with a creative new use—a climbing gym, one of the nation's largest, with simulated cliff faces and boulders to provide weather-free practice. When climbers reach the highest "peak," they are rewarded with a view of Seabright Beach and the bay from the room's high windows. (Photograph by Joe Michalak.)

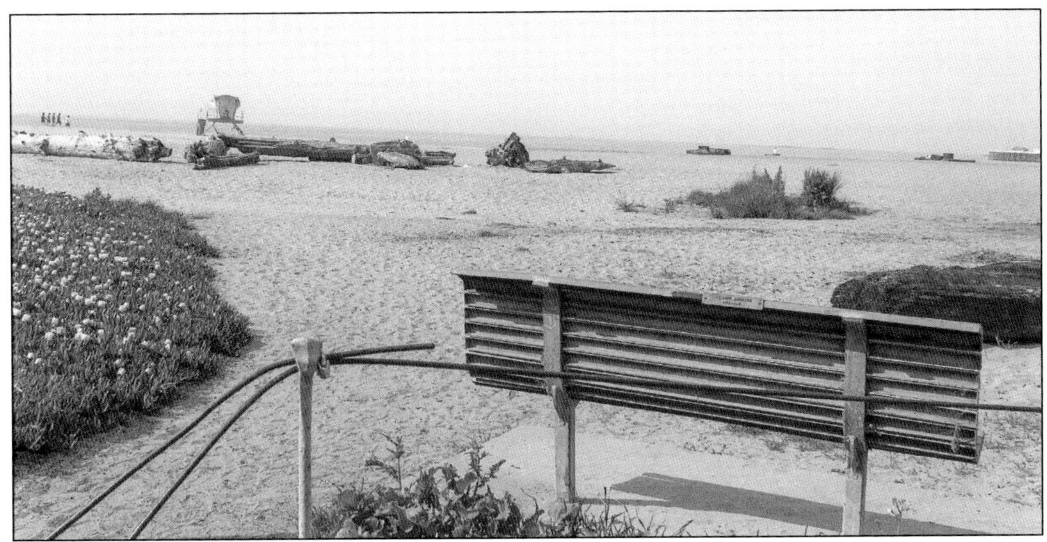

Attorney Stewart Cureton served as president of and legal advisor to the Seabright Beach Improvement Society for more than 20 years. He spearheaded beach cleanups, hosted bonfires for children, and fought to keep the Castle family-oriented and alcohol-free. When Stewart passed away in 1971, his beach volleyball buddies (see page 98) installed a galvanized steel bench on Castle Beach in his memory—evidently without permission. Eventually, accumulated sand made it an ugly and unusable seat, just inches off the ground. Stewart's son John worked with California State Parks to rescue the bench and, in 2013, gave it a permanent concrete foundation with all the required permissions. (Photograph by Joe Michalak.)

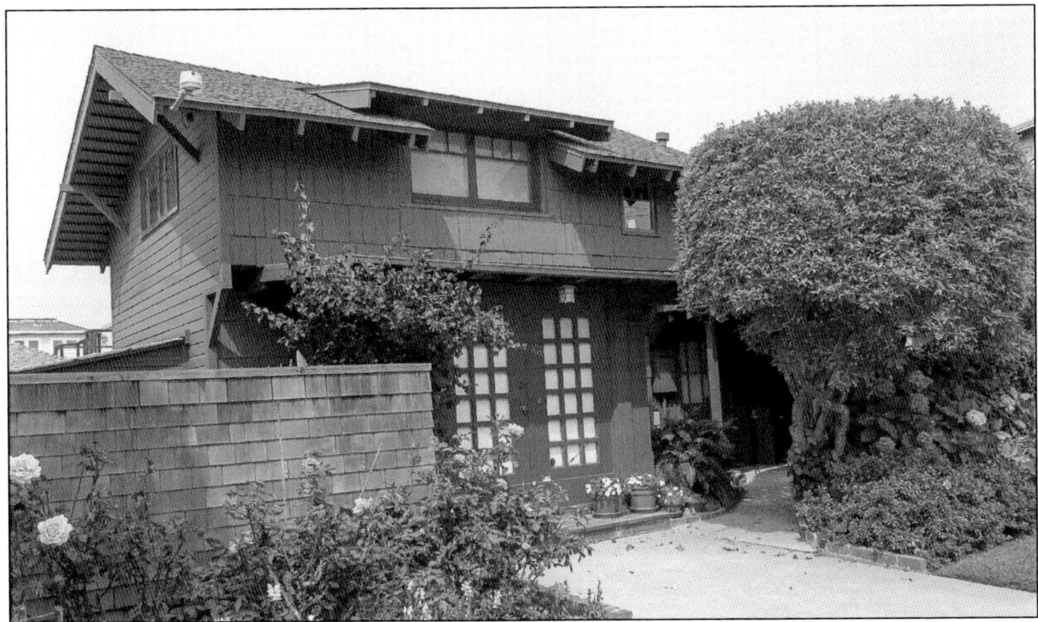

Beginning in 1905, architect Marie B. Thompson constructed several houses on her Seabright property, expressing the ideals of simplicity and beauty advocated in the magazine *Craftsman*. At 109 Alhambra Avenue, her two-story design provided clear views of Monterey Bay. Only slightly altered, the home remains in place today, tucked behind the relocated Van Kaathoven house and is listed in the *Santa Cruz Historic Buildings Survey, Vol. 1.* (Photograph by Joe Michalak.)

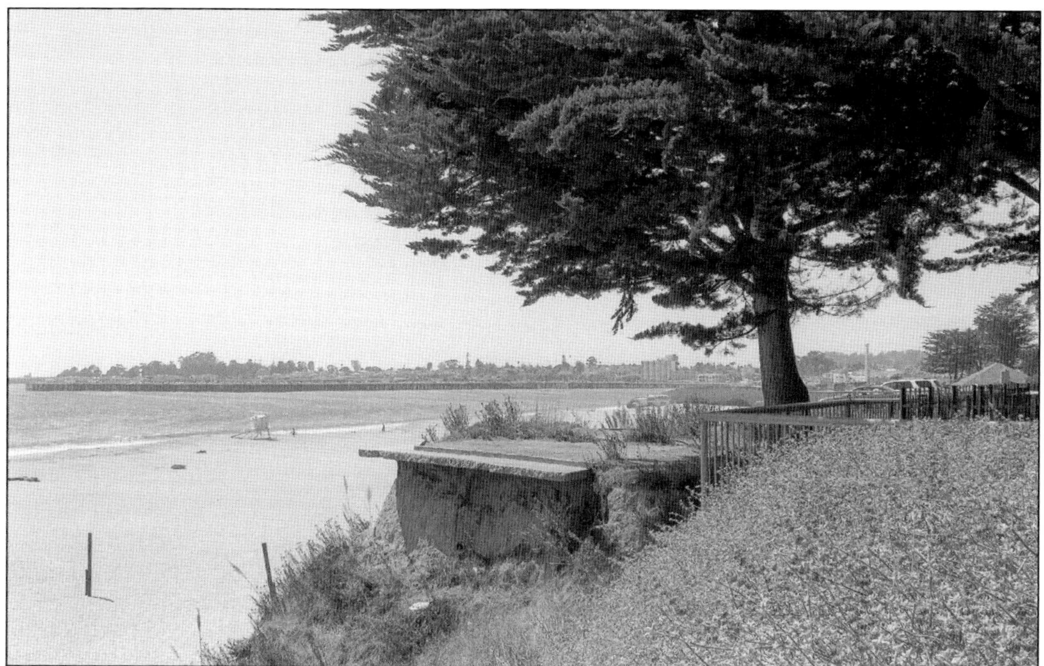

East Cliff Drive, the pride and joy of the old-time Seabright Improvement Society, originally ran from one end of the neighborhood to the other, offering drivers spectacular views. Today, however, due to persistent cliff erosion, the road east of Seabright Avenue consists of remnants. Hundreds of feet of land have fallen away since 1925, leaving some sections, such as the end of Second Avenue (pictured) hanging in the air. (Photograph by Joe Michalak.)

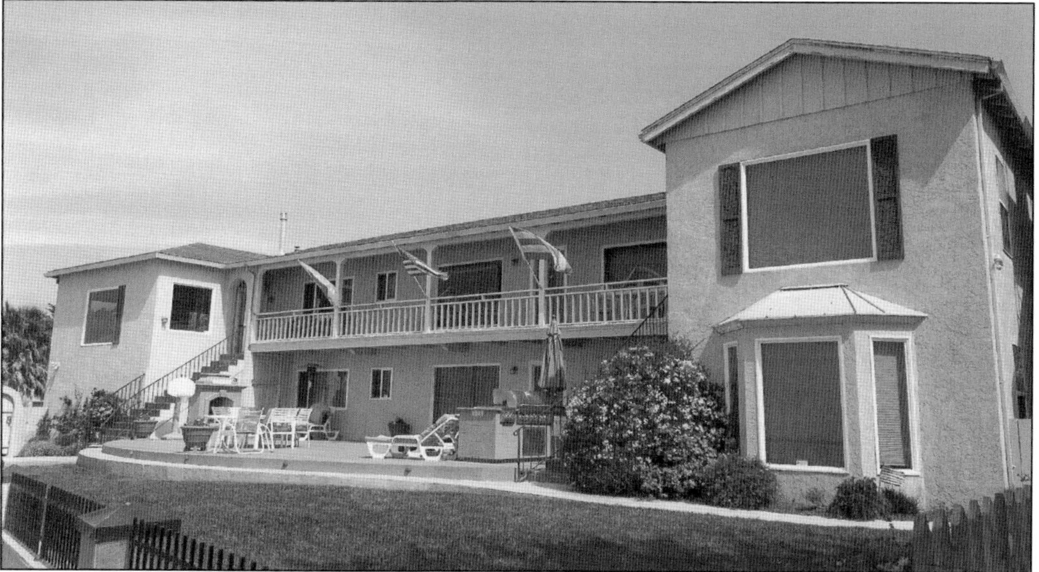

For decades, the McEnery family of San José enjoyed Castle Beach, their summer home just a short walk away. Then, in 1986, they bought the elegant apartment complex at 1703 East Cliff Drive (see page 79) and converted it into a family compound. La Solana, built in the late 1930s, was the first Seabright residence to have an attached garage, which still accommodates five cars. (Photograph by Joe Michalak.)

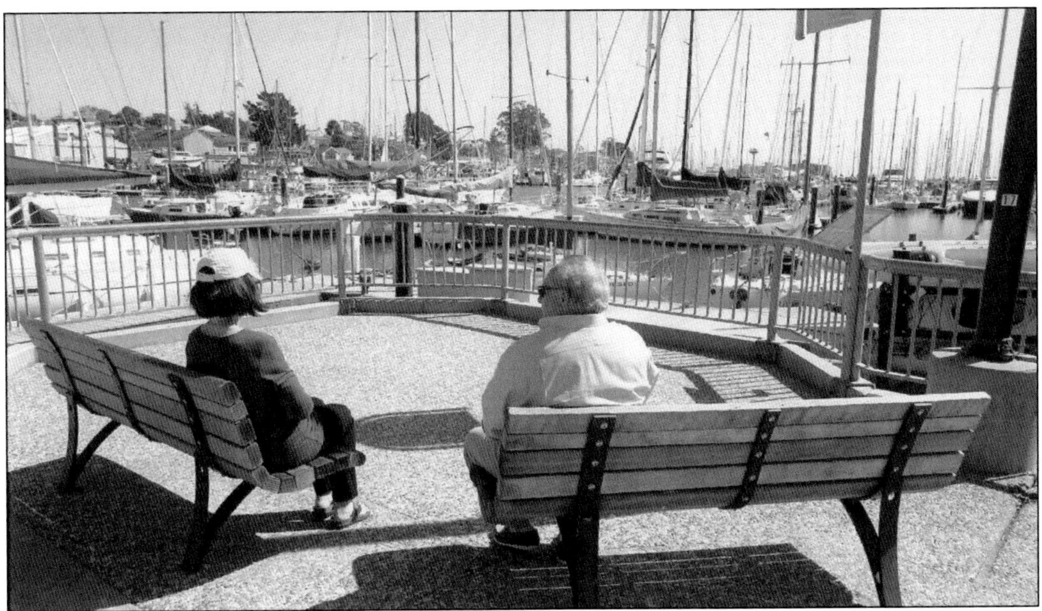

At the plaza beneath Murray Street Bridge, locals get a ringside view of the Small Craft Harbor thanks to strategically placed benches near FF Dock. A total of 70 outdoor benches beautify the nearly two-mile walking path around the harbor. Many feature commemorative plaques with familiar Santa Cruz names such as Canepa, Faraola, Larson, Norman, Randall, and Rideout. (Photograph by Bill Lovejoy.)

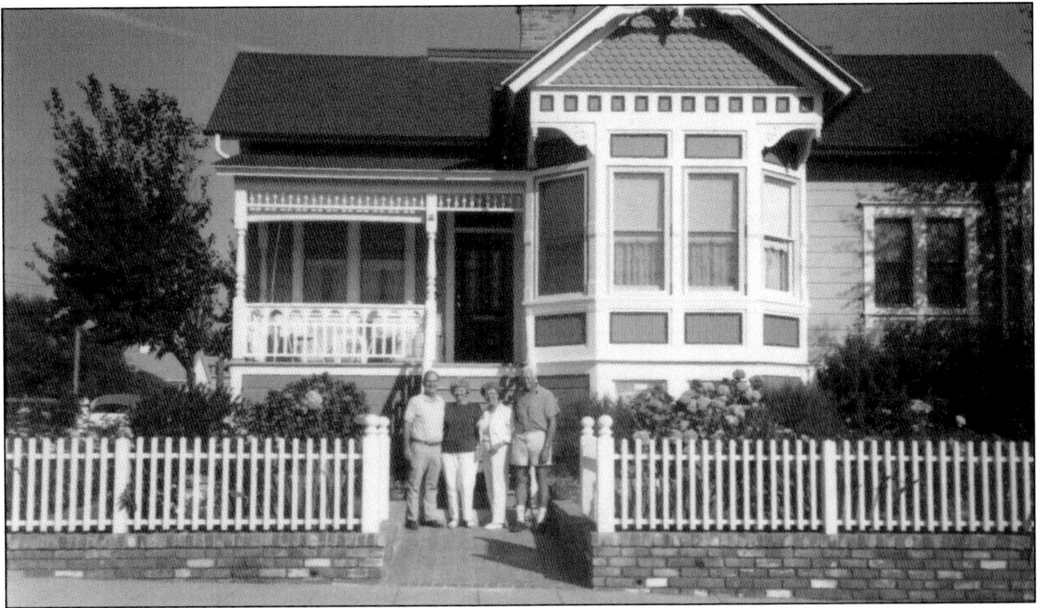

In 1973, when Richard and Joyce Dannebaum became owners of the c. 1890 home at 122 Seabright Avenue, their goal of authentic restoration would make fine use of Richard's skills as an architect. In raising the foundation and adding such features as a front porch and chimney, they diligently maintained the original structural facade and Eastlake style (see page 31). The Dannebaums received a SCOPE (Santa Cruz Organization for Progress and Euthenics) Award for outstanding restoration in 1986. (Courtesy of SNA.)

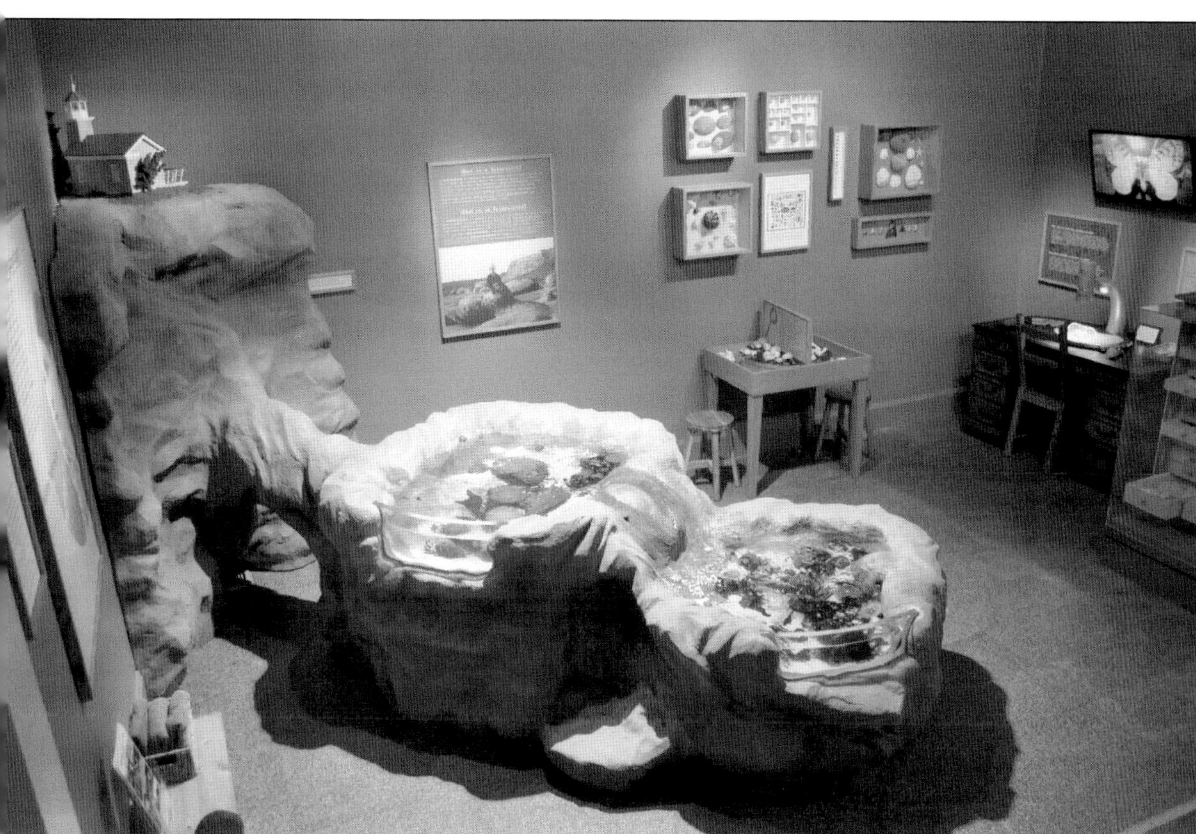

For over a century, the Santa Cruz Museum of Natural History has served residents and tourists alike. Originally run by the City of Santa Cruz, the museum became a fully independent, community-supported nonprofit in 2009. From its humble beginnings in the basement of the Santa Cruz Library, the museum's core mission—to connect people with the region's natural wonders and to inspire a love of them—has evolved in new and exciting ways. In 2016, the museum transformed its intertidal exhibit into a fresh, dynamic experience, which shares the remarkable story of 19th-century Santa Cruz naturalist Laura Hecox while encouraging patrons to roll up their sleeves and try on the role of a naturalist themselves. These new rocky touch-pools introduce visitors to the real tide-pooling experience along Lighthouse Point on West Cliff Drive. When Hecox gave her entire lighthouse museum collection to the city, she envisioned a rich, educational experience—one that seems more fully realized today than ever before. (Courtesy of SCMNH.)

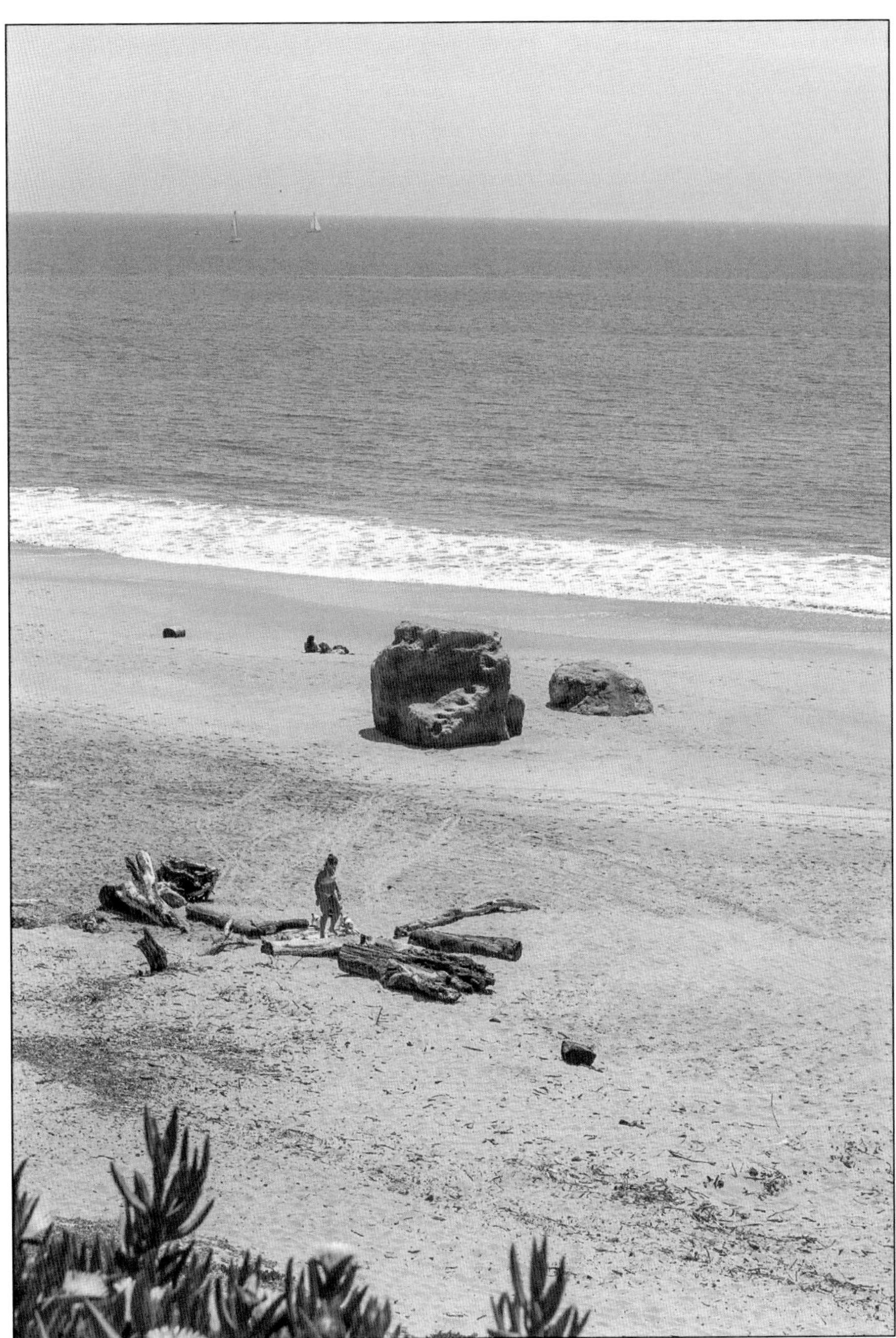

Pinnacle Rock had been a prominent landmark since the Pilkingtons first settled in the area in the 1860s. Over the decades, the sea stack acquired various names, including the "Monument," "Bird Rock," and the "Stone Sentinel." A sight as familiar to locals as the Castle, Pinnacle Rock also came to a dramatic end. As described by Prof. Gary Griggs, it "split and partially collapsed during the 1989 Loma Prieta earthquake." Today, visitors often climb up the remaining stump for a special view of the Monterey Bay National Marine Sanctuary, established in 1992; it is one of the largest such refuges in the United States. (Photograph by Joe Michalak.)

INDEX

Consistent with our mission to preserve history on a local level, this book was printed in South Carolina on American-made paper and manufactured entirely in the United States. Products carrying the accredited Forest Stewardship Council (FSC) label are printed on 100 percent FSC-certified paper.

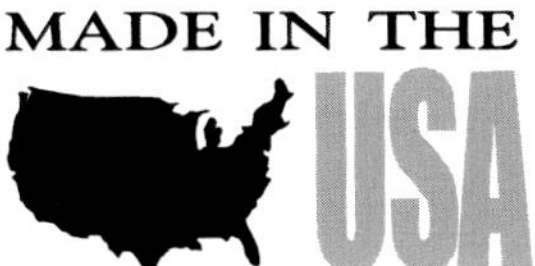